OUR CHILDREN'S CRIPPLED FUTURE

Also by Frank E. Armbruster

THE FORGOTTEN AMERICANS
CAN WE WIN IN VIETNAM?

OUR CHILDREN'S CRIPPLED FUTURE

How American Education Has Failed

FRANK E. ARMBRUSTER

with contributions by PAUL BRACKEN

and the assistance of JOYCE LIND
and ROSE MARIE MARTIN

 Quadrangle/The New York Times Book Co.

Designed by Beth Tondreau

Library of Congress Cataloging in Publication Data

Armbruster, Frank E
  Our children's crippled future.

  Published in 1975 under title: The U.S. primary and
secondary educational process.
  Bibliography: p.
  Includes index.
  1. Educational sociology—United States. 2. Educa-
tion—United States. I. Title.
LC205.A75 1977   370'.973   76–50814
ISBN 0–8129–0666–7

CONTENTS

ACKNOWLEDGMENTS

We gratefully acknowledge the following sources for permission to use their copyrighted material.

The American Psychological Association for material from "The Army General Classification Test" by the Staff, Personnel Research Section, Classification and Replacement Branch, Adjutant General's Office, *The Psychological Bulletin,* Vol. 42, 1945. Copyright 1945 by the American Psychological Association. Reprinted by permission for one-time use.

Read D. Tuddenham and the American Psychological Association for material from "Soldier Intelligence in World Wars I and II" by Read D. Tuddenham, *The American Psychologist,* Vol. 3, Feb. 1948. Copyright 1948 by the American Psychological Association. Reprinted by permission for one-time use.

New Society, London, for one-time permission to reprint excerpts of "Remember, Remember" by Andrew Mayes from the Nov. 1, 1973, issue. Copyright 1973 by *New Society.*

Science for material from "Inequality in Adult Capacity—From Military Data" by Walter V. Bingham, Vol. 104, Aug. 1946, pp. 147–52. Copyright 1946 by *Science.*

Fred M. Hechinger and *Saturday Review/World* for material from "What Happened to the Best and the Brightest?" by Fred M. Hechinger from the Feb. 9, 1974, issue. Copyright 1974 by *Saturday Review/World* and Fred M. Hechinger.

Dr. Donald Ross Green, CTB/McGraw-Hill, for excerpts from a personal communication, and Richard A. Shaffer, *The Wall Street Journal,* recipient of the communication.

Dr. Karl Shapiro for excerpts from his article "Is This Really the Brightest Student Generation?" *Human Events,* July 11, 1970.

Dr. Joseph R. Sligo for material from his doctoral dissertation, "Comparison of Achievement in Selected High School Subjects in 1934 and 1954" for the College of Education, Graduate College of the State University of Iowa, Aug. 1955.

Dr. Stephen A. Roderick for material from his doctoral dissertation, "A Comparative Study of Mathematics Achievement by Sixth Graders and Eighth Graders, 1936 to 1973, 1951–55 to 1973, and 1965 to 1973," for the University of Iowa, July 1973.

Professor Morris Kline for material from his book *Why Johnny Can't Add: The Failure of the New Math,* published by St. Martin's Press. Copyright 1973 by Morris Kline.

The College Entrance Examination Board, New York, for tabular material from

"Mean Scores on the College Board Scholastic Aptitude Test" (mimeographed).

The University of Minnesota Press for material from *Who Goes to College?: Comparison of Minnesota College Freshmen 1930–1960* by Ralph F. Berdie et al. Copyright 1962 by the University of Minnesota Press.

Dodd, Mead & Company, Inc., for material from *The Role of the School in American Society* by V. T. Thayer and Martin Levit. Copyright 1966 by Dodd, Mead & Company, Inc.

The University of North Carolina Press for material from *The Impact of the War Upon American Education* by I. L. Kandel. Copyright 1948 by The University of North Carolina Press.

Alfred A. Knopf, Inc., and Random House for material from *The Transformation of the School* by Lawrence A. Cremin. Copyright 1961 by Vintage Books, Division of Random House.

A. N. Hieronymus, The University of Iowa, and Houghton Mifflin, Inc., for material from *Manual for Administrators, Supervisors, and Counselors,* Levels Ed., *Forms 5 & 6, Iowa Tests of Basic Skills* by A. N. Hieronymus and E. F. Lindquist. Copyright 1974 by The University of Iowa.

Teachers College Press for material reproduced by permission of the publisher from Arthur I. Gates, *Reading Attainment in Elementary Schools: 1957 and 1937.* (New York: Teachers College Press, copyright 1961 by Teachers College, Columbia University).

Basic Books, Inc., and Diane Ravitch for material from *The Great School Wars: New York City, 1805–1973: A History of the Public Schools As Battlefield of Social Change,* by Diane Ravitch, © 1974 by Diane Ravitch, Basic Books, Inc., Publishers, New York.

Los Angeles Times for material from "The Decline of American Education," by Jack McCurdy and Don Speich. Copyright 1976, *Los Angeles Times*. Reprinted by permission.

AUTHOR'S NOTE

I am deeply indebted to Paul Bracken for the specific sections he wrote and his outstanding contributions and assistance throughout the study as a whole without which this book would not have been possible. I am also indebted to Joyce Lind for her suggestions and invaluable assistance throughout all phases of the initial study, from the preliminary research to the editing and production of it. I likewise owe much to Rose Marie Martin, who played a similar role in updating the original study, for her suggestions and indispensable assistance. I would also like to express my appreciation to my wife for her assistance in the research effort and on the production of the manuscript.

Jane Newitt's patience, encouragement, and assistance throughout the initial project were of great value. Other members of the Hudson Institute staff were also helpful and generous in their advice, particularly Herman Kahn, Rudy L. Ruggles, Jr., Mildred Schneck, and Doris Yokelson.

Maud Bonnell, Ruth Ann Crow, Carolann Roussel, Yvonne Swinton, and Audrey Tobin were of great assistance in the graphic work, editing, and production of the study.

I also want to thank the many people from all over the country—professionals from all phases of the education and testing processes, school board trustees, journalists, and private citizens—who brought to my attention much valuable data.

Except for the signed sections by Paul Bracken, none of those named here is responsible for conclusions and interpretations in this study; they are, of course, entirely my own.

This book is a considerably expanded updated version of a Hudson Institute study printed in July 1975, "The U.S. Primary and Secondary Educational Process," HI–2308–RR. The material has in many cases been brought up to date as of mid-Autumn 1976, but the general thrust of the study has not been significantly altered.

OUR CHILDREN'S CRIPPLED FUTURE

INTRODUCTION

Over the past decade, many fashionable premises significantly influenced the policies of our school systems. We entered the 1960s with the theme that we were shortchanging education and educators, despite the fact that expenditures on primary and secondary education had almost tripled between 1950 and 1960 from $6.7 billion to $18 billion. That figure had reached $75 billion by the 1976–77 school year, more than quadrupling the 1960 figure and increasing the 1950 figure by more than eleven times. This approximately triples the 1950 cost even in *constant* dollars *per pupil* (eliminating the effects of inflation and fluctuations in the number of pupils), and doubles that of 1960. In our most expensive school districts, the cost to the taxpayer for tuition for a high school student often is about $4,000 per year, about that of Ivy League colleges.

Since 1950, for all forms of education, including college, we have gone from 4 to 8 percent of the gross national product. The 1976–77 school year's total cost for education was $130 billion, far outstripping the defense budget and many of the other high-cost budget items usually considered in the top spending category.

About two-thirds, and in some cases almost three-quarters, of the cost of primary and secondary education these days is in educators' (including administrators') salaries and fringe benefits. We have an ever-increasing number of educators per pupil in our schools. In 1950 the pupil/teacher ratio was about 27 to 1; in 1960 it was about 25 to 1; by the 1974–75 school year it had fallen to about 1 educator for every 18 pupils, a 28 percent drop. At the same time the salaries and fringe benefits of teachers and administrators have been soaring and their work hours and days shrinking. Currently, the average compensation they receive equals or exceeds the average hourly rate for all college graduates, even though current educators are, on the average, younger, less experienced, and have less graduate school time.

Much of the other one-quarter to one-third of current school budgets goes to pay off debts incurred by building new, often lavish schools, and to purchase and maintain vast amounts of laboratory, audio-visual, and other equipment, and even computer terminals.

These inputs to our schools over these time periods, and particularly since the mid-1960s, have been impressive and even startling. The output over this last decade of spectacular increases in spending, however, has been anything but impressive. An examination of the results of academic achievement tests (administered to all grades in most states) shows an almost unremitting fall in pupil academic ability during the second half of the 1960s and the first half of the 1970s.

This is true for all grades except the first through the third or fourth grades, which generally consistently maintain the levels of achievement they demonstrated in the mid-sixties, almost regardless of the state or socioeconomic area examined. The sample examined in this study covered school systems containing over half the entire primary and secondary pupil population of the United States, spanning from Rhode Island to Hawaii and from Michigan to Texas. In general, the average achievement scores for all grades above the third or fourth grade in a state not only fell but fell simultaneously, and each year the same children dropped further and further behind the old achievement norms as they progressed through the grades. Many graduates of some of those $4,000-a-year-tuition high schools mentioned earlier could barely read at a level normally demanded of eighth graders.

It was during this same period, 1963–76, that the much more publicized results of the Scholastic Aptitude Test (SAT—College Board Test) showed a consistent decline in verbal and mathematical aptitude of high school pupils who intended to apply for college. This decline continues, though the number of pupils taking the test has declined since the late 1960s, while high school pupils and graduates have increased, which, under normal circumstances, should have brought a more select group to the test. (In 1976 approximately 1 million out of 3 million high school seniors and about 300,000 juniors took these tests.)

In general the evidence indicates that, from the fourth grade up, during the past decade, the better pupils—those in the upper 10 and 25 percent of their class—were losing ground faster than the worst ones—those in the lower 10 and 25 percent. There is other evidence that core-city students from our metropolises seem to be falling more slowly than students from our smaller cities and even from some of the better suburbs of large cities. Some recent, very short-term, evidence coming from two years of SAT results shows that the very tiny minority of the very brightest high school graduates also may now have begun to improve; but this same evidence indicates that that great body of the more intelligent high school graduates, which traditionally made up the bulk of our successful college people, may have slipped further. It would be disturbing if such a split became a trend.

We have had drops in achievement in our schools before. Apparently achievement was low in the 1920s, but it peaked again in the mid- and late 1930s, then fell precipitously in the 1940s. It bottomed out about 1950 and climbed steadily during the "silent fifties" and apparently peaked again in the mid- and late 1960s. By the end of the 1960s, however, it was generally in decline, apparently with but few exceptions across the country. These general trends also applied to private schools, though here, too, there were some exceptions and, as a rule, academic and discipline standards seem to continue to remain above those of the public school systems.

According to some scattered short-term evidence, and even more "feeling" among educators, the trend in academic achievement scores may be beginning to bottom out again, possibly because the tendency to question the recent innovations, and even to get "back to basics," is showing up again. It remains to be seen, however, whether a large body of statewide test evidence will reveal a continuing leveling out or upward trend. As already indicated, the SAT scores, which are based on a relatively unchanging test, fell again in 1976, so if the trend in achievement had started to bottom out, the effects had not yet reached the high school juniors and seniors. The author and the main contributor to this book both "feel" that academic achievement scores are, or will soon be, bottoming out. But at least in my case, this feeling is based largely on a belief in the system in this country that I feel will cause, or is already causing, actions such as discussed in this book, which should tend to turn the situation around. Failure to pressure for initiating or continuing such actions, however, could, in my opinion, significantly delay or even preclude a general improvement in academic achievement.

An examination of the general IQ of the United States public over time, based largely on "mental competence" tests of Army draftees, shows a great increase in the average IQ level, according to the Army's alpha test, between World War I and World War II. There may be a relationship between this increase in IQ and the rise in academic achievement of high school freshmen in the 1930s (these men would have been in the service in 1943); but, though the samples are smaller, the Army General Classification Test scores of draftees since 1948 show no such fluctuations to coincide with the fluctuations in academic achievement since the 1930s. Some recent but short-term data from one state do show a consistent and, in total, significant drop in average IQ for pupils, particularly for the students in the upper IQ range, over the first few years of the 1970s. Over the past decade, however, the average IQ of our pupils, nationally, apparently did not fall as their achievement scores did.

Throughout this most recent period of academic decline, although there was much emphasis on the need for more money for education, we could find no positive correlation between spending trends and trends in pupil academic achievement.

As in other such surveys, including those of the city of New York, we could not find correlations between a lower student/teacher ratio and higher achievement. In fact, since the mid-1960s, nationally, the reverse trend has generally been true; as student/teacher ratios dropped, achievement dropped, too. There was also no relation between the age of school buildings or even money spent per pupil and academic achievement. In fact, as money spent increased at an ever-faster rate since the mid-sixties, achievement consistently fell. The districts that were holding their own during this period often spent much less per pupil than those experiencing severe declines. West Virginia, for example, spends less than half what New York spends per pupil, and also less than California.

There continued to be a difference in achievement between children from affluent and those from lower-income districts, but traditionally there also has usually been a significant difference in average IQ of students from such diverse areas. The better-educated, better-paid parents with higher IQ tend to cluster in the more affluent neighborhoods—which may largely explain the higher *average* IQ offspring. When comparing *like* neighborhoods and school districts, or the *same* school districts today with themselves in the mid-1960s, however, we find that as more money has been spent, academic achievement has generally declined. In fact, historically, there has not been a standard pattern of achievement score trends related to spending; during the 1950s achievement went up along with increased spending per pupil, but in the past decade, when even more money was spent, the achievement scores declined with alarming consistency.

The same difficulty arises with the argument that the "changing pupil population," together with a lack of education funds, are the causes of pupils being unable to handle the fundamentals and of the disruption in our schools.

We began by examining the urban school systems at the beginning of this century, the last period when large numbers of predominantly rural people swarmed into our northern cities. During this time, northern-city schools saw vast numbers of pupils who spoke no English. In New York 53 percent of the children came from families where no English was spoken, and 72 percent of the city's entire population was first- or second-generation immigrants. Similar situations existed in Philadelphia, Chicago, Cleveland, Boston, Milwaukee, and Buffalo, as well as many smaller coal, iron, and mill cities throughout the East. Most of these new arrivals were Polish, Italian, and primarily Jewish Russian peasants and village dwellers. The majority of their children were over age for the school grade they were in, and in the cities mentioned the heads of families of these pupils earned lower salaries than those of any other large identifiable group of citizens.

Classrooms housed up to eighty or ninety pupils. Teachers were from earlier immigrant groups but spoke only English in class and often as not are said to have despised the unwashed newcomers. Yet the schools upheld the standards and taught the essential subjects of middle-class America. The pupils learned to read and write, and learned basic grammar, arithmetic, history, and geography by the sixth grade—which was as far as most children went in those days. With little but our educational system to help them, Americans of Russian, Polish, and Italian descent, within about two generations, had the highest incomes of any racial or ethnic groups in the country, and their level of education equaled or exceeded the average for the country as a whole.

The Great Depression era again saw high student/teacher ratios (about 30 to 1); many schools with second-generation immigrants whose parents couldn't speak English (and those who could had generally gone only to the sixth grade); and little money for education "specialists" or for schools in general. Yet pupils who couldn't read by the seventh grade in those days were virtually unknown. They could also do long division, knew history, geography, could write compositions, and scored some of the highest grades on ninth-grade academic achievement tests we have ever seen. Most states had strictly enforced laws that kept pupils in school until they were sixteen, but these big, tough kids were orderly, for slum, or mining patch, behavior, grammar, and dress were left at the schoolyard gate. Middle-class standards were maintained, and even "Manual Arts" program students had to take and pass one year of algebra, one year of geometry, two years of a foreign language, three years of real history, and four years of English, including composition and American and English literature. During World War II, these were the boys who had those high aptitude test scores. After the war, when the GI bill gave hundreds of thousands of them a chance at college, they were ready—and they had one of the most consistent records of high academic achievement in the history of American higher education, despite the very crowded conditions and the spectacularly high professor/student ratios.

During the 1940s, a period of relative affluence and increasing expenditures for grade and high schools, there began a de-emphasis of specific disciplines and subject matter and increasing emphasis on educating "the whole child," as in the work-study programs where pupils spent less time in school and more time on part-time jobs, for which they were given academic credit. The "innovators" were enjoying considerable influence, but by 1950 obvious low student achievement had sparked a reaction by parents, taxpayers, academicians, and responsible educators, and the "innovative" movement collapsed.

During the 1950s, expenditures on schools continued to rise and pupil/teacher ratios to fall, but the schools tended to return to normal, and academic achievement rose rapidly until the mid-1960s.

During the 1960s, the moderates in our school system lost their prominence and some apparently injudicious activist educators gained influence and began once more to alter the standard educational curriculums, structure, and teaching methods. When achievement and behavior happened to begin to deteriorate in the mid-1960s, educators found they often had a sympathetic audience among the media, and even school boards, when they tried to direct the search for the reasons outside the schools. This sympathetic attitude may have been a spinoff from the Kennedy era and later emphasis on such programs as the "War on Poverty," which were receiving so much attention at the time. In any event, the home and neighborhood "environmentalists" were influential in many schools of education and local, state, and federal education establishments.

These critics, many of them members of a school system that had successfully educated children who emerged from the unspeakably impoverished conditions of the immigrant slums and the Great Depression, suddenly said this system was incapable of teaching the fundamentals to children from comparatively much better economic conditions. The same school system that had taught the fundamentals to the children of immigrants from provinces in southern Italy where from 67 to 79 percent of the adult populations could not read or write Italian, now presumably could not do the same for children of native-born American in-migrants, all of whom spoke English and most of whom were at least literate. The critics even complained of a parental lack of concern, though public opinion surveys show attitudes of parents and the public as a whole unchanged from those of similar adults in the past. When a relatively few Spanish-speaking pupils appeared, many educators claimed that our school system could not function without "English as a second language" programs; yet this is a system within which teachers who spoke only English traditionally had taken in their stride up to half a dozen different tongues among their pupils. Furthermore, this school system, which over the decades had used teachers from earlier immigrant groups of vastly different ethnic and racial backgrounds to teach the newer ones, was now said to be incapable of teaching the new in-migrants without teachers of the same race and ethnicity.

Perhaps worst of all, many educators broke a cardinal rule of the past: they opened the schoolyard gate to the language, grammar, habits, dress, and values of the slums. Middle-class values, correct grammar and word usage, careful, meticulous arithmetical operations, even the banning of gutter language, were no longer stressed as much as they once were. Some teachers emulated the slum students in language, habits, and dress, and many told the other students these just represented another, and presumably equally valuable, culture. The bad grammar and habits spread to all groups; permissiveness caused disruptive conditions in suburban schools and violence entered the core-city schools. This was a particularly bad time for the school to let down its guard. Other restraints outside the school were being weakened, and acceptance of improper behavior, and even some types of criminal acts, were becoming commonplace. Adults, even police, could be ignored with impunity. In underprivileged urban areas, hustlers, pimps, loafers, and prostitutes lived off the community with less pressure on them from the authorities than there had been in decades. Furthermore, many teachers began to treat children as if they were little adults and had the experience and judgment of grown-ups; they yielded to them the responsibility of determining when, if, and, within a disturbingly questionable range, even what they would study.

The cutting edge of this whole movement was the class of "innovator" writers on education of the late 1960s and early 1970s. Some saw the current problems as unique and invulnerable to any past approaches to solution. Many attacked everything from homework and rote learning to curriculums that included the standard academic disciplines. They again were out to "educate the whole child"—they used the same terms as the 1940s "innovators." Tending to undervalue middle-class standards and having seemingly lost their perspective on the role of the school, they apparently underrated the effect of lowering academic standards, and put social engineering on a level with teaching basic academic skills.

The popularity of these writers among certain educators and others, and much of the trend in education in the late 1960s and early 1970s, may not stem entirely from the seductive logic of their philosophy. For many less than totally responsible educators (which, of course, excludes the many good teachers) were quick to learn that down this road lay the good life. With no one looking closely at what was happening in the schools, it was possible to press the point that if the public wanted "quality education," more money would be needed. If, after spending much more money, the quality wasn't there, it was because, on the one hand, we still weren't spending enough and, on the other, we as parents weren't doing enough for our children. The home and neighborhood environment were to blame.

In writing this study, we found that many of the accepted clichés regarding outside causes of poor pupil performance will simply not stand the light of day. The lack-of-money claim faded long ago. Given the recent series of spectacular budgets and costs per pupil, we find it difficult to agree that those who felt we could simply spend our way out of our difficulties have not had their day in court. The arguments that place the primary blame on the home conditions of the underprivileged pupils also fade considerably when we look at the much worse conditions of past slum children who did learn. The same holds true for parental attitudes of present and past slum children. To both, basic education was and is viewed as a means to upward mobility; and though today's underprivileged parents may be ill-equipped to help their children with difficult schoolwork, so were such parents in the past. Significantly, the traditionally underprivileged state of West Virginia does well, and on comparatively little money. Furthermore, slum children also do well through the third or fourth grade; their blighted backgrounds should show up before then.

Most illuminating is the greater drop in achievement among students from more affluent homes full of books and encyclopedias, with parents with college educations, good vocabularies, and all the other advantages. Interested parents will attest that many schools only want parental involvement to the extent that they underwrite the actions of the educators. Pressing for detailed information on what the study program is and what is going on in the classroom, or even on how one's underachieving child is doing, is often likely to get the response that the parent is too "grade conscious," and worse.

Of course, there have always been parents, some of them very vocal activists, who have made less than reasonable demands. But the great majority have consistently, though perhaps quietly, pursued a sensible course. Surveys show that three out of four parents, other adults, and high school juniors and seniors as well, want national achievement tests given to local students so that they can be compared with students in other school districts. A large majority also want teachers to be held responsible for students' progress and to be paid on the basis of quality. By about three to one, adults also disapprove of teacher tenure; most, but far from all, professional educators differ with the public at least on this issue.

Parents and other adults have wanted children to be taught the basics, and recently they have been demanding more discipline in the schools. No one wants school to be an unnecessarily harsh or unhappy place, but people also see schooling as a serious enterprise. They see education as the way to a better life and have been consistent in their far from ill-conceived ideas about schooling over the years.

The recent search outside our educational system for the causes of its ills can, and apparently in many cases may have, result in important indirect effects inside the school. Perhaps this should not in itself be surprising. Some educators' objectivity is likely to suffer if they are left to choose whether to lay the blame for poor pupil achievement at the school's doorstep, and take on much additional hard work with increasingly annoyed children, or to suggest that the fault lies elsewhere, or even that the children are learning a lot but the tests given them are inappropriate.

For those less-responsible educators, the approach makes sense. Blaming the parents, the neighborhood, the "establishment," or other external factors for children's inability allows one to rationalize continuing "rap sessions" with the pupils, which is a lot easier than developing and carrying out a structured instruction program. One can show a movie rather than have the children write a theme, which a teacher must correct. One can just give them the "concepts" in math and science rather than the many homework problems necessary for correctly using the concepts—problems that must also be corrected by teachers. Similar excuses can be used to avoid quizzes and tests, which many teachers don't like to correct, staying after school to help a child who is behind, or even having pupils spend time at the blackboard during class so that the teacher can find out who is behind and give quick, individual attention. Obviously, with a much less demanding process, the children, too, have a much easier time. Furthermore, teachers often make "general criteria reference" judgments about how much certain children are capable of learning, although we have seen no general drop in their average IQ. The children then are not pushed to learn beyond a level previously decided on by the educator.

These don't look like bad ideas at first glance, but they can give less-than-dedicated teachers an out when it begins to take much hard work for them to teach increasingly difficult subject matter. There is always the temptation —and it is much easier for both teacher and pupil—to say that the pupil inherently can go no higher. These days some schools grade on general criteria reference factors, giving a pupil the same satisfactory marks in a subject for achieving much less than other pupils and thus promoting him through the grades. Perhaps as troubling is the not infrequent practice of general inflation of marks, which has led to some unrealistic expectations and bitter disappointments for many ill-prepared high school graduates.

Now that "work/study" programs and reducing the compulsory age of schooling are being brought up again, we may see the difficult-to-teach children, including late-bloomers, simply being tossed out by the less conscientious educators.

Without close scrutiny of activities inside the schools, educators can also resort to expensive but unproductive gimmickry, and can claim to be wrestling with the school problems, rather than face difficult education issues head on. "Modular scheduling," "open classrooms," "classrooms without walls," "nongraded schools"—these are sometimes heralded as great, new, and exhausting, efforts by educators to raise our children's achievement.

But although some people, many educators among them, prefer to look outside the school for the causes of our problems with education, we feel that looking inside the schools will be more rewarding, both from the point of view of improving academic achievement and reducing costs. The recent drops in achievement of the same children as they go up through the grades have occurred so suddenly that their parents, home life, environment, or any outside factor are highly unlikely to have been the causes. Most indications seem to point toward curriculum changes and lowering of standards. For example, the academic curriculum of Manual Arts students in the 1930s, outlined earlier, is no longer required of high school students in many states. Low-academic-content electives and grade-school-level arithmetic take up dwindling high school time once spent on the more difficult disciplines. Throughout the school system, moreover, fewer hours per day and fewer days per year are spent in school, and even less time on demanding academic subjects. Lowering standards in the schools is one thing that *could* lower achievement rapidly; if we demand less, children most likely quickly achieve less.

One of the most discouraging facets of this issue is that over the past decade many schools have tended to educate children for a nonexistent world. Certain things in life simply cannot be avoided or blamed on someone else; actions have personal consequences; outside the school environment one normally has to produce to be promoted; work must satisfy the needs of the economy to be profitable to the worker; many trades and professions require work that gives no credit for good intentions or being nearly accurate—much work, and advanced study, must be explicit, meticulous, and correct every time; it is important to be well-informed and logical, not just spontaneous and talkative; and not everything is relative. Furthermore, young people's ideas, too, can often be simply incorrect and even worthless.

But we the citizens and parents pay for the schools; we control them; and with the more responsible, and often frustrated, educators, we can change them. Through pressure on our school boards and our elected local, state, and federal officials, we can influence those who run our education systems to concentrate on the output of our schools—our children's academic competence. We must, however, know enough about the educational process to sort out the competent, dedicated educators from the not-so-dedicated, and to cut through the jargon and get the pertinent information.

We must know how to find out how our schools are progressing on the basis of student achievement, usually according to trends in standardized achievement test scores.

We must determine, in detail, what is being done in our schools: what the curriculums are like; how much teacher-corrected writing, mathematics homework, and other specific work is assigned; and whether standards of learning and behavior are being maintained or improved.

We must know how to find out what the spectacular amounts of money used by our school districts are being spent for; how to determine if specific types of heavy spending are related to academic achievement; how to influence our superintendents and school boards before they present us with virtually unchangeable budgets, locked in by contracts; how to counteract their often questionable claims of huge amounts of "mandated" monies over which the parents-voters-taxpayers have no control.

If the student makeup has not altered and achievement scores are down, and particularly if costs per pupil in constant dollars are up, the school district should take a close look at its curriculums, teaching methods, and even its administrative and instructional personnel. For the welfare of the children must be considered first, then that of the parents and taxpayers, and then of other interested parties.

Equally important, we must know enough about what can be, and traditionally has been, expected of our school system and its personnel, so we can support our position and get the actions we need before too many more children pay the price of inadequate educational systems. That is what this book is about.

1

SCHOOL BUDGETS

Much about the innovations in our school systems over the recent past is unclear. What is clear, however, is that education has become increasingly and alarmingly expensive. The local, state, and federal expenditures on public and private primary and secondary education in the United States rose from $6.7 billion in 1950 to approximately $75 billion by 1976.

ELEMENTARY AND SECONDARY SCHOOL EXPENDITURES, 1950-1976

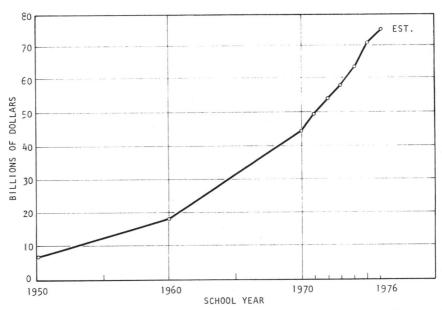

SOURCES: U.S. Census Bureau, *U.S. Stat. Abst.: 1975*, p. 111, table 176. HEW, *Dig. of Educ. Stat.: 1975*, p. 24, table 21.*

*Throughout the book the following abbreviations have been used:
Dig. of Educ. Stat.: Digest of Education Statistics
HEW: U.S. Department of Health, Education and Welfare
U.S. Census Bureau: U.S. Bureau of the Census
U.S. Stat. Abst.: Statistical Abstract of the U.S.

While expenditures increased more than tenfold during this period, student enrollment rose only from 28.6 to 49.6 million. Indeed, since 1970, total enrollment has been declining.

PUBLIC AND PRIVATE ELEMENTARY AND SECONDARY
SCHOOL ENROLLMENT, 1950-1975

Sources: U. S. Census Bureau, *U. S. Stat. Abst.: 1975,* p. 111, table 175, HEW, Dig. of Educ. Stat.: 1975, p. 6, table 1; *1974,* p. 6, table 1.

Furthermore, between 1960 and the 1975–76 school year, when elementary and secondary student enrollment increased from 42 to 49.6 million, a gain of only 18.1 percent, the expenditures rose from $18 billion to an estimated $75 billion, a gain of 317 percent.[1]

The largest part of this expenditure of course is, and has been, for public schools: $67.9 billion in the 1975–76 school year to educate 44.94 million children, or $1,511 per pupil.[2] In the 1974–75 school year it was $1,431.[3]

Private schools are estimated (fall 1975) to have spent $6.9 billion for 4.67 million children, or $1,477 per pupil.[4] By far the largest single group of private school students attend less expensive Catholic parochial schools, at an estimated cost per elementary school pupil for the 1972–73 school year of about $310. Catholic high schools, which contain less than one fourth of parochial school pupils, had a per pupil cost for the same school year of about $700.[5]

The average cost per pupil in current dollars for public schools in 1973–1974 was $1,364; in 1950–51 it was about $227, which in constant 1973–74 dollars is the equivalent of $490. Costs per pupil, in constant dollars, rose

TOTAL EXPENDITURES PER PUPIL IN AVERAGE DAILY ATTENDANCE IN PUBLIC SCHOOLS, 1929-1930 to 1973-74, IN CONSTANT DOLLARS

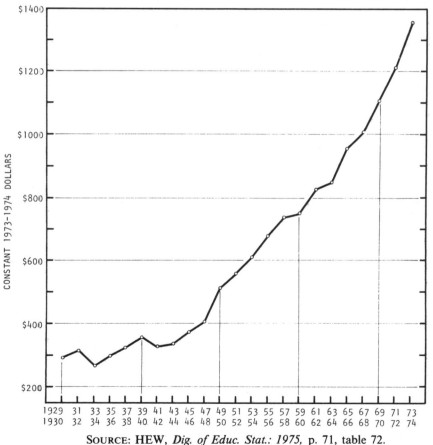

SOURCE: HEW, *Dig. of Educ. Stat.: 1975,* p. 71, table 72.

over 61 percent in the ten years between the 1963–64 and 1973–74 school years alone.[6]

The increase in educational expenditures in the country—including higher education, that is college—has truly been spectacular. In percent of GNP it rose from 3.4 in 1950 to over 8.0 percent in the 1971–72 school year.

TOTAL EXPENDITURES FOR EDUCATION AS A PERCENTAGE OF THE GNP: UNITED STATES, 1929-30 TO 1971-72

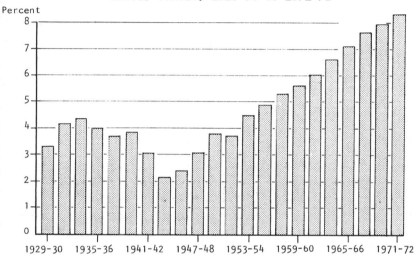

The large percentage of the GNP spent on education in 1930–41 was the result of the plummeting GNP. Even though the World War I baby boom was swelling school population to unprecedented proportions, expenditures on education, like all spending, actually decreased compared to the 1920s.
NOTE: Reprinted from HEW's *Dig. of Educ. Stat.: 1975,* p. 25.

The cost for 1974 was 7.8 percent of the GNP.[7] In 1971, costs of all types of education, including higher education, passed those of national defense; the Department of Defense budget was $77.7 billion, while education costs were $83.3 billion.[8] The estimated 1976–77 expenditures for all types of education were $130.3 billion,[9] and for national defense, $104 billion. An estimate for 1975–76 expenditures for primary and secondary schools alone was $75 billion.[10]

The trend toward increased expenditures has been strongest in the densely populated, industrialized northern areas. In New York State between 1951 and 1976, expenditures on primary and secondary public education rose from about $800 million[11] to a figure that may be as high as $8 billion.[12] During 1973–74, expenditures were $6.93 billion.[13] This increase was at a considerably higher rate than for the nation as a whole. In New

York State enrollment in the public schools rose from about 2 million[14] to about 3.52 million between 1951 and 1972.[15] In 1974–75 this figure was 3.43 million.[16] Yearly expenditures per pupil rose from about $400 in 1951 to $2,241 in 1974–75.[17]

California, in the 1974–75 school year, spent $1,373 per pupil; Connecticut, $1,596; Illinois, $1,637; Massachusetts, $1,504; Michigan, $1,770; New Jersey, $1,713; Ohio, $1,270; Pennsylvania, $1,587. The national average was $1,431. New York had the highest cost per pupil of any state, including Alaska, which spent $2,228.[18] For reasons that will become apparent later, it is interesting to note that for the 1974–75 school year, West Virginia spent $1,020 per student, Nebraska $1,378 per student, Iowa $1,400, and South Dakota $1,062.[19]

In downstate suburban areas of New York State, 1975–76 budgets reflect a spectacular rise in costs. The average cost per pupil per year for primary and secondary public schools, including kindergarten, is now about $3,000 or more. The secondary, or high school, portion of these budgets, therefore, must reflect a cost of about $4,000 per pupil,[20] which is close to tuition costs at our most prestigious universities, such as Harvard, Yale, Princeton, and Columbia. Even considering the endowments of these latter schools, this is an impressive figure for high school tuition. Nor is this pattern confined to New York State.

We are all aware of the large, and some say excessive, number of new schools that have been built in recent years to meet both the increased student body and the drive for smaller classes. They are often lavishly equipped. The author once delivered a lecture in a huge, extremely expensive auditorium theater in a New York State high school that was superior to most on Broadway, then retired to a principal's office with appointments and decor more luxurious than is to be found in many a corporation executive's Fifth Avenue office. There is no evidence that this is completely atypical for new high schools in the suburban areas of industrialized states.

We are also aware of the proliferation of electronic and other gadgets in the schools, as in one school in Washington, D.C. with 247 children, grades three through six, in twelve classrooms, that Mark Arnold writes had ". . . 10 television sets, 10 filmstrip projectors, 3 overhead projectors, 4 calculators, 10 record players, 1 copy machine and 2 primer typewriters."[21] In 1971 HEW investigators "charged that 'considerable amounts of equipment' had been purchased through Title I with 'no evidence' that it contributed to meeting the needs of Title I children."[22]

Such activities help expand the great costs of capital outlay. According to an HEW report, they accounted for $4.5 billion of a $45.5 billion primary and secondary school budget for 1970–71, with plant operation accounting for $3.1 billion and interest on debts $1.3 billion.[23]

But these expenses, though large, often excessive, and even unnecessary, are small compared to the huge and greatly increasing amounts of money spent on instructional and administrative staff salaries and benefits. With the decrease of school-age children and the closing of schools we see today, school construction and even maintenance should not increase significantly in the near future. Increases in future costs, even more than in the past, will reflect increases in costs of salaries. These salaries, therefore, are worth examining.

In 1973–74, out of the total $56.97 billion expenditure in the United States for public primary and secondary education, $32.61 billion went for "instruction" (teachers' salaries), almost $2.28 billion for "administration"

TEACHERS IN PUBLIC ELEMENTARY AND SECONDARY SCHOOLS, 1955-1975

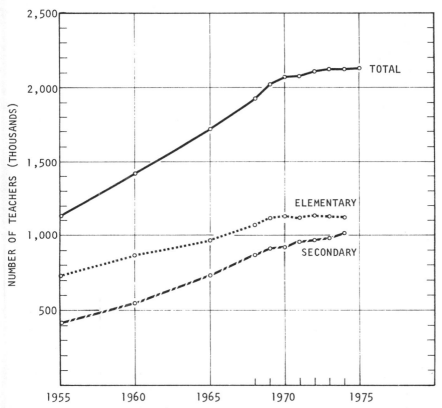

SOURCES: U.S. Census Bureau, *U.S. Stat. Abst.: 1975,* p. 129, table 212. HEW, *Dig. of Educ. Stat.: 1975,* pp. 49, 50.

(mostly for salaries of school superintendents and assistants, but some also for intermediate administrators, state commissioners, and assistants), and almost $5.63 billion for "fixed charges,"[24] which includes a lot for fringe benefits for the instructional and administrative staffs.

These numbers reflect two factors: the number of teachers and the average salary and fringe benefits per teacher. The number of teachers employed is indicated on the previous graph.

New York State's per pupil expenditure in 1973–74 on instruction (teachers' salaries $1,078) and administration ($78) was far higher than that of other states. Her nearest competitors were New Jersey, $874 and $56; Connecticut, $873 and $44; and California, $822 and $61. In fixed charges per enrolled pupil New York, with $310, surpassed the other industrial states by an even wider margin: Pennsylvania $166, New Jersey $159, California $141, Connecticut $134, Illinois $113.[25] As mentioned earlier, these charges in part reflect fringe benefits to teachers. In New York a pension plan accounts for the lion's share; it was already $94 per pupil in 1965–66.[26]

Overall, the increased costs are often likely to result from factors such as the number of pupils per teacher in a given school—which usually have no proven effect on pupils' academic achievement. The student/teacher ratio is not the number of pupils assigned to a classroom teacher, but the number of pupils in a building divided by the number of teachers in that building, including all nonclassroom teachers; this is a very different thing.[27] Nationally, as a result of the greater percentage increase in teachers than in pupils over the years and, recently, due to a drop in school enrollment that was not accompanied by an equivalent percentage decrease in teachers, the student/teacher ratio has continued to fall.

In New York, the number of professional staff per 1,000 students rose from 44.5 in 1951 to 61.2 in 1971, or one such staff member for every 16.3 pupils. Principals and assistant principals are included in these figures. The absolute number of such staff members in New York State in 1951 was 86,000. In 1971 it was 213,000.[28] By the 1973–74 school year this pupil/teacher ratio had fallen to 15.9 pupils enrolled per instruction staff member. This is one staff member for every 13.7 children in average daily attendance. The instructional staff had risen to 217,489.[29] New York State has a higher ratio of instructional staff to pupils than any of the states listed earlier and, with the exception of Alaska, pays instructional staff more than any other state in the union.

In New York City, in fall 1973, there was one teacher for every 18.4 pupils enrolled, and one teacher for every 15.0 pupils in average daily attendance (note the high absenteeism), while the national average was one teacher for every 21.4 pupils in enrollment and 19.8 pupils in average daily attendance.[30] If we were to add the thousands of principals and assistant

NATIONAL PUBLIC ELEMENTARY AND SECONDARY SCHOOL STUDENT-TEACHER
RATIO, 1929-30 to 1974-75

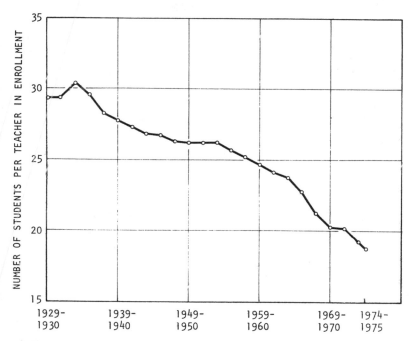

SOURCES: HEW, *Dig. of Educ. Stat.: 1975*, pp. 6 (table 1), 49; 1973,
pp. 33-35. HEW, *Statistics of State School Systems: 1969-70*, pp. 5, 7.
HEW, *Stat. of Pub. Elementary & Secondary Day Schools: Fall, 1973*, pp. 12, 14, 16.

principals, consultants and supervisors of instruction, librarians, guidance
and psychological personnel, and other nonsupervisory, instructional personnel—to say nothing of security personnel and the like—we would no
doubt find that the staff had begun to approach one instructional employee,
or at least one adult employee, for every 10 or 12 public school pupils in
average daily attendance. For the 1974–75 school year, the estimated average salary for instructional staff in New York State was $15,000, while the
national estimated average was about $12,070.[31]

Educators' salaries—that is, salaries of teachers, principals, and supervisors—are about 20 percent above the overall national average for all workers, "$12,070 versus $9,400 in the 1974–75 school year."[32] The average
salaried "professional, technical, and kindred" man, including salaried
physicians and surgeons, earned $14,139 in 1973, and the salaried profes-
sional woman earned $9,103. Male primary and secondary school teachers

earned $12,019 in 1973 and female teachers, who comprise two-thirds of the force, earned $9,108.[33] Other professional people, however, work different amounts of time for their salary. Teachers have extended Christmas and spring vacations as well as all holidays and the entire summer free. This is so because of the way our schools function and in no way reflects any connivance by school instructional staff. Indeed many teachers so supplement their salaries by working on other jobs during the summer that their yearly days worked approach those of the average worker. On the other hand—and important from the viewpoint of the taxpayer—the adequacy of the remuneration from the taxpayer for time spent rendering teaching service is often challenged by educators and others.

It may be of interest to note how teachers' salaries compare with those of all college graduates on a day-for-day, money-earned basis. The average college-educated person must be at his place of business approximately 240 days a year, 8 hours a day. The national average school term is 178.7 days per year.[34] Instructional personnel in our schools are supposed to work approximately 6 hours a day. Many teachers actually teach an average of only 4 hours a day, while few teach more than 6, even including extra teaching assignments. In the 1971–72 school year, in upstate New York, time taken off by teachers—"particularly before and after weekends"—reduced teaching days by another 2.5 percent, or four and one half days, on the average. In New York City in the 1972–73 school year, it was 6 percent[35]—almost 11 days. Even if we assume that all teachers work all the required days, use any free time during the day, and spend up to an additional 2 hours daily at home doing school-related work (averaging an 8-hour day 5 days a week), the time spent by nonteacher college graduates on the job is still about one-third more than on-the-job time for teachers. So the $10,100 national average salary for teachers and principals for the year beginning in September 1971[36] was earned, in the overwhelming majority of cases, at a daily rate equal to $13,433 for a full year's work, which apparently compared favorably with the average yearly income for all college graduates, $13,200 in 1971.[37] This trend apparently continued with the estimated average teacher's salary of $12,070 in September of 1974,[38] a daily salary rate equivalent to that of a $16,053 yearly salary, compared to $16,494 for all college graduates for that year. The 1974 income breakdown for all full-time workers with college degrees in the United States was: males, $18,751; females, $10,382.[39]

The average age of that segment of college graduates found among educators is likely to be lower than that of members of other professions, for though the number of college graduates rose by about 5 percent between 1960 and 1971,[40] the number of grade and high school teachers rose by 90 percent.[41] In 1964, 16.9 percent of public elementary school teachers had only one to three years of experience, and 14.3 percent had only 4 to 6 years' experience. In 1974, those figures had risen to 19.3 and 21.8 percent. In the

INCOME, ALL COLLEGE GRADUATES, 1974

	4 Years College	5 Years College or More	Combined Average of 4/5 Years College
18-24-year-olds			
Males:	$ 8,800	*	$ 8,868
Females:	7,297	*	7,282
25-year-olds and older			
Males:	$18,011	$20,582 (46.0%)	$19,198
Females:	9,975	11,962 (36.0%)	10,787

*Full-time employees in this peer group with 5 or more years of college represented a base of less than 75,000 for the country.

SOURCE: U.S. Census Bureau, *Current Population Reports,* Jan. 1976, "Money Income in 1974 of Families and Persons in the U.S.," pp. 113–14, 116–20.

same time period, those with twenty or more years' experience dropped in elementary schools from 31.8 percent to 17.2 percent. The median years of experience dropped from 12 to 8.[42] The fact that teachers are likely to be younger on the average than other college graduates is significant, for, as we have seen, among all college graduates in the country the older people drive the average up. Even the over-24 group is significantly higher in salary than those below 24.

This brings us to a subject that, in my judgment, is raised too often these days—the years of higher education and even the average intelligence of primary and secondary school teachers. Regardless of teachers' *average* academic achievement—and even IQ—they number in their group many very intelligent, capable, and dedicated people, though, as we shall see later, there seems to be evidence that the number of such teachers is dwindling. In any event, one is well advised not to count academic achievement and IQ alone as measurements of teaching ability. Teachers require personalities suitable for dealing with often trying youngsters, as well as the ability to impart their knowledge to someone else—an ability obviously absent in many very intelligent people. On the other hand, since this topic of teachers' higher education, particularly years of graduate school, is often brought up by educators and may even be considered as a basis for comparison of salaries of teachers and other college graduates, we perhaps should touch on it.

Teachers still seem to have less graduate school work than the average

American college graduate. In 1974 among all male working college graduates, 46 percent had five or more years of college; among all working female college graduates, the number was 36.0 percent.[43] For the same year, among working teachers the figure for males was 50.8 percent and for females 32 percent.[44] But women outnumber men by about two to one on our public school instructional staffs,[45] so overall this averages out to about 38.3 percent of *all* teachers having five or more years of college. Among *all* working college graduates, men outnumber women by three to one. The whole group averages out to 43.5 percent with five or more years of college. For college-educated workers this is significant as far as income is concerned. For example, among the 25- to 34-year-old group of male college graduates working full time, the average income for those with undergraduate degrees was $13,582, while for those with five or more years of college, it was $16,176. For women, the comparable figures were $9,126 and $10,811.[46]

Some would argue that comparing university school of education graduates, to say nothing of state teachers college graduates, with graduates in other fields from other colleges and universities is misleading. Institutions of higher learning that educate potential teachers vary, as do any other schools; some are better than others, and it is wrong to condemn them all. It seems true, however, that the school of education in any given university, particularly among those of higher academic standing, is not likely to rank high scholastically among schools within that university. One also gets the impression that the average scholastic aptitude of students in these schools of education is normally low among the disciplines at any given college or university. There apparently may be more to this suspicion of average relative scholastic weakness among education majors than the almost universal impression of those who have attended college. After some comparison of statistics, James B. Conant concluded emphatically (in italics) in 1963, "... *it is clear that in many institutions many of those graduated as teachers must have scholastic aptitudes well below that of the top 30 per cent of the graduating high school class on a national basis.*" He adds, "This corresponds to my observations on the intellectual level of the bottom portion of the class preparing to be teachers in certain institutions."[47] One must remember that in this time period, less than 30 percent of those graduating from high school graduated from college; for example, 1.9 million people graduated from high school in 1960 and only .5 million graduated from college in 1965.[48] To have large numbers of college graduates in a discipline coming from "well below" the upper 30 percent level of high school graduates must place the group as a whole low on the scale of average scholastic aptitude among college graduates.

Even omitting the low-paid college graduates under 25, who comprised an increasing number in this group in recent years and a large segment of teachers, and whose income is counted into the teacher's average salary for

1974, only one category of college graduates under 34—males with five or more years of college[49]—matched the average daily salary rate for teachers, and certainly such income for all college graduate full-time employees between 18 and 34 is considerably below it. Furthermore, if we were to take a sample of all college graduates based upon a mix of men and women of all ages similar to that of instructional staff in primary and secondary schools, the educator's average daily rate of pay would be considerably higher than that of the other college graduates, including those with five or more years of college.

Also, there is a degree of security in a teaching job once a teacher acquires tenure—an almost automatic procedure after a few years of teaching in many school districts[50]—that is hard to measure in dollar value, but is unmatched in the overwhelming number of professional fields. Then there are the fringe benefits, which *are* measurable in dollars, to the taxpayers at least, for they can amount to as much as an additional 30 percent or more of the teacher's salary. The argument, therefore, that in general most teachers would be likely to have trouble getting the kinds of degrees held by most other college graduates with which we are comparing them may, for some purposes, no longer be completely invalid. Such information may be useful when the charge is made that, in general, private industry still stands ready to steal our teachers unless we raise their salaries even higher. In addition, there may be some merit in the argument that the majority of college graduates have led more precarious lives in business and industry. Most have no tenure, and money available for salary is based on company funds that have definite, obvious, and—particularly during dips in the economy—often restrictive limits. Teachers' salaries are based on tax sources and are backed by the power of the state. This situation is most obvious in states like New York, with its nonvoted austerity budgets, where, in effect, taxpayers have little or no opportunity to vote down the constantly escalating teachers' and administrators' salary portions of school budgets.

In any event, although it may once have been so, it apparently is no longer true that, considering their education, talent, and efforts, teachers are vastly underpaid. Furthermore, among large groups of professional employees, teachers hold a unique position. They are not only represented by a powerful National Education Association lobby, which had 1,470,000 members in 1974,[51] but are members of two unions. The combined membership of these three groups, despite some possible overlapping between the unions and the NEA, probably make up the largest group of organized craft workers in the country; they may even outnumber the largest single union in the country, the monster Teamsters Union conglomerate, which had 1,973,000 in 1974.[52] They wield impressive power in local communities, statewide, and nationally. It was estimated by the New York *Times* in 1974 that their campaign contributions that year would exceed $2 million, making them "one of the best financed special interest groups in the nation." Most of the money was said to be earmarked for candidates for state and local offices, but $600,000 to $750,000 would probably go to candidates for Congress. By comparison, "the American Medical Association and its state affiliates, which have long been considered one of the richest of the special interest groups and one of the most powerful lobbies in Washington, gave $475,000 to candidates for Congress in 1972." Senator Pell of Rhode Island was said to owe his position to the teachers, and candidates for local, state, and federal offices across the country seek their money and support.[53] Teachers' organizations have also been known to work through other channels to affect directly the educational process. For example, the New Jersey Education Association, for various reasons, brought suit in court and, apparently, at least temporarily, blocked the release of statewide student achievement test scores for 1973.[54]

Teachers' union locals, represented by tough professional negotiators, often deal with inexperienced, sometimes intimidated, local school boards, whose members cannot get over the idea that they must depend on the "professional educators" to outline "quality education" for the children. In effect, therefore, educators not only exercise absolute control over the union side of the bargaining table, but, wearing their other hat as the only professionals qualified to hold forth on quality education, exert significant influence on the management side. This is truly an odd, perhaps unique, situation in union-management negotiations. Nor are many school superintendents, who are themselves usually educators and ex-teachers, necessarily much help these days, particularly with regard to increases of teacher productivity as measured by student achievement.

In such circumstances, it is little wonder that teachers' union representatives have been so successful in their legitimate mission to get the best possible conditions for their members. The author knows of a board of education that began negotiating with a teachers' union without having developed a negotiating position. They entered the bargaining with no demands on the teachers, but merely an inquiry as to what the teachers wanted. They then tried to whittle down the demands, which probably came in with much whittling cushion. One can but sympathize with those who ask, "Who is looking out for the welfare of the children and the taxpayers?" In many cases, one gets the impression that this consideration may not be of the importance to either party in the negotiations that many think it should be. The same school board just mentioned apparently had never examined the achievement scores of the children and compared them with past performances of the school system, nor examined IQ scores over the years. This elected board was not unique in this respect, it would seem. The time when bad school performance could be blamed on underpaid and overworked teachers seems long past, if it ever existed at all.

There is ample evidence that while the average citizen continued to have high regard for education as a means of upward social and economic mobility, and respect for teachers and the educated person per se, he was becoming pinched for money and perhaps no longer saw exactly eye to eye with some educators. By the 1970s, opinion polls showed he was unwilling to pay more taxes for public schools (1970, 56 percent against, 37 percent for; 1972, 56 percent against, 36 percent for); he wanted national achievement tests to be given and the children of his district compared with others (1970, 75 percent for, 16 percent against); he wanted teachers and administrators held responsible for students' progress (1970, 67 percent for, 21 percent against); and their salaries to be based upon the quality of work rather than a standard scale basis (1970, 58 percent for, 36 percent against); he was in favor of more discipline in the schools (1970, 53 percent for, 35 percent against; 1972, 61 percent for, 28 percent against).[55] His attitude may reflect a reaction to what has recently been happening to pupils. Children's achievement scores, as we shall see, apparently left much to be desired.

2
STUDENT ACHIEVEMENT

A standard question that arises when discussing education is whether students are academically as well equipped today when they leave grade or high school as they were ten or more years ago. At least until recently, the answer was often not readily discernible from newspaper articles that rate individual districts, schools, or classes as being above or below the "national average" in achievement, for though this does indicate a comparative standing of districts or schools at the particular time, it does not indicate how any one district is doing over time, or whether the national average itself has risen or fallen over time.

Actually these national averages today are not current national averages at all; they are averages of the last time an achievement test was developed and/or normed. "Norming" a test consists of selecting a large typical sample of American students—perhaps 200,000—administering the test to them, then getting the distribution of scores from this sample. This very expensive procedure, which costs about $1,000,000, is not done too frequently by testing organizations. The result is that tests administered in 1974 usually were normed in the mid-1960s. Therefore, what one sees in the newspapers, at least up to 1974, is often the comparison of a district or state with the national average of the mid-1960s.

This result has advantages, however, lending itself as it does to longitudinal studies of our school system. As we shall see, it is possible to gather enough data from such tests to produce some rather good evidence as to whether the overall national average in achievement has gone up or down since the tests were last normed. Of course, assuming a state continues to administer the same standardized tests for several consecutive years, the trend in achievement will be quite apparent from the record of the test results. There are indications that many of the standardized tests administered to our children have been, or are going to be, largely rewritten and renormed in the near future, so that the chain of comparative results will be broken for a few years until a new trend line can be established. At least in the past, however, the comparisons of the new raw score distribution for the test with those established years earlier give a trend of the norms themselves. If, for example, a test was normed in 1964 and the fiftieth percentile—that is, 49 percent of students scored below that point and 49 above it—fell on a raw score of 50 answers correct out of 100, and the test was renormed in 1974 and the fiftieth percentile fell on a raw score of 45 answers correct out of 100, the national average can be assumed to have declined about five points on the raw score.

Some states give their own tests, administered only to their own students, which makes comparison to a national average more difficult, but the ability to compare the state to itself over time, of course, still remains.

The real difficulty arises when the content of the tests is changed, which does occur. Despite such breaks in the chain, however, and despite the paucity of data as one goes further back in time, one can still derive a feeling for the trend of scholastic aptitude, or at least expectations of scholastic aptitude, for a given grade or grades. These hints are valuable in many ways, not the least of which is for comparing what they imply with the accepted notions about educational standards. Of course, as standardized testing became more prevalent over the past two decades, data points emerged in such numbers and with such consistency that trends, particularly in state-wide achievement, became much more discernible.

There are those who attack achievement tests on many grounds; they charge, for example, that they are culturally biased and do not test for the correct things. (They normally test for basic verbal and mathematical skills —reading, grammar, word definition, mathematical computation and methodology—and often for social studies and science.) We will not attempt to debate the issue of test validity here since we feel that for our primary purpose, which is to seek trends in average achievement-test results for a vast number of pupils made up of the same cultural groups over the years, the objections are less valid. Despite our awareness of the imperfection of achievement tests and testing, not only are these tests in some sense the only objective evaluators of our schools, but arguments contesting the claim to any validity in the trends they show over time are far from conclusive, particularly in light of other evidence. We therefore examined the data on achievement test results, beginning with "then and now" studies that have gone back into the history of our schools to recover tests given "then" and administered the tests "now" to students in the same grades.

3

A LONGITUDINAL STUDY
OF ACADEMIC ACHIEVEMENT
by Paul Bracken

One of the earliest comparisons between pupils of different times resulted from the readministration in 1919 of a test originally given to the top eighth-grade students in selected Boston schools of 1845. The pupils tested in 1845 were attempting to win an "honors medal." The 1919 comparison group was unselected but again was made up of eighth graders from Boston as well as several other cities. The test contained sections on history, geography, arithmetic, grammar, definitions, natural philosophy (that is, the sciences), and astronomy. For obvious reasons this test proved hard to administer to eighth graders in 1919. In fact, the 1919 test contained only 18 percent of the questions asked on the 1845 version. A full 82 percent of the original questions were screened from the test primarily because they were too difficult for the 1919 children.[1] The test results indicated that the 1919 group had a median score 21 percent higher than the Boston children of 1845.[2] Although this exam was designed for honor students, the belief among many that today's youngsters or even current honor students are more knowledgeable than same-grade children or honor students of a hundred years ago is unconvincing.

The next comparisons of changes in educational achievement stem from several studies of reading ability.

PREWAR READING ACHIEVEMENT COMPARATIVE STUDIES

Period	Indicator	Achievement Changes
1924/1934	Woods study of grade 6	+ 6 months [*]
1927/1939	Davis and Morgan study of grade 6	+ 2 months[†]
1916/1938	Boss study of grades 2-8	- gains in grades 4-8[‡]

[*]Reprinted from Elizabeth L. Woods, as cited in Gerberich, p. 346.
[†]Reprinted from Percy R. Davis and M. Evan Morgan, as cited in Gerberich, p. 346.
[‡]Reprinted from Mabel E. Boss, *School and Society* 51 (1940), pp. 62-63.

From the foregoing table it seems that school achievement was rising in the 1920s and 1930s—progress was being made. An interesting feature, however, is that in the Boss study, which compared about 9,000 1916 St. Louis children with approximately 1,100 1938 St. Louis pupils, the 1916 pupils outscored those of 1938. The results, of course, are not necessarily true for the nation as a whole. However, it would be risky to say they are not representative, for experience has shown, at least in recent years, that achievement generally fluctuates nationally in the same way that it does locally. The mean scores for the 1916–38 St. Louis students are:

AVERAGE SILENT READING QUALITY SCORES 1916 and 1938

Grade	2	3	4	5	6	7	8
1916	37	45	34	38	44	30	34
1938	38	45	29	28	36	24	31

Source: Mabel E. Boss, *School and Society* 51 (1940), pp. 62-63.

Since it is difficult to rely on old data when we do not know the detailed experimental design, we are fortunate that the trend between 1916 and 1938 for all grades above grade 3 is obvious. It seems plausible that reading achievement in 1916 was superior to that in the late 1930s.

If we accept that achievement was higher in 1916 than in 1938 and that it was lower in the 1920s than in the 1930s, even though it appears it was increasing in the second half of the 1920s, then there appears to have been a trough between 1916 and the mid-1920s. Unfortunately, we have no more data on this, making it impossible to pinpoint this fascinating social indicator. It is just as likely that 1916 was on a declining trend as it is that it was a peak year, but it is not so likely that it was increasing, unless the drop was precipitous just prior to 1924.

A gain in reading ability as measured by achievement tests was found in a study of Lincoln, Nebraska, that compared 1921 pupils with those of 1947.[3] These gains were recorded for students in grades 4 through 7 who, at identical grade positions in 1947, were from six to eight months younger than their counterparts in 1921.

There seems to be a broad consensus of education opinion that large gains in achievement were made in the 1920s and 1930s. For example, Arthur Gates, a renowned specialist in reading achievement, in describing the gains found in Lincoln, Nebraska, in the 1921–1947 comparison study, notes:

It is possible that the greater gains shown by the Lincoln study in comparison with those obtained in the present one are a valid illustration of what some students of reading have suspected, namely that the period from say 1920 to 1935, or thereabouts, was one in which relatively great advances were made in methods of teaching reading in American schools, and that progress has slowed down somewhat during recent years . . . but no conspicuous advance in either has appeared during the past decade. . . . Many educators would not be surprised to find that reading attainment today [December 1960] is even somewhat less than it was twelve years ago, or at approximately the time of the final tests in the Nebraska study.[4]

Gates's surmise that reading achievement in 1960 was lower than that in the late 1940s is incorrect, however. He does express the feeling that achievement does *not* continually rise generation after generation but may well follow more complex patterns. Another impression that the 1930s was probably a period of very high educational achievement comes from a history of education in New York City by Diane Ravitch:

Academically able pupils moved in fast tracks and enriched classes into academic high schools, and, if they passed the entrance examination, into the city's elite high schools. Competition for excellence was keen, and from these schools came a generation of remarkable professionals, scholars, writers, scientists, and intellectuals—many of them the children and grandchildren of the new immigration that ended in 1924.[5]

Comparisons of later periods with the 1930s also indicate that achievement apparently was high during this period.

The available data—and one must remember the scarcity of such data until three or four decades ago—therefore seem to suggest that achievement was high in the immediate immigrant era and that some declines apparently occurred after this. They also seem to suggest, however, that from lows in the mid-1920s to the late 1930s, there was a broad increase in achievement as revealed by several indicators.

In the late 1930s and early 1940s again there is evidence of a gradual erosion of achievement in the nation's schools. This evidence in the main derives from comparisons between the 1930s and 1950s that show the 1950s to be inferior in all subject areas involving basic skills. Very good evidence indicates that achievement was increasing in the early 1950s, so declines must have occurred chiefly in the 1940s. Some direct evidence from one state also supports this last premise. In Minnesota, statewide testing results of all high school seniors between 1939 and 1948 show an overall downward trend. The trend, which is reflected on an English achievement test, shows up among all groups of students: men, women, the college-bound, and so on. For our purposes the results for the frame of all high school seniors is most relevant.

MEAN SCORES OF HIGH SCHOOL
SENIORS ON COOPERATIVE
ENGLISH TEST, 20 PERCENT SAMPLE

	Men	Women
1939	131.6	155.7
1940	130.1	152.6
1941*	127.1	148.2
1942	127.4	147.4
1943	126.7	148.3
1944	131.5	147.8
1945	129.0	146.6
1946	126.2	141.4
1947**	119.5	140.2
1948	118.7	140.9

*   Total Sample   **   17% Sample

SOURCE: Ralph F. Berdie et al., *Who Goes to College?* pp. 30–31.

Scores describing pupil intelligence over this same time period indicate little change. Thus, no evidence that incoming Minnesota students were "less bright" and hence failed to do as well on the English achievement test exists. At no time between 1939 and 1948 did mean scores reach the 1939 level for men or women. Although there was a rise for 1944 and 1945, the general trend was downward. There is little likelihood that using a 20 percent sample instead of the complete sample had any effect on the outcomes. This decline undoubtedly had a complex of causes.

Some results from statewide testing in Minnesota are available after 1948.[6] Data from the mid-1950s to 1972 show "that mean scores increased until about 1961–1962, where they plateaued until about 1969–1970 when the mean scores began dropping approximately ½ a raw score point annually."[7]

That achievement tended to rise in the 1950s above the level of the 1940s is demonstrated from the renorming of the General Test of Educational Development (GED). This test renorming showed achievement gains between 1943 and 1955 in all subject areas for a sample of high school seniors numbering approximately 36,000 each year. The overall conclusion derived from this comparison was that the entire distribution of 1955 scores had shifted up by approximately 5 percentile points over the twelve-year period.[8] Gains were particularly large for mathematics but increases were noted in *all* areas.

However, even though achievement levels were rising nationally in the early and mid-1950s, they were still *below* the 1930s levels. The Gates study of comparative reading achievement in 1937 and 1957 shows the earlier pupils to be superior by grade level. It turned out that 1957 students were better insofar as achievement for a given chronological age was concerned, but for equal years of schooling, perhaps the more interesting variable, the 1930s elementary students were more advanced. The following data were generated from comparisons of the Gates reading test, which involved approximately 31,000 pupils in 1957.

MEAN AMOUNTS BY WHICH READING GRADES OF 1937 PUPILS
AT A PARTICULAR GRADE LEVEL EXCEEDED READING GRADES OF 1957 PUPILS
EXPRESSED IN TENTHS OF READING GRADE

Grade	Mean	Grade	Mean
3.5	.07	6.0	.21
4.0	.09	6.5	.24
4.5	.11	6.9	.25
5.0	.14	7.5	.28
5.5	.18	8.5	.34

Source: Arthur I. Gates, *Reading Attainment in Elementary Schools: 1957 and 1937.*

In a grade-to-grade comparison 1937 pupils were superior to 1957 pupils at all levels. In fact, the higher the grade, the more the 1930s students outperformed the 1950s students. As noted, when comparing children of the same age, the 1957 children did better—that is, for a given age they outperformed the earlier pupils—but this is mainly a function of the 1950s students starting school much earlier. As far as amount of exposure time to the school system is concerned, or given equal "doses" of the same factor, the 1930s schools appear to have been more effective than those of 1957.[9]

While the Gates comparisons examine a fundamental skill for a national student population, a study by Joseph Sligo looked at achievement differences in more advanced subjects for 1934 and 1954. This study was restricted to selected Iowa high schools, and we note in passing that Iowa high schools have historically been among the best in the nation as far as achievement is concerned. The general approach was to use old tests for which records of the performance of past groups were still available.[10] In order to check for possible differences in mental ability between the two groups, intelligence test results were examined. In this area the 1954 pupils were considerably higher. In achievement, on the other hand, the 1934 pupils performed better in all areas:

DISTRIBUTIONS OF IOWA HIGH SCHOOL PUPIL SCORES

Subject Matter Test	1934 Group Mean	1954 Group Mean	Differences
1934 Ninth Year Algebra	14.3	10.9	3.4
1934 General Science	43.9	42.9	1.0
1934 English Correctness (Ninth Grade)	61.9	45.6	16.3
1934 United States History	42.4	37.3	5.1
1933 United States History	47.0	39.3	7.7

SOURCE: Joseph R. Sligo, "Comparison of Achievement in Selected High School Subjects in 1934 and 1954," p. 152.

The results of this selective study seem to coincide with Gates's perception of achievement levels in the 1950s compared to those of the 1930s. However, as noted earlier, steady advances were being made in the 1950s although during this decade these apparently had not raised achievement enough to equal the levels of the thirties.

A broad comparison of achievement from the early 1950s to the early 1960s by William B. Schrader[11] showed gains of approximately .2 of a standard deviation over this period. It is interesting to compare this with the Minnesota high school data for the 1939–48 period, which give a .3 standard deviation loss. Both studies concentrate on approximately a ten-

IOWA TESTS OF BASIC SKILLS
SUMMARY OF DIFFERENCES IN 1956, 1964 AND 1971
EDITIONS OF NORMS OF PUPIL SCORES
(GRADE EQUIVALENT IN MONTHS*)

90TH PERCENTILE GRADE		VOCABULARY	READING	LANGUAGE SKILLS					WORK STUDY SKILLS				MATHEMATICS SKILLS			COMPOSITE
				SPELLING	CAPITALIZATION	PUNCTUATION	USAGE	TOTAL	MAPS	GRAPHS	REFERENCES	TOTAL	CONCEPTS	PROBLEMS	TOTAL	
8	'71-64	0.0	-1.5	0.0	1.4	0.0	-2.2	0.0	1.0	1.6	0.8	1.1	-0.9	-3.6	-2.1	-0.4
	'64-56	-1.4	-0.5	5.0	3.0	0.0	3.0	2.8	5.0	3.8	1.8	3.5	7.3	0.9	4.1	1.7
7	'71-64	-1.6	-1.8	1.5	1.2	0.0	-1.3	0.0	0.0	2.3	1.6	1.3	-0.7	-2.6	-1.8	-1.0
	'64-56	3.5	4.0	6.0	4.8	0.0	2.0	3.2	4.4	3.0	4.5	4.0	6.0	2.9	4.5	3.8
6	'71-64	-1.7	-1.9	-2.3	-1.5	0.0	-2.2	-1.6	1.0	0.2	0.6	0.7	-1.9	-2.3	-2.3	-1.2
	'64-56	3.0	1.5	5.5	6.1	2.0	3.5	4.3	5.0	4.4	5.5	5.0	7.8	2.0	4.9	3.7
5	'71-64	0.3	-1.0	-1.1	-2.0	0.7	-1.3	-0.9	1.8	0.9	0.7	1.1	0.9	-1.6	-0.4	0.0
	'64-56	1.0	1.5	1.5	6.7	-4.0	0.0	1.1	0.4	4.5	5.0	3.3	6.6	6.4	6.5	2.7
4	'71-64	-0.5	-0.8	-1.5	-1.7	-0.8	-1.1	-1.4	2.1	0.6	0.5	0.9	1.5	-0.7	0.4	0.0
	'64-56	-0.2	0.5	5.3	7.0	6.0	3.5	5.5	0.7	1.0	4.5	2.1	4.5	2.8	3.7	2.3
3	'71-64	0.8	0.7	-1.0	-1.3	0.8	-1.4	-0.7	1.2	0.0	1.1	0.8	2.0	2.0	2.1	0.5
	'64-56	2.5	4.5	9.0	7.3	6.5	3.3	6.5	3.6	3.7	5.0	4.1	2.0	2.2	2.1	3.9
Mean Diff.	'71-64	-0.4	-1.0	-0.7	-0.6	0.1	-1.6	-0.8	1.2	0.9	0.9	1.0	0.2	-1.5	-0.7	-0.3
	'64-56	1.4	1.9	5.4	5.3	1.8	2.6	3.9	3.2	3.4	4.4	3.7	5.7	2.9	4.3	3.0
50TH PERCENTILE																
8	'71-64	0.4	-2.1	1.0	0.6	-1.6	-3.1	0.0	0.8	0.9	1.4	0.9	-1.7	-3.1	-2.4	-1.1
	-64-56	-0.8	2.5	2.1	3.3	-2.0	1.6	1.3	2.0	3.2	1.8	2.3	3.4	1.6	2.5	1.6
7	'71-64	1.0	-1.4	1.1	-0.9	0.0	-1.6	0.0	1.2	2.3	2.0	1.7	-2.2	-4.1	-2.8	-0.4
	'64-56	1.8	1.5	4.8	6.6	-2.4	1.4	2.6	3.8	3.7	2.8	3.4	3.5	4.6	4.1	2.7

Grade	Period	1	2	3	4	5	6	7	8	9	10	11	12	13	14	15
6	'71-64	0.9	-2.6	-1.4	-2.8	-1.4	-1.6	-1.4	0.7	2.2	0.3	1.1	2.4			
	'64-56	0.8	2.2	1.5	4.5	-0.2	2.4	2.1	2.0	1.2	3.8	2.3	4.4	2.5	3.4	2.2
5	'71-64	1.4	-0.7	0.4	-2.3	0.0	-0.8	-0.5	1.4	3.4	0.7	1.5	0.8	0.6	0.6	0.6
	'64-56	0.8	2.6	4.0	4.4	1.8	2.0	3.1	1.4	1.6	1.8	1.6	3.6	2.6	3.1	2.2
4	'71-64	0.6	-0.6	-1.0	-1.6	-0.6	-2.2	-1.4	1.2	3.5	1.0	1.9	0.6	0.3	0.7	0.3
	'64-56	3.6	2.5	3.4	6.6	3.4	3.2	4.2	1.5	0.5	2.8	1.6	1.9	0.6	1.3	2.6
3	'71-64	1.3	0.5	0.0	-0.6	1.0	0.0	-0.6	0.9	0.3	1.0	0.9	0.7	1.9	1.6	0.4
	'64-56	2.4	4.3	3.0	4.6	1.8	0.5	2.5	1.6	2.5	2.2	2.1	2.8	0.6	1.7	2.6
Mean Diff.	'71-64	0.9	-1.2	0.0	-1.3	-0.4	-1.6	-0.6	1.0	2.1	1.1	1.3	-0.8	-1.2	-0.9	-0.2
	'64-56	1.4	2.6	3.1	5.0	0.4	1.8	2.6	2.0	2.1	2.5	2.2	3.3	2.1	2.7	2.3

10TH PERCENTILE

Grade	Period	1	2	3	4	5	6	7	8	9	10	11	12	13	14	15
8	'71-64	2.3	-1.0	0.0	0.0	-0.7	-0.9	0.0	0.0	1.5	0.6	0.5	0.0	-3.3	-1.7	0.0
	'64-56	1.2	-1.0	-2.9	-0.6	-4.2	-1.2	-2.2	3.3	2.1	-3.4	0.7	1.8	4.9	3.4	0.4
7	'71-64	4.4	0.0	0.0	0.0	-1.1	0.0	0.0	0.0	4.6	0.7	1.6	-1.6	-3.3	-1.9	0.0
	'64-56	1.1	1.0	2.1	1.1	-1.0	-1.8	0.1	2.5	1.8	5.0	3.1	2.6	4.6	3.6	1.8
6	'71-64	1.7	-1.0	0.0	-0.4	0.0	0.0	0.0	1.0	3.3	1.2	1.3	-2.0	-2.0	-2.2	-0.5
	'64-56	0.0	2.9	1.4	1.6	-0.8	0.4	0.6	0.6	-1.6	3.6	0.9	1.6	3.6	2.6	1.4
5	'71-64	1.6	0.0	0.7	0.0	0.0	0.0	0.0	2.1	2.9	0.2	2.0	1.4	0.9	1.3	1.1
	'64-56	0.0	0.0	1.4	0.0	-1.3	-0.6	-0.1	-0.9	-0.2	0.5	-0.2	2.0	1.2	1.6	0.3
4	'71-64	2.1	0.2	0.0	0.0	0.0	-1.2	-0.3	1.2	1.6	0.1	1.6	0.5	0.8	0.6	0.6
	'64-56	2.4	1.5	1.6	3.4	-1.5	2.2	1.4	0.7	1.2	3.4	1.8	2.0	-1.5	0.2	1.5
3	'71-64	1.1	0.9	0.0	0.0	-0.6	-0.7	0.0	1.6	0.0	0.2	0.5	0.0	1.0	0.8	0.1
	'64-56	1.0	1.5	1.5	2.6	0.1	-0.4	0.9	-0.2	1.1	1.4	0.8	0.0	1.4	0.7	1.0
Mean Diff.	'71-64	2.2	-0.2	0.1	-0.1	-0.4	-0.5	0.0	1.0	2.5	0.5	1.2	-0.3	-1.0	-0.5	-0.2
	'64-56	0.9	1.0	0.8	-1.4	-1.4	-0.2	0.1	1.0	0.7	1.8	1.2	1.7	2.4	2.0	1.1

*Expressed in months of a school year gain or loss, e.g., in June sixth grade children should test sixth year, ninth month, or 6.9.

NOTE: Reprinted from *Manual for Administrators, Supervisors, and Counselors, Forms 5 & 6* by A. N. Hieronymus and E. F. Lindquist, p. 67, table 6.8.

year period. If we assume that the Minnesota study reflected a national trend—and there is evidence, as mentioned earlier and as we shall see, that this is a not completely unreasonable assumption—it appears that achievement is likely to have been falling faster in the 1940s than it was gaining in the 1950s. The Schrader comparison was based on a number of renorming studies undertaken by several well-known standardized-test publishing organizations, and the comparisons involved all of the basic-skill subject areas.

During the 1960s the growth in academic achievement under way since World War II seems to have topped out. Although it is naturally impossible to pin down the change to a single year, many achievement indicators show a turning point after the middle 1960s. For this period there are two sources of data: nationally administered and statewide tests. The national indicators are useful for a broad picture of this turning point and the state data allow a close look at local achievement losses. For example, the national renorming studies of the Iowa Tests of Basic Skills (ITBS) carried out in 1955, 1964, and 1970 show the changes indicated below and on the previous page:

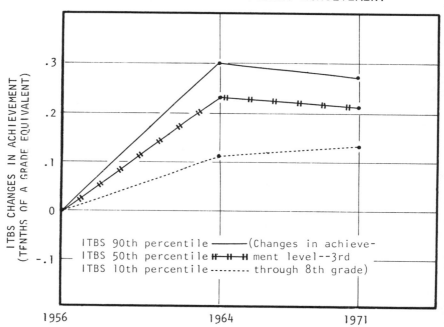

NATIONAL TRENDS IN STUDENT ACHIEVEMENT

SOURCE: Hieronymus and Lindquist, *Manual for Administrators, Supervisors, and Counselors, Forms 5 & 6,* p. 67, table 6.8.

These tables have several interesting features. First, note that mean losses in achievement took place over the 1964–71 period in contrast to the gains picked up over the 1956–64 period, and then that the losses were the greatest for the better students—.3 for the ninetieth percentile students and .2 for the fiftieth percentile students. The tenth percentile pupils actually gained +.2 over the 1964–71 period. This is not good news for the lower tenth percentile, however, for, as the chart indicates, during the 1956–64 period, it gained *1.1* compared to the 1964–71 gain of only .2.

Another trend in these ITBS data reflects the traditional split between the achievement in the lower and upper elementary grades, in this case the tendency for the lower grades to have improved over the 1964–71 period while the upper grades declined. Thus the mean loss is in a sense misleading because it masks the true decline in the upper grades. The ITBS data show the following gains and losses in the three upper grades:

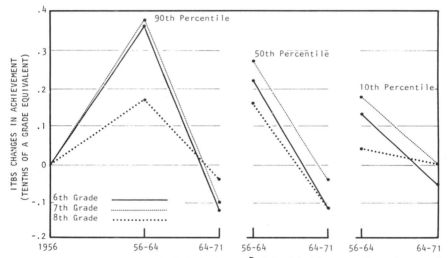

SOURCE: Hieronymus and Lindquist, *Manual for Administrators, Supervisors, and Counselors, Forms 5 & 6* p. 67, table 6.8.

As we will demonstrate, this decline in the higher grades is, in general, also a strong signal in the analysis of statewide data. Over the past few years, the ITBS data seem to indicate that nationally the lower grades have been improving or at least holding steady and the upper grades declining. The higher the grade, the more the decline is likely to have been. A. N. Hieronymus and E. F. Lindquist, the designers of the current edition of ITBS, conclude:

Between 1955 and 1963 achievement improved rather consistently for most achievement test areas, grade levels, and achievement levels. The average change for the composite was 3.0 months at the 90th percentile, 2.3 months at the 50th percentile, and 1.1 months at the 10th percentile.

Overall, between 1963 and 1970, differences in median composite scores were negligible. However, there were some small but fairly consistent qualitative differences among achievement areas, grades, and achievement levels. In general the changes were positive in the lower grades and tended to balance out in the upper grades. Gains were fairly consistent in vocabulary and work-study skills, but fairly consistent losses occurred in reading and in some of the language skills. Mathematics achievement appears to have improved in the lower grades, but in the upper grades losses in both concepts and problem solving are consistent and sizable.[12]

A good indicator of the achievement peak in the mid-1960s and a drop thereafter comes from the results of renorming the Comprehensive Tests of Basic Skills in 1973, making possible comparisons of 1973 versus 1968 such as this one by Donald Green:

The Comprehensive Tests of Basic Skills, Form Q, was standardized on a national probability sample of more than 200,000 students in February and March of 1968. A year ago this test was given again to a similar but smaller sample of over 10,000 students. The grades covered were 2 through 10. The data show largely negligible and inconsistent differences in average performance in grades 2, 3, and 4 but lower scores for the 1973 sample thereafter in all areas of the test (reading, mathematics, language, and study skills). The drop is larger the higher the grade.[13]

Again we see the tendency for the lower grades to be performing better over time and the higher grades to be declining in achievement.

Another indicator of the current achievement drop is a study by Stephen Roderick of mathematics skills in Iowa for grades six and eight. Tests from 1936, 1951–55, and 1965 were given again to pupils in the same schools in 1973.[14] The results from each year were compared to the 1973 results and were analyzed item by item. This study is probably important because it takes place in Iowa, where many of the problems associated with such factors as worsened home environment, student body socioeconomic status, and racial strife are at a minimum compared with the large eastern states. It should be remembered that this study focused exclusively on mathematics achievement.

The outcome of the study was that 1973 pupils were worse than *all* other students of the previous periods, and in some cases the differences in achievement were massive. Consequently the following significant conclusions were reached:

1. Student mathematics achievement in grades six and eight in 1973 is clearly inferior to the achievement of similar students in 1936 in the areas of problem solving, whole number computation, fractional number computation, and decimals, percentages, and fractional parts.
2. Student mathematics achievement in 1973 is inferior to the achievement of similar students in 1951–55 in the areas of whole number computation and fractional number computation at grade six, and decimals and percentages and problem solving at grade eight.
3. Student mathematics achievement in grades six and eight in 1973 is inferior to the achievement of similar students in 1965 in the area of problem solving.
4. There is a general trend apparent indicating that 1973 student achievement in problem solving is at the lowest level of any of the years included in this study.
5. There is an indication that 1973 student achievement in whole number computation and fractional number computation is inferior to the level of achievement in 1936 at both grade levels and in 1951 at grade six. Such topics were not included for testing in 1965.[15]

The students in 1936 were superior at both grades six and eight in all areas tested. This conforms to the earlier observations on the high state of academic achievement found in the schools of the Depression era.

Studies that compare the very early 1960s with the 1970–71 period show very small changes. The reason for this seems to be the concavity of the achievement curve during this decade, making it possible for the latter comparison to be slightly higher. However, when comparisons are made between the mid-1960s and the 1970–71 period, significant declines are always noted. Renorming of the Iowa Tests of Educational Development in 1971 shows this. Gains between 1962 and 1971 were found for high school students in grades 9 through 12.[16] Reports indicate the scores since 1971 have been steadily falling. Another example is the reading test in the "Progress in Education" study by John Flanagan and Steven Jung of Project Talent. The reading test given to eleventh graders in 1960 was readministered to eleventh graders in 1970. A tiny gain of 0.04 standard deviations was found compared with the .2 standard deviation increase in the 1950s and early 1960s found in the Schrader study. It is very doubtful if such a small gain is statistically significant by the analysis of variance. The Project Talent report concludes:

> During this period [the 1960s] billions of new dollars have been poured into new reading texts, materials, procedures, enrichment projects, Head Start programs, and a host of other "improvements." The lack of a substantial increase in measured reading comprehension, then, is especially discouraging.[17]

4
TRENDS IN RECENT ACHIEVEMENT TESTS

Not all states administer individual achievement tests, but the results among those that do often seem to bear out our conclusions. We collected such results from twenty-one states and the District of Columbia, from Hawaii to Rhode Island and from Michigan to Texas—states that account for approximately half the country's population (see the Appendix).

Data from several states did not lend themselves to our analysis, but for the others, though the tests and the number of years over which they were administered differ—in some cases only for two or three years—where there are any "longitudinal" data, we see a pattern. Few states exceeded in whole or in part a national norm in achievement for grades four or five and above, particularly a norm established in the mid- or early 1960s, and a majority of students covered seem to be declining in achievement.

The better state records were as follows:

In 1972 Nebraska eleventh and seventh graders exceeded 1971 norms in all categories.[1]

Rhode Island's 1972 eighth graders surpassed national achievement norms, established in 1964, in reading, mathematics, and language and equaled the norm in vocabulary.[2]

South Dakota consistently surpassed national norms throughout the sixties in both ninth and eleventh grades, usually by wide margins. In 1972, however, the ninth grade exceeded 1970 norms in only two of four subjects tested, and the eleventh grade equaled one norm, exceeded two, and scored less in a fourth. Furthermore, even though they still exceeded the norm, the amount by which they did so fell; in all cases the pupils scored worse in 1972 than in 1970.[3]

Utah reported that in 1971 the average for all grades lumped into one exceeded the national average in mathematics, science, social studies, and total achievement.[4]

Though West Virginia consistently showed scores just below the national norm for the STS Educational Development Series test, practically no decline in achievement showed up in the data covering the 1970–71 through

1973–74 school years. Furthermore, contrary to the general national trend, the upper grades held up just about as well as, and the eleventh grade better than, the lower grades.[5]

Mississippi also seemed to be holding steady. Under new testing programs, achievement in the fifth and eighth grades rose between the 1972–73 and 1973–74 school years, although it had fallen under the previous program between 1970–71 and 1971–72.[6]

Some states, such as Ohio and California, record only achievement scores for public schools; others, like New York, Idaho, Iowa, and West Virginia, record test results for both private and public schools. There seems to be no consistent pattern of difference between the achievement trends of states that include private school data and those that do not. Where broken out, academic achievement records of nonpublic schools are higher and may fall more slowly over time in the upper primary grades than do those of public schools, but generally the trend is also down in states recording tests results of *all* schools.[7]

In other states for which the full data also will be found in the Appendix, we believe a consistent pattern emerges. First, in the late 1960s and

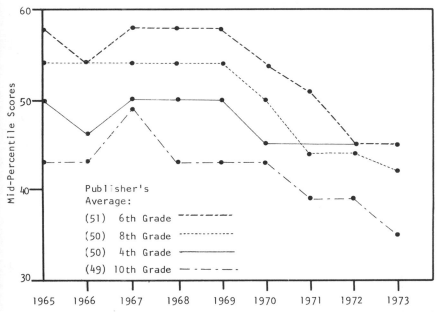

HAWAII
TRACES OF READING ACHIEVEMENT SCORES FOR THE FOURTH,
SIXTH, EIGHTH AND TENTH GRADES, 1966-1973

Publisher's
Average:

(51) 6th Grade
(50) 8th Grade
(50) 4th Grade
(49) 10th Grade

Source: Hawaii State Dept. of Education, "Summary Report of Statewide Testing Program 1972–73," p. 19.

early 1970s pupils generally tended to fall below achievement norms established in the mid- and late sixties in grades four or five and above. Second, in almost all states where achievement test score data exist for a sequence of years, a downward trend is apparent in these upper grades, regardless of whether the scores were above or below the norm during the first year recorded.[8] Finally, declines occurred more or less simultaneously in all the upper elementary and all high school grades of any given state or district.

In states like New Jersey and Texas, where "criterion-referenced" tests are given, it is very difficult to trace trends. In such a test a judgment is normally made by a committee as to whether percentages of students should be rated as "excellent," "good," or "poor" achievers. The judgments are based on many issues and may be assumed to be less finite measures of achievement, and particularly trends in achievement, than those possible

IOWA
TRACES OF READING ACHIEVEMENT
SCORES FOR THIRD THROUGH EIGHTH
GRADES, 1966-72
1965 "BASE-YEAR" PERCENTILE RANKS*

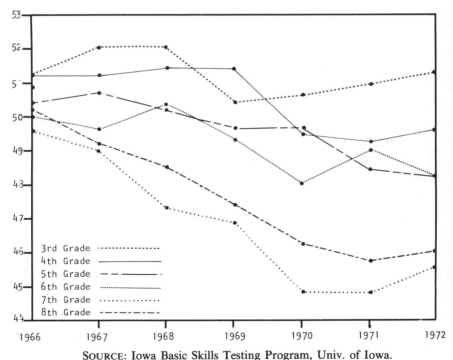

SOURCE: Iowa Basic Skills Testing Program, Univ. of Iowa.
*The fiftieth percentile point for each grade in 1965 is the starting point.

with norm-referenced tests. Nonetheless, samples of raw data—and data from major cities in such states, like Newark, which will be discussed later in this section—and observers' comments seem to indicate a low or dropping achievement level in these states as well.[9] (Detailed data, which will be discussed later, indicate that large-city school districts apparently can no longer be lightly disregarded as barometers for declining scores for whole states.)[10]

The graphs here, based on data expressed on a percentile basis in the Appendix, show the fall-off in reading skills in the upper elementary and lower secondary grades since the mid-1960s. Similar data exist for mathematic skills, as well as for reading skills for other grades mentioned in the Appendix; in general, for the upper grades—with the exceptions mentioned earlier—the trends are similar.

One should note that in state after state all these grades fell in academic achievement almost simultaneously. This could hardly be the result of a particularly unintelligent group of children moving through the schools, causing one grade after another to fall in achievement.

NEW YORK STATE
TRACES OF READING ACHIEVEMENT TEST SCORES
FOR PUBLIC AND PRIVATE SCHOOLS,
THIRD, SIXTH AND NINTH GRADES, 1966-1973
PERCENTILE RANK OF MEDIAN RAW SCORES, BASE YEAR 1965

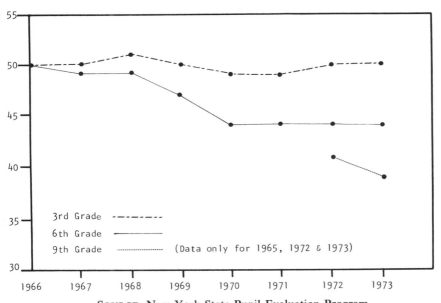

SOURCE: New York State Pupil Evaluation Program.

A word of explanation might explain part, but by no means all, of the continuing ostensible contradiction in the patterns just mentioned—that is, over these years we usually find simultaneous stable or even rising mean scores in the lower grades, particularly among first through third grades, and declining mean scores in the upper grades.[11] First of all, mean scores, particularly when given in grade equivalent figures (for example, average reading skill in fourth grade is fourth year fifth month—4.5), can be significantly affected in the lower grades by some students achieving exceptionally well. For example, it is not uncommon for several children in a class to read several years above the norm for the lower grades. In computing the *average* scores, one such child, of course, tends to cancel out the effects of several poor readers' scores in the very low grades, since by definition a third grader cannot be more than three years below the norm. As these children advance through the grades, however, two things

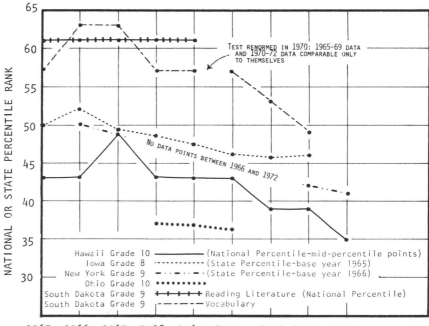

HAWAII, IOWA, NEW YORK, OHIO, SOUTH DAKOTA
READING ACHIEVEMENT SCORES OF
EIGHTH THROUGH TENTH GRADES, 1965-1973

SOURCES: Hawaii, "Summary Report of Statewide Testing Program 1972–1973," p. 19. Iowa Basic Skills Testing Program. New York State Pupil Evaluation Program. Ohio Survey Tests, 1968–73. South Dakota Education Dept. Testing Program.

happen. First, the poor readers fall farther behind, and second, the "canceling effect" of the superior students decreases—for example a tenth grade "overachiever" cannot score more than twelfth grade level, two years above the norm, but a tenth grade "underachiever" can, and often does, score considerably more than two years below the norm.[12] Even though the dropouts reduce some of the pressure, it is not enough to cancel out this effect, particularly prior to the ninth grade, because of compulsory school attendance to age sixteen in almost all states. This account, however, does not explain all the reasons for the stability in achievement levels in the first through third or fourth grades; nor does it explain why the achievement levels in lower grades have in several instances risen. The children apparently bring considerable competence and initiative with them to the schools.

Of course, one explanation for the drop in average scores in the upper grades is simply that subjects get harder, particularly for those not grounded in the fundamentals, and the teaching job is more demanding. A child can get by with little knowledge of the multiplication tables in the lower grades, but when he must learn long division in the fifth grade, his inability to multiply readily tends to incapacitate him. Nor should we

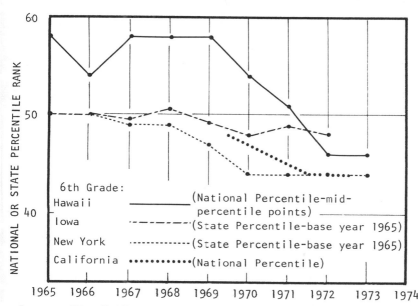

HAWAII, IOWA, NEW YORK, CALIFORNIA
READING ACHIEVEMENT SCORES OF SIXTH GRADES, 1965-1973

SOURCES: Hawaii, "Summary Report," p. 19. Iowa Basic Skills Testing Program. New York State Pupil Evaluation Program. *California State Testing Program 1971–1972 and 1972–73.*

overlook the possibility that by the fourth grade children have begun to learn the "facts" from pupils in the upper grades. The little ones may come to school with a built-in respect for the advice of parents and teachers, but once they learn that there is no penalty for not doing homework, or even skipping school, that one is promoted regardless of achievement levels, they may stop trying to do this more difficult work. Children a decade ago showed no greater aptitude than these pupils in the first through third grades, but they did not fall in achievement beyond third grade when asked to do equally, or even more, difficult work.

Another interesting pattern that may be emerging, as we have seen in the previous chapter, is the apparent decline of scholastic achievement of the brighter children and, as we shall see, in the less turbulent schools of the often more affluent suburbs and small cities. We may have another interesting case if we assume the "bottoming out" of the achievement in some of our larger cities, for which we have data, is a pattern that applies to most metropolises. The reason for the bottoming out in the upper grades in these cities is not known. Among the possibilities, however, one should not overlook the chance that in certain cases the scores are so low that they are reaching the theoretical lower limit for multiple choice tests. For example, in 1972, on arithmetic tests normed several years earlier so that 50 percent of nationwide samples of pupils fell below the *fiftieth* percentile level, 50 percent of Philadelphia public school seventh graders scored below the *thirteenth* percentile and the same percentage of eighth graders scored below the *fourteenth* percentile level.[13] Between 1974 and 1976, on a different test normed in 1970—which means the skills of the national sample of students had probably declined—Philadelphia student raw scores looked better on math, reading, and language skills compared to the new norm. Perhaps of more significance, however, each year they generally increased the percentage of pupils scoring in the higher percentile brackets.[14] New York City sixth grade averages for public and private schools in 1972 were at the twenty-ninth percentile point in mathematics and at the thirty-second percentile point in reading.[15]

In any event, in New York City in 1972, 71.3 percent of the junior high school students, and 66.3 percent of the elementary and junior high students in 1965, were reading below grade level.[16] High schools in other big city systems at that time showed similar trends. In the District of Columbia, writes Mark Arnold:

> . . . every objective measurement points to a slow and steady deterioration in the performance level of students.[17]
> . . . ninth graders in September 1971 were a month behind the reading level recorded by ninth graders in September 1970. The average was a grade equivalent of 6.4 years in September 1971. . . .[18]

Washington, too, only checks its students against themselves, as it does not administer standard national tests. Like New York, these tests reflect the drop in achievement in District of Columbia schools, not how they compare with schools in other states.

It was reported unofficially that in 1972, 75 percent of Washington's pupils were reading below grade level.[19] In 1973, in Newark, New Jersey's largest city, the high school seniors' median reading score was equal to the eighth grade average nationally. Many were at a fifth grade level, though Newark's student body was said not to be below average intelligence.[20] In 1974 after new test results were recorded, Newark's scores went down again.[21] In 1972, unofficial sources said that, in Baltimore and Philadelphia, 75 percent of the pupils were reading below grade level.

Nor was this problem confined to the big cities on the east coast. According to the same sources, in the Midwest, 70 percent of Chicago and Cleveland pupils were reading below grade level that year.[22]

On the other hand, in 1973 the entire New York City school system from the first through ninth grades, with the exception of one grade, showed improvement in reading achievement test scores compared to 1972.[23] In 1974 there were claims of some fraud in the 1973 administration of the test, though supposedly not enough to affect scores greatly, and the 1974 scores were about the same as in 1973. Actually they apparently were slightly below those of 1973,[24] and in 1975 fewer New York City sixth and ninth graders scored above the "reference point"—previously called "minimum competence"—level than in 1974.[25] Such "minimum competence" data alone, however, do not give one as firm a feeling of how a school system is doing as do raw score averages or percentile data. People above the minimum competence level could increase while the overall average declined. Indeed, the improvement in Iowa Test of Basic Skills scores for the lower tenth percentile, which accompanied the decline in scores for the ninetieth and fiftieth percentile children (see p. 38) could support such a phenomenon.

If we accept the number of pupils reading below minimum competence levels as an indicator of overall average reading scores, then New York City, as well as New York State, pupils beyond the third grade are still falling, and falling faster in large cities in upstate New York than in New York City.[26] New York City students above third grade may be slowing down in their decline (see following chart), but they have yet to reverse the downward trend. In California, Los Angeles pupils' reading and math scores generally continue to decline, and statewide twelfth graders had the "largest drop" in 1975.[27] On the other hand, as we have seen, the number of Philadelphia school children scoring in the upper national percentile brackets in reading, language, and math skills increased between 1974 and 1976, according to the type of test administered to them since 1974.[28]

If we assume that the big cities are bottoming out or have stabilized in a slight decline while whole states continue to fall, however, then, as mentioned earlier, the rural districts, suburbs, and smaller cities must be falling, and in many cases falling rapidly. Indeed, at least between 1966 and 1972, in New York State, as the following chart indicates, the rate of decline in the average achievement level (based on a percentile level achieved in 1966) in public and private schools in all other districts, rural areas, suburbs, and small and other "large" cities was greater than in New York City.

NEW YORK STATE, 1966-73
AVERAGE PERCENTILE TEST SCORES,
READING AND MATHEMATICS, GRADE 6

	1966	1967	1968	1969	1970	1971	1972	1973
Reading								
New York City	37	36	37	34	32	32	32	NA
Large Cities	47	44	42	40	38	35	35	NA
Medium Cities	54	52	51	48	47	46	45	NA
Small Cities	53	52	52	50	48	47	47	NA
Vl & Lg Central	59	58	57	56	54	53	53	NA
Large Rural	55	53	54	51	51	49	48	NA
Small Rural	52	50	50	50	48	47	46	NA
Total State	50	49	49	47	44	44	44	44
Mathematics								
New York City	34	30	32	30	28	30	29	NA
Large Cities	49	48	46	39	37	33	33	NA
Medium Cities	51	50	48	46	43	43	42	NA
Small Cities	54	52	51	48	46	44	43	NA
Vl & Lg Central	58	56	54	54	51	50	49	NA
Large Rural	59	54	53	51	50	47	45	NA
Small Rural	59	56	54	52	50	47	45	NA
Total State	50	47	47	44	42	41	41	39

NOTE: Reprinted from New York State Pupil Evaluation Program.

Data for California, which also publishes such testing details, show a drop in the seventy-fifth percentile—the upper twenty-five percent of the class—as well as the twenty-fifth percentile—the lower twenty-five percent —between the 1969–70 and 1972–73 school year in all subjects. Indeed, in grade twelve the seventy-fifth percentile fell faster than the twenty-fifth percentile in *all* subjects. These latter data coincide with the national ITBS data primary grades mentioned on pp. 36–39, where the ninetieth percentile was faring worse than the tenth percentile. With California twelfth graders, however, other factors, such as a reduction of legal dropouts, could affect the scores.

GRADE 6

	Reading				Language				Spelling				Arithmetic			
	1969-1970	1970-1971	1971-1972	1972-1973	1969-1970	1970-1971	1971-1972	1972-1973	1969-1970	1970-1971	1971-1972	1972-1973	1969-1970	1970-1971	1971-1972	1972-1973
75TH PERCENTILE																
State Raw Score	71.8	71.4	70.5	70.6	68.4	67.9	66.5	66.7	25.7	25.7	25.5	25.4	84.8	83.2	81.5	81.6
Publisher's Percentile Rank	74	72	72	72	68	68	65	65	73	73	73	64	74	68	65	65
25TH PERCENTILE																
State Raw Score	45.7	45.3	43.7	44.3	44.3	43.2	41.0	41.2	17.6	17.3	16.4	16.3	58.9	56.1	52.9	53.6
Publisher's Percentile Rank	24	23	21	21	21	19	17	17	22	19	16	16	24	21	18	19

GRADE 12

	Reading				Expression				Spelling				Quantitative			
	1969-1970	1970-1971	1971-1972	1972-1973	1969-1970	1970-1971	1971-1972	1972-1973	1969-1970	1970-1971	1971-1972	1972-1973	1969-1970	1970-1971	1971-1972	1972-1973
75TH PERCENTILE																
State Raw Score	29.8	29.4	28.8	28.1	50.8	49.8	48.4	47.3	11.1	11.0	10.7	10.5	19.0	18.7	18.4	18.3
Publisher's Percentile Rank	74	71	71	67	68	65	60	57	72	72	72	72	77	77	74	74
25TH PERCENTILE																
State Raw Score	15.4	15.1	14.9	14.6	30.3	29.6	28.6	27.7	5.4	5.3	5.2	5.0	8.8	8.6	8.5	8.4
Publisher's Percentile Rank	24	24	24	24	22	22	21	19	26	26	26	26	25	25	25	20

NOTE: Reprinted from *California State Testing Program 1971–72 and 1972–73.*

None of all this is meant to imply that all school districts throughout the country, without exception, are or have been declining in academic achievement. In recent years some urban and suburban districts have showed improvement at least in some subjects in the upper primary and secondary grades, and this seems to hold true for California too. For example, in the Oakland City Unified District, where 60.2 percent pupils are Negroes and 8.5 percent are Spanish surnamed, reading ability improved in both the sixth and twelfth grades between the school years 1971–72 and 1972–73. Furthermore, in the twelfth grade, language and spelling also improved.[29] (It is interesting to note, however, that second- and third-grade achievement dropped in this district over this period, a rather rare occurrence these days.) There was also improvement in the Sacramento City Unified District, and here twelfth grade mathematics also improved.[30] We find sixth graders improving in all subjects in some school districts in non-urban areas such as Contra Costa County,[31] and even in some urban districts in San Francisco[32] and San Diego,[33] while twelfth graders improved over this time period in all subjects in some nonurban high school districts in some areas, such as Shasta.[34] These are short time periods to use for trend purposes, but if such achievement has continued, the samples become significant for these specific districts. If the downward trend for the state as a whole has continued, it also becomes more significant.

By and large, however, over the recent past, data on academic achievement trends in primary school upper grades and throughout secondary schools, as measured by the scores of standardized tests administered by the individual states, are too consistent to be ignored. The prudent man should entertain the thought that in general our school pupils have declined in scholastic achievement and that this decline can no longer be blamed solely on our largest cities and shifting pupil populations.[35] In fact, it would have been difficult for most individual states to have blamed declining achievement on changing populations, for it apparently has been widespread throughout the country, including many states and areas within states where the population change was negligible.

Claims persist, however, that because of in-migration some school districts and states may have experienced a drop in natural ability—perhaps reflected in the average IQ—among students. Nationwide, of course, this effect should cancel out, but perhaps one should mention a less probable phenomenon that could cause problems in trying to determine what is happening to individual segments of our school system. For example, if we are transferring students of IQ levels *below the mean* from one district to another district with a *higher* mean IQ, the results should be obvious. The mean IQ of the district to which these children relocate should decrease, and the one from which they came should rise. If, however, we transfer students whose IQs are somewhat *above* the mean for their district but still *below* the mean for the district with the higher IQ level into which they transfer, then the mean IQs of both districts should fall. If this were true for whole states or regions, it might be confusing, but one doubts that it would be the case consistently; even if so, however, and if *it* were the principal cause of falling academic achievement, one would think the lower grades should be affected as well.

It may be useful at this point to mention private schools again. We said earlier that states including these pupils in computing achievement records also generally show drops in academic achievement levels, but it is also worth adding that the number of private school pupils has decreased, particularly in high school. In California, between 1969–70 and the 1972–74 school years, private school pupils decreased from 8.1 percent of the student population to 6.7 percent, and the private high school population fell from 7.3 to 4.0 percent. In Hawaii, the same figures for all private schools were 13.1 percent of the school population in 1969 and 10.5 percent in 1973; private high school figures were 20 percent in 1969 and 8.5 percent in 1973. Nationally, private school enrollment fell from 15.5 percent of the total in 1960 to 13.4 percent in 1970 and 13.1 percent in 1973; the figures for private high school pupils were 9.8 percent in 1960, 8.2 percent in 1970, and 7.8 percent in 1973.[36] One would assume that a diminishing private school population should decrease any distorting effect due to the exclusion of these pupils' achievement scores from state data.

Educators like to point out that the better pupils with the most interested parents are leaving the public school system, which they claim reduces median achievement scores for public schools. Even with the dropping enrollment in private schools, particularly high schools from the mid-1960s through 1972,[37] however, this claim might still have some merit—a shrinking but increasingly elite nonpublic school student body—if it were not for the drop in achievement among *private* school students, too, where they are identified, and the drop in overall state scores where private school scores are included.

There are some other, perhaps even more interesting, data that probably should be mentioned. These concern large peer groups ("cohorts") of children with barely changing or virtually unchanging membership, moving up through the grades together. These groups, which consistently showed a certain level of achievement—normally thought to reflect a certain mean IQ level and, often, a socioeconomic level—have tended suddenly to show a lower achievement level when the achievement level record of the *grade* they entered was lower. Perhaps most important, when achievement scores of a grade were in *decline,* a subsequent peer group that in the lower grades had been *consistently comparable* in academic achievement to its predecessor according to identical tests suddenly tested significantly *below* the preceding group when it took an identical test for the new "declining" grade. The elapsed time for such a cohort to fall behind its previously comparable predecessor was as little as one year and, at most, three years. In other words, at least in these cases, the data indicate that the trend of the *grade* mean percentile score seemed to control achievement independently of the characteristics of each cohort.

The following traces of reading achievement scores of pupil cohorts from the third through the eighth grades in one state, the fourth through tenth in another, and the third through ninth in a third state, superimposed on the *grade* score traces indicated earlier, demonstrate this phenomenon.

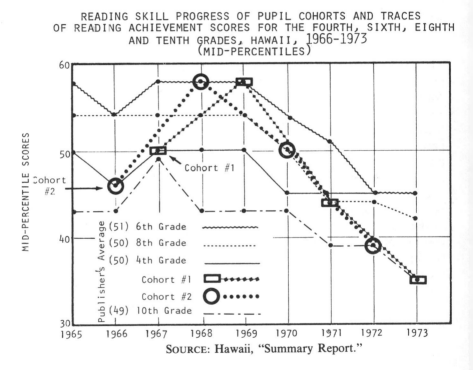

READING SKILL PROGRESS OF PUPIL COHORTS AND TRACES OF READING ACHIEVEMENT SCORES FOR THE FOURTH, SIXTH, EIGHTH AND TENTH GRADES, HAWAII, 1966-1973 (MID-PERCENTILES)

SOURCE: Hawaii, "Summary Report."

The conventional explanations that the fundamental characteristics of the peer groups changed significantly in the span of, in one case, one year, and in the worst case, three years, seem a little weak. Socioeconomic status and IQ, or attitude of the parents, of an entire cohort in Iowa should not change much in a year, or even in three or four years. The same should hold true for Hawaii. Even in New York, since the private schools are included in the study and upstate scores are falling faster than those in the city, the rationale of changing population is somewhat feeble.

READING SKILL PROGRESS OF PUPIL COHORTS AND TRACES OF
READING ACHIEVEMENT SCORES FOR THIRD THROUGH EIGHTH GRADES,
IOWA, 1966-1972
1965 "BASE-YEAR" PERCENTILE RANKS*

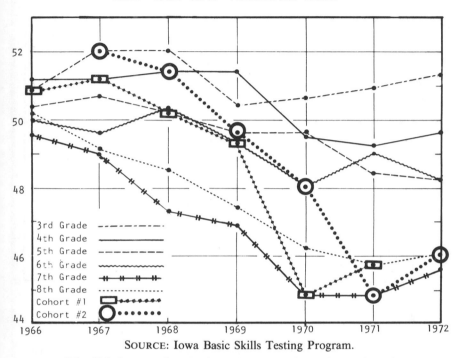

SOURCE: Iowa Basic Skills Testing Program.

*The fiftieth percentile point for each grade in 1965 is the starting point.

Moreover, in examining the data one is struck by the apparent importance, at least in these instances, of the trend in the *grades* over the years, despite the characteristics of the children in them. It should also be noted that these data, with the possible exception of the tenth grade in Hawaii, all came from within the realm of traditional pre-dropout student cohort groups. Since long before World War II children have been forced by law in most states to remain in school until the age of sixteen. Changes in dropout rate could therefore not have affected these average scores.

The often cited factors of changing population, poor socioeconomic conditions, ethnically incompatible teachers, or excessively high pupil/teacher ratios, which in fact fell throughout this period, do not explain the decline in academic achievement of entire cohorts over a short period. We must look to other causes. We must now look at the schools themselves. We must look at the teachers and curriculum, at teaching methods, at discipline, and at the amount of teacher effort expended in that period. Perhaps only the

READING SKILL PROGRESS OF PUPIL COHORTS AND TRACES OF
READING ACHIEVEMENT TEST SCORES FOR PUBLIC AND PRIVATE SCHOOLS,
THIRD, SIXTH AND NINTH GRADES, NEW YORK STATE, 1966-1973
(PERCENTILE RANK OF MEDIAN RAW SCORES, PUPIL EVALUATION
PROGRAM, BASE YEAR 1965)

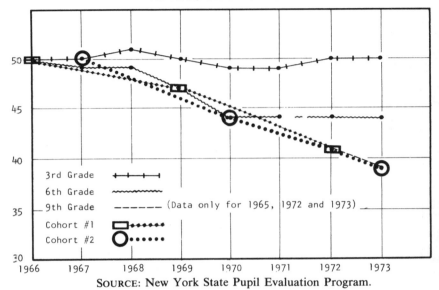

SOURCE: New York State Pupil Evaluation Program.

schools themselves could have caused such rapid change, reducing relative
percentile academic achievement levels of given cohorts in a single year or
two.

More than any other, the College Board Scholastic Aptitude Test (SAT) is
the final publicized, standardized achievement test taken by our high school
students who feel they may enter college. The trend of the SAT, which is
in some sense a test of the fruits of eleven to twelve years of education for
our most intelligent students, is clear. There has been a consistent drop in
the mean SAT scores over the past thirteen years.

"Between 1964–65 and 1973–74 a general decline also was shown on
scores on the ACT. . . ," according to the Los Angeles *Times,* Aug. 15,
1976, p. 3. The ACT is a test similar to the SAT, used primarily in the
central part of the country for the same purposes, as a "college board" test.

Although educators have advanced many reasons to account for this
drop in SAT and ACT scores, none has considered the drop in the context
of other achievement trends. But given the achievement data we have cited,
it would be surprising if the SAT scores did not decline.

MEAN SCHOLASTIC APTITUDE TEST (SAT)
SCORES FOR ALL CANDIDATES, 1956-76

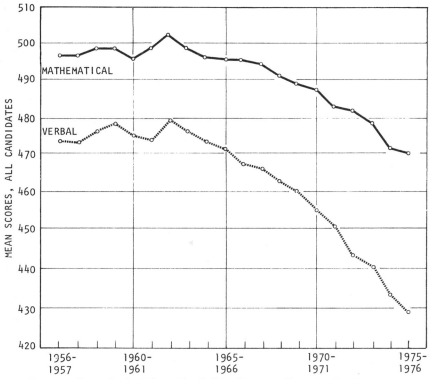

SOURCE: Data obtained from the College Entrance Examination Board, New York, N.Y.

Many educators have suggested that the main reason for the decline was that with the increasing number of students encouraged to take the test, those tested no longer represented just the "cream" of the student body, so the average scores were bound to fall.

There are two objections to this explanation. First, while it is true that the number of test-takers increased in the 1960s—from 933,000 candidates in the 1962–63 school year to 1,606,000 in 1969–70—the number of candidates declined to 1,354,000 in 1973–74.[38] Yet the scores continued to drop. During this period, the verbal aptitude scores dropped at about twice the rate of the mathematical scores, but both plummeted at a *faster* rate than they had during the prior five years, when the number of students taking the test was increasing. It also seems that the spread of candidates over the years had not changed very much. For example, in 1959–60 the standard deviation on the SAT verbal was 108 points, and in 1968–69 it was also 108 points.[39]

Second, during this decline, even the "cream-of-the-crop" students in primary and secondary schools were also declining in achievement. As we have seen in the comparison of scores on the Iowa Tests of Basic Skills, the top students suffered the greatest decline in achievement. Similarly, in California, we saw a decline in the seventy-fifth percentile of twelfth graders that exceeded the twenty-fifth percentile pupils. By definition such a test as the SAT should make the top-scoring students readily identifiable; the absolute number of top-scoring students should remain about the same— or actually increase, since the high school student body expanded during this time—regardless of how many of the lower scoring students were included. This was not consistently the case; for example, in the year between 1972 and 1973 the number of male high school seniors scoring between 750 and 800, the highest possible score, on the verbal portion of the test declined from 1,573 to 987.[40] On the other hand, among high school seniors who took the test in 1976, the number scoring above 600 on the verbal score—about 82,000—had increased by 4 percent over 1975. Those scoring between 400 and 600—about 520,000—had decreased by 4 percent and those scoring between 200 and 400—about 397,000—had increased by 6 percent. In mathematics, those scoring over 600 increased by 5 percent and those scoring below 400 increased by 3 percent. "The trend toward an increase in the number of relative low scores in both sections of the test continues," a report from the College Entrance Examination Board stated, "but it has been moderated somewhat this year by an increase in scores above 600."[41] According to the Educational Testing Service, this examination "changes little from year to year in the kinds of questions asked."[42]

Between 1975 and 1976, the average score of the English Composition Advanced Placement Test, taken by about the top 20 percent of those seniors taking the SAT rose by 17 points. But at the same time, on a three-digit basis, there was a one-point drop in the average Standard Written English Test score, and a two-point drop in the average reading test score, both of which are taken by *all* students taking the SAT.[43]

Some educators and testers still seemed reluctant to admit that these youngsters are not as well educated as those in the past; and some gave, as reasons for the poorer scores, explanations from the hardly plausible to the somewhat plausible. For example, some claimed that the declining scores resulted from the fact that there was a yearly variation in the students taking the test.[44] This would logically mean that the scores should vary, going up one year and down the next, but they have not behaved this way since the late 1950s and early 1960s. The declines from the mid-1960s to the present have been consistent: thirteen consecutive years of drops on the average score of the SAT verbal test, with the exception of 1966, when the score remained the same as in 1965; the same is true for the mathematical test (see the graph on p. 57). A well-known rule of thumb from the field of statistical quality control asserts that seven consecutive drops in a trend probably mean that the process under observation is out of control. In the late 1950s and early 1960s the mean SAT scores fluctuated as if the changes were truly random—up and down over time. Since then, the consistent drops contrast sharply with the formerly random pattern. The drop in SAT scores is statistically significant—there is some assignable cause that accounts for the drop.

Another explanation offered for the decline is that more juniors are taking the SAT and fewer are repeating the test as seniors.[45] Juniors, on the average, traditionally score lower than seniors. This could cause a downward trend in scores if the number of juniors compared to seniors taking the test had been *constantly* increasing, but one doubts even this explanation. Juniors usually take this test in the spring; if they repeat it, they usually take it the following November or December. About 25 percent of the scores made on the test by seniors are *lower* than those they made as juniors. About a decade ago, it was expected that, on average, repeaters would improve their SAT scores by about 20 or 30 points in their senior year. Even the absence of repeaters, however, would not explain the drop, for we know that the average increase in the scores made by repeaters on their SATs in the senior year over the junior year has also been steadily declining over this same time period.

Time magazine reported that "many parents fear, that American schools just are not doing as good a job of developing verbal and mathematical skills as they used to do. . . ."[46] All the arguments against this conclusion have grown less convincing with time, and will continue to do so if College Board scores continue to fall. By 1973 it appeared that the theory of increased numbers taking the test causing the scores to drop was losing credence among the experts, and some, according to a New York *Times* article, seemed ready to consider that the drop in achievement may stem ". . . from an education that does not equip them well for the test, which measures developed abilities."[47]

We would argue that national achievement levels above grade three or four in primary and secondary schools in the last twenty years probably took approximately the shape of the first of the following curves.

If we were to speculate further on that achievement curve from the late 1930s to the present, we would argue that, based on all data mentioned in this and the previous chapter, it would look somewhat like the second.

APPARENT ACADEMIC ACHIEVEMENT CURVE

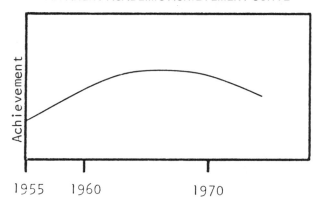

APPARENT CYCLICAL ACHIEVEMENT CURVE

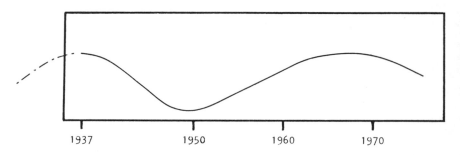

In addition to the plethora of statistical evidence, much anecdotal evidence by university professors, some of it very emphatic, indicates that the high schoolers we have been sending to college in recent years have not measured up. As Karl Shapiro said back in 1970,

> Students in similar creative writing programs today, according to my experience all over the United States, can no longer spell, can no longer construct a simple English sentence, much less a paragraph, and cannot speak. We have the most inarticulate generation of college students in our history. . . . But what is really distressing is that this generation cannot and does not read. I am speaking of university students in what are supposed to be our best universities. Their illiteracy is staggering.[48]

The accuracy and the prophetic nature of this observation was proven by the increasing linguistic incompetence of college students. In 1976 at Johns Hopkins, Ohio State, and the University of California (statewide) the impressions of educators are that the students' abilities in reading and writing are down.[49] The Council on College Composition and Communication seems to have lowered its standards for technical craft skills of writing.[50]

The Los Angeles *Times* in August 1976 summarized its own findings as follows: "According to interviews with scores of educators across the country—persons who deal with students rather than statistics—the answer is 'yes,' today's students are lagging behind yesterday's."[51] Even four-year colleges have discovered that many high school graduates entering college these days cannot understand the textbooks that high school graduates used to be able to read. Textbooks are now being scaled down to this lower capability with "fewer abstractions and more repetition of concepts," according to a New York *Times* article.[52]

Many schoolteachers and college professors feel current students are not as well grounded in mathematics as they used to be.[53] One noted educator, Joseph Schwab, warned in 1969 of general "privation" in thinking and decision-making ability among recent products of our secondary school system.[54] Such observations are quite common when one talks to almost any group of thoughtful professors about students in the late 1960s and early 1970s.

Nor are these observations the only evidence of recent educational decline. In mid-1973 The New York *Times* reported, for example, that an estimated "19 million Americans over 16 were functionally illiterate," unable "to read job application forms, drivers license examinations and newspaper want ads" or to distinguish between medicine bottles by reading simple labels.[55] This statement agrees with results of a Harris survey for the Department of Health, Education, and Welfare in 1971, in which each person was given a test on this kind of subject matter. The survey showed that 15 percent of people over 16 years of age were illiterate by these standards. Blacks showed 32 percent illiterate, whites 11 percent. Among high school graduates, 13 percent were illiterate, and among those with some college and college graduates, 7 percent. Those 50 and over and 16-year-olds had particularly high illiteracy rates.[56]

Perhaps more disturbing are the results of an earlier survey of literacy (by test) of 12- to 17-year-olds between 1966 and 1970, and reported in December 1973 by the U.S. Department of Health, Education, and Welfare. The data indicate that 4.8 percent of the adolescents tested could not read at "the beginning of the fourth grade level." More than one in five black boys, or 20.5 percent, in that age bracket could not read simple paragraphs such as:

> It was spring. The young boy breathed the warm air, threw off his shoes and began to run. His arms swung. His feet hit sharply and evenly against the ground. At last he felt free.[57]

Furthermore, some claimed, like Wallace Roberts, that functional illiteracy "has shown no sign of abating with illiteracy levels remaining constant for the past 20 years."[58] If true, this would be very disturbing, considering the fact that by 1972 the percent of the population over 25 years of age that had received eight full years of schooling had risen to over 88 percent, and those with five to seven years to almost 92 percent. Of those between 25 and 29 years of age, 99.2 percent had five or more years of school.[59]

However, the New York City school system's Bureau of Educational Research, in explaining why the city showed up badly in 1971 when compared to the national reading ability average, apparently taken in 1970, stated, as reported in the New York *Times,* that "In general, the pupils in the 1970 national sample were better readers than pupils in the 1958 sample [used for comparison purposes prior to 1971]."[60] This may have been a true description of the ability of the two samples of students at the different dates when the test was normed, but New York City reading scores continued to decline in 1972 below the 1971 achievement levels, even though both results were compared to the same new 1970 national norm.

Such well-meaning statements have tended to confuse parents and policy makers alike. In fact, this comparison of pupils' relative achievement at different time periods becomes quite philosophical. According to Jerome Kagan:

> . . . every two or three generations the level of mastery that will be regarded as poor, average or advanced is likely to change.
>
> The amount of knowledge possessed by the 10-year-old son of a doctor living in 17th-century rural Massachusetts was probably far below that possessed by a 10-year-old boy in Harlem in 1973. Yet the former was probably classified as intellectually precocious in 1690 because he was compared with Indian children living outside the village, while the black New York child is classified as retarded with respect to the white middle-class child living in Forest Hills.[61]

There is validity to the point that it is unjust to compare achievement of different groups of children—among other things, their average IQ scores may vary—but it is cause for concern when any group of children falls below a certain traditionally recognized minimum competence. In any event, the preceding statement seems a little too stark. One doubts that a doctor's ten-year-old son, even in 1690 rural Massachusetts, would be considered "intellectually precocious" if his ability to read or do simple ciphering were as limited as that of countless ten-year-olds in today's Harlem. The obvious discrepancies become very worrisome when we compare the low academic achievement of children who all are "in the village" with the higher academic achievement of children who were in the same village ten years previously, often under worse economic conditions and with far "inferior," far cheaper, education systems.

This is not to say there are no problems in judging how effective our present schools have been, particularly past ninth grade, compared to schools of thirty-five or forty years ago. Many more students go through senior high school these days than in the past. And more important, children have been promoted through the grades who used to be kept back until they knew the subject matter.

PERCENT OF COHORT KEPT BACK
ONE YEAR AND/OR DROPPED OUT
BY THE ELEVENTH GRADE

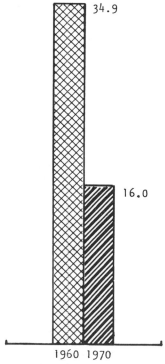

34.9

16.0

1960 1970

SOURCE: U.S. Census Bureau, *U.S. Stat. Abst.: 1973*, p. 121.

High schools these days often are actually judged on their "holding power," that is, what percent of the children who entered ninth grade graduate with their cohort four years later. The smaller the dropout rate, the better the school is considered.[62] Under these conditions, and under any method of teaching, the quality of the average student is bound to fall. But eventually the students must pick up the upper grade skills or become poorer students; the SAT and Iowa test scores seem to bear this out. Since almost half of all high school students now go on to college, the quality of the average college freshman is bound to have fallen too.

Evaluating school effectiveness over time is not quite as difficult with elementary and junior high school pupils, who for several decades by law have had to remain in school until they were sixteen years old. Students are not held back in these grades anymore either, so many an eighth grader of today may have only been equal to a sixth grader of the same age in the old system, if that.

PERCENT OF COHORT KEPT BACK AT LEAST ONE YEAR
BY THE SIXTH GRADE

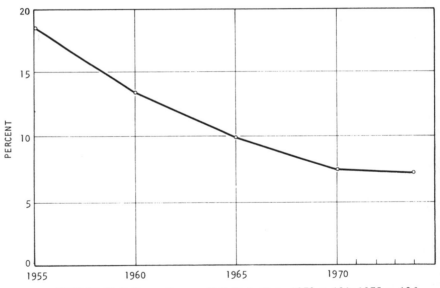

SOURCE: U. S. Census Bureau, *U. S. Stat. Abst.: 1973*, p. 121; *1975*, p. 126.

This new promotion policy cannot, of course, account for the drop in achievement scores since the mid-1960s, nor the degree of acceleration of the drop. First of all, as the graph indicates, the easy promotion policy was well under way in the late 1950s and early 1960s, when average academic achievement was *rising*. Since 1970 the pass-on rate reached about 93 percent at the sixth grade level and remained there to 1974. Clearly other factors are at work here.

In 1976 there apparently still are educators who challenge the idea that the scores are really declining.[63] Indeed, some use the oldest and most questionable excuses. One educator was reported to have contended still, in addressing a state school board association in fall 1976, that achievement scores were lower because we were now carrying more students in our high schools who formerly would have dropped out (which does not explain lower scores in primary and junior high school —before dropout rates significantly affect scores), and that "College Board scores are going down because more young Americans are taking the test."[64] The latter part of the statement has been demonstrably inaccurate since 1970, as pointed out earlier. Furthermore, according to a New York *Times* article on November 8, 1976 (p. 18), a recent report to the U.S. Office of Education states that high school pupils spend too much time on academic work and recommends that they spend only two to four hours per day on it.

There does seem to be some evidence on a national scale that at least some of the very lowest achievers may have begun to bottom out in recent years. Based on a "mini-assessment" test given in 1974 to 17-year-olds enrolled in school, it was concluded by the Education Commission of the States: "Overall functional literacy scores improved an average of 2 percentage points between 1971 and 1974. In general, groups with the lowest scores in 1971 gained the most in 1974: those whose parents had no high school education gained 4.7 percentage points, blacks gained 3.6 percentage points and those who lived in the inner city gained 3.6 percentage points."[65]

In comparing reading skills of 9-, 13-, and 17-year-olds between the 1970–71 and 1974–75 school years, according to a National Assessment of Educational Progress Test, the following results were reported:

> Nine-year-olds during the second assessment read significantly better than did 9-year-olds four years earlier. The improvement was recorded in all reading skills, but most noteworthy in reference skills.
>
> The reading ability of 13- and 17-year-olds changed little over the four-year period. Both ages recorded slight improvement in literal comprehension, but slight decline in inferential comprehension. Thirteen-year-olds declined in their performance of reference skill items, 17-year-olds improved on the reference skill items.
>
> Students of all ages demonstrate little difficulty in comprehending basic, literal, straightforward written material. But comprehension drops off quickly as soon as the reading tasks become more difficult.

The following test scores were presented in the document:[66]

COMPARATIVE SCORES ON LITERAL COMPREHENSION SECTIONS OF TEST

9-year-olds		13-year-olds		17-year-olds	
1970-71	1974-75	1970-71	1974-75	1970-71	1974-75
(%)	(%)	(%)	(%)	(%)	(%)
64	66	33	31	47	49
40	32	63	57	60	60
53	52	18	16	29	26
NA	NA	60	54	70	76
NA	NA	68	74	72	79

COMPARATIVE SCORES ON INFERENTIAL SECTIONS OF TEST

9-year-olds		13-year-olds		17-year-olds	
1970-71	1974-75	1970-71	1974-75	1970-71	1974-75
(%)	(%)	(%)	(%)	(%)	(%)
43	37	64	64	81	82

COMPARATIVE SCORES ON REFERENCE SECTIONS OF TEST

9-year-olds		13-year-olds		17-year-olds	
1970-71	1974-75	1970-71	1974-75	1970-71	1974-75
(%)	(%)	(%)	(%)	(%)	(%)
57	60	42	40	63	59

The press recorded these results with front-page column heads such as "Monitors Find No Deterioration in Reading of U.S. Schoolchildren."[67] The headline is not necessarily inaccurate, but the statement in the booklet just cited concerning the nine-year-olds might be considered by some to be too optimistic. According to the test results contained in the document and listed here, 9-year-olds in the 1974–75 school year improved by two points over 1970–71 9-year-olds in one section of the literal comprehension portion of the test, but fell by 8 points in another section and 1 point in a third. On the "inferential" portion of the test, 9-year-olds dropped 6 points, but on the "reference" skills portion they rose 3 points. Apparently, the weight given to each section is primary in deciding how much improvement, if any, there has been.

On the literal comprehension portion between the 1970–71 and 1974–75 school years, 13-year-olds' scores dropped from 2 to 6 points in four out of five sections, and gained six points in one section. They remained the same on the inferential portion of the test and fell two points on the reference skills portion. For the same time period, 17-year-olds gained from 2 to 7 points in three out of five sections of the comprehensive portion of the test, remained the same in one and dropped 3 points in another. They gained one point in the inferential section and dropped four points in the reference skills portion.

We must also insert one caveat here. According to the Los Angeles *Times* ". . . Wiley pointed out that the gain [among 17-year-olds] may be relatively insignificant since the reading material on the National Assessment Test was much simpler compared to that on school tests for the same age level."[68]

But an earlier comparison of writing skills between the 1969–70 and the 1973–74 school years had virtually no bright spots: 9-, 13-, and 17-year-olds all dropped in skills. The Education Commission of the States found: "In 1974 the percentage of coherent paragraphs written by 17-year-olds declined from an average of 85 percent to 76 percent, with the biggest decline occurring among the poorer writers."[69] And a comparison of basic science knowledge between the pupils of the 1969–70 and the 1972–73 school years showed 13- and 17-year-olds having "fewer correct answers in 1972–73 than in 1969–70."[70]

Leaving aside for the moment the achievements of the "9-year-olds"— for they may simply fit into the traditional stable and rising achievement pattern for children at the lower end of the elementary grades, referred to throughout this book—possibly, at least in reading, the lower achievers in the upper elementary and high school grades have begun to decline less rapidly, and perhaps to "bottom out."[71] This trend was not reflected, however, in the reading tests given to high achievers in the top grade, along with the SAT. Between 1974–75 and 1975–76 school years, the average score on this standard reading test taken by the college-bound upper third of the senior class dropped two points.[72]

It is still too early to tell, but we may be seeing a repetition of the phenomenon that apparently occurred in the ITBS renorming data, where the lower tenth percentile children actually improved somewhat between 1964 and 1971, but the ninetieth, or upper tenth, percentile, and the overall average for all children, fell (see pp. 36–39). This pattern may also be discernible in the California data, which show that between 1969–70 and 1972–73, the seventy-fifth, or upper twenty-fifth percentile children fell faster in academic achievement than the lowest twenty-fifth percentile (see pp. 216–217), and in New York State data, which shows upstate achievement falling faster than in "core-city" New York.

The improvement of the low achievers is very important and must always be sought; but historically the way to raise this group efficiently has been to upgrade the whole student body.[73] Currently it is possible that, inadvertently, we may not be doing this. And if further data confirm this situation, it will mean that our most recent efforts at education may be a failure, in that the slowing of the descent, or perhaps in some cases even the leveling off, of the achievement of lower achievers has been accompanied by a precipitous drop in the academic skills of our higher achievers.

There could conceivably be even another factor involved if the above-600 verbal scores—about 3 percent of high school seniors—on the SAT and the English Composition Advanced Placement tests scores—7 percent of seniors—continue to rise in the coming years, as they did this past year, but the Standard Written English test given to all those who take the SAT, and the *average* SAT scores themselves, continue to fall, as the former did for the past year and the latter for the past thirteen years.[74] Since the number of people taking the SAT has stabilized, a trend like this, along with the other achievement score trends, may mean that only the *very* highest and the lowest achievers are holding their own or rising, while the great center and high achievers fall further toward the lowest achievers. This situation, too, would represent a school system that failed. However, as yet there is no real evidence of such a trend among the very highest, center, and high achievers.

The skewing of the SAT scores of the great mass of high- and middle-achieving college-bound high school seniors toward the down side between the 1974–75 and 1975–76 school years, despite the increase in the few highest achievers, is apparent from the following stylized distribution curves.

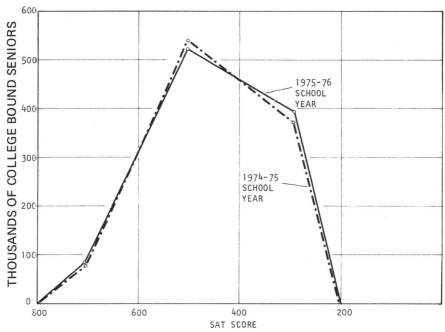

SOURCE: College Entrance Examination Board, *National Report, 1975–76,* pp. 6–7.

5

IQ LEVELS FROM WORLD WAR I TO THE PRESENT
by Paul Bracken

The preceding data, which seem to imply an almost cyclical change in academic achievement characteristics over the decades—at least for the upper primary grades and high school—tempt one to consider the possibility of a changing national mean IQ. This is a difficult assumption to substantiate, but the available data should perhaps be examined to see whether changes in mean IQ can be traced nationally.

The primary source of information in the area of mental competence comes from repeated mass testing programs. The most notable example of this is the testing performed by the military. For example, the U.S. Army first administered mental ability tests during World War I, and continued its testing during World War II and afterward. (Psychometricians generally use levels of scores on these tests as indicative of IQ levels.) Although different tests were used for many of the administrations, it is possible to equate the scores from different tests. This allows a very long-term look at mental ability amid the young adult male population of the United States. As with all studies that consider real data, caution must be used. Errors due to sampling, changes in test score equating, scoring variations, and other factors too numerous to mention are all present. However, two facts make analysis of the data worthwhile: the large sample sizes involved, and the fascination associated with even crude estimates of national mental ability.

A comparison of ability levels of World War I and World War II groups was made possible by a readministration of the World War I Army alpha test. A sample of 768 white enlisted draftees was chosen to be statistically representative of the entire 1943 draft.[1] This sample was given both the Army alpha test and the World War II Army General Classification Test (AGCT), both of which seemed to be measuring the same skills and functions. The correlation coefficient between the results was .9. The results indicated a truly dramatic rise in mental ability when the scores on the alpha were compared to the scores of a large group of World War I white enlisted soldiers. The World War I group, with a sample size of 48,102, obtained only a twenty-second percentile score in terms of the World War II group. The average World War II soldier would have placed at the eighty-third percentile in terms of the original alpha group. Note also that the 1943 group was probably much more representative of the nation than the 1917 sample. In 1917 only the "cream" of the Army was included among the 48,102 soldiers, since illiterates and those who originally did badly on the alpha test were screened from the sample.[2] It is easy to show that both samples were representative of the underlying populations from which they were drawn.[3]

Some further results of Army testing are also available. Scores from sample groups taking the Armed Forces Qualification Test (AFQT) in 1955, 1962, and 1970 can be equated to scores on the World War II AGCT. Since the World War I scores can also be transformed into World War II categories, a stream of mental ability estimates for most of the twentieth century can be obtained. Using the following definitions, it is possible to make comparisons of this ability for very large sample sizes.

WORLD WAR II MENTAL CATEGORY DEFINITIONS

Category I	93.3 - 100.0 percentile
Category II	69.1 - 93.3 percentile
Category III	30.9 - 69.1 percentile
Category IV	6.7 - 30.9 percentile
Category V	0.0 - 6.7 percentile

The equating of data to the World War II categories shows the following: (All numbers give percentages of soldiers falling in the respective baseline World War II category.)

TWENTIETH CENTURY TRENDS IN MENTAL ABILITY
BASED ON MILITARY TEST DATA

	World War I (1917-1918)	1941	1943	All World War II*	1955	1962	1970
Category I	1%	9%	6.4%	8.8%	6.9%	5.9%	3%
Category II	8	36.4	28.6	28.5	20	24	33
Category III	31	29.0	31.1	30.7	36	37	36
Category IV	50	17.0	28.5	26.2	23	28	20
Category V	10	8.6	5.4	5.8	14.1	5.1	4

This table shows the massive increases in mental ability between the world wars. The results after World War II are based on smaller sample sizes. Taking the midpoint of each category and multiplying it by the obtained percentages permits a crude estimate of the mean. The results yield the following:

	1917	1941	1943	1941-45	1955	1962	1970
Mean score	31.8	55.4	51.1	51.2	44.6	49.5	55.5

While these must be considered crude estimates, the implications are fascinating. Why did the tremendous growth of the pre-World War II era top out? It is difficult to suggest any explanations that can be backed up with data. Some experts suggest that industrialization, the introduction of radio broadcasts, improvements in nutrition, and mass education are all important factors in the pre-World War II gains. The postwar scores came from samples that were much smaller. The drop of 1955 could therefore be a sampling anomaly, caused by the inherent variability of any sample. Other estimates of mean AFQT score trends for the postwar era give:

1952:   52   1957:   53.3
1953:   52   1963:   53.1
Source: "Successive AFQT Forms—Comparisons and Evaluations." Technical Research Note No. 12, May 1963, U.S. Army Personnel Research Office.

We do not know the sample sizes of these studies (each number given represents the results of a different individual study) or any other details, but these scores are much closer to the total World War II score and to the 1970 estimate. Furthermore, 1952 was a heavy manpower year for the armed forces and, assuming no defects in the study that produced the figure for that year, it would lead us to doubt the trough indicated by the previous 1955 and 1962 estimates and to assume they were probably biased below the true mean value. If this were the case, then the postwar mean scores would lie in the range of 51 to 55 points. However, because of their large samples, the estimates for World War I and World War II are still valid.

In summary, there were large gains in mental ability between the world wars as measured by Army mental examinations. Other indicators of mental ability almost invariably show increases when similar populations are tested some years apart.[4] It is possible that the slope of this curve in IQ improvement was even steeper in some areas and/or in some years of this time span. For example, children from Tennessee mountain areas were tested in 1930 and 1940. The 1940 results showed a gain of about .6 standard deviations.[5] Considering the time span involved, this seems to be an even greater rate of gain than that found in the military data. The trend since the war, however, does not continue the large increases apparent in the previous era but shows a stabilization of the increase. Assuming that the trough apparently indicated by the initial set of AFQT scores was an invalid indicator, there is no significant evidence that mental ability of men of military age has declined from the World War II mobilization base levels to the present mid-1970s. In any event, the changes from year to year in the postwar Armed Forces Qualification Test scores are quite small compared to the changes in the prewar era.

We have a less encouraging indication, however, from at least one school system for the years 1969 to 1973. These data reflect the IQ of a very large sample of pupils—about a quarter of a million twelfth graders tested each year and about a third of a million sixth graders—from a very large, cosmopolitan state, California. The statewide mean IQ of twelfth and sixth graders decreased through four school years as follows:[6]

	Twelfth Graders	Sixth Graders
1969-1970	101.5	98.1
1970-1971	101.0	97.2
1971-1972	99.1	96.6
1972-1973	98.8	96.3

SOURCE: *California State Testing Program 1971–72 & 1972–73.*

Furthermore, these falling IQ scores for both grades track the achievement scores in both the California twelfth grade data and the Iowa Tests of Basic Skills data in that the drop is greater among the seventy-fifth percentile, or more intelligent, students than among those in the twenty-fifth percentile:[7]

	Twelfth Grade		Sixth Grade	
	75th Percentile	25th Percentile	75th Percentile	25th Percentile
1969-1970	113.2	90.5	109.0	87.9
1970-1971	112.8	90.2	108.2	87.4
1971-1972	110.5	88.7	107.5	87.0
1972-1973	110.1	88.3	107.0	86.9

SOURCE: *California State Testing Program 1971–72 & 1972–73.*

6

SOME INTERPRETATIONS OF IQ DATA

California apparently is not unique in showing this possible drop in IQ in recent years. Many other states—for example, Idaho, New Mexico, Ohio, West Virginia—now list test results in such categories as "abstract reasoning," "academic aptitude," and "total ability." With the exception of West Virginia, where "total ability" held steady and even demonstrated some improvement in the eleventh grade between the 1970–71 and 1973–74 school years, and New Mexico's first grade, which increased its "mental ability" score and the eighth grade, which held steady, while the fifth grade fell, in "academic aptitude" between the 1971–72 and 1973–74 school years, all other states showed a decrease in such "ability" test results.[1] As mentioned earlier, changing populations or shifts to private schools apparently do not solely account for these trends.

If we assume these test results show mean IQ trends, we still hesitate to generalize from this significant sample of states, even when it includes our largest and one of our most diversified states (which clearly indicates its data are IQ test results), particularly when West Virginia data apparently contradict this trend. On the other hand, we have found so much similarity between states as regards trends in the academic achievement area that one also hesitates to ignore the possibility that in mean IQ we may once again be seeing a general trend reflected in statistics from several different types of IQ tests, and possibly IQ indicative tests, from various states, including our most populous. West Virginia's "total ability" scores may be somewhat atypical, as apparently are its almost stable academic achievement scores. In any event, the possibility of the mean IQ going down in recent years among the many states with extended periods of declining academic achievement scores should not be ignored. Yet a 1972 study by a team led by Thorndike showed 10-, 15-, and 18-year-olds to be superior in IQ to similar groups in the early 1930s. The 1972 study included ethnic minorities; the earlier one did not.[2] Ten-year-olds in 1933 were twenty-year-olds in 1943, the high achievers in the Army alpha test, the high achievers in ninth grade in 1937. If 1972 ten-year-olds were more intelligent than the 1933 ten-year-olds were, then the sixth graders who preceded these 1972–73

sixth graders must have been even more brilliant, for 1972–73 sixth graders
in California, and perhaps elsewhere, had a lower IQ than their predecessors. Furthermore, California 1972–73 sixth graders' IQ was not that high
—96.3. Obviously, plotting a clear line of IQ trends over time is impossible.

If, however, one were forced to plot the military mental ability scores on
a graph, it would probably indicate a likely broad band in mental ability
that would show a sharp upward slope for the population of military age
between World Wars I and II. Then the band would plateau with perhaps
a less dramatic rise in the late 1960s, while some Armed Forces Qualification Test data,[3] Navy Trainability data,[4] and the Minnesota high school
senior data might suggest a possible dip in the mid-1950s when these high
school boys entered the service.

Our speculative national mean IQ curve for adults of military age, therefore, may look like this:

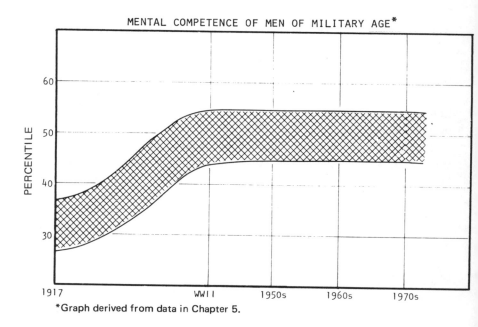

MENTAL COMPETENCE OF MEN OF MILITARY AGE*

*Graph derived from data in Chapter 5.

One is even more reluctant to speculate about reasons for apparent
changes in mental ability, although, as indicated earlier, many have been
offered. For example, Read Tuddenham, who first brought the impressive
change between World Wars I and II to the attention of scholars, felt it was
the direct result of more and better primary and secondary education
enjoyed by World War II draftees.[5] For longer-term trends, others speculate
on genetics and even home environmental effects. We do not claim to know

much about causes of changes in IQ, and particularly short-term changes. Cultural bias in tests and other issues may make a difference, but they probably cannot fully explain changed results of repeated administrations of the same IQ test over a period of years amid the same cultural group. We do not necessarily know, in each case, if there is cause and effect between IQ and academic achievement, and if so, which is which. There is no conclusive evidence that the apparent drop in academic achievement in primary and secondary schools in the late forties was reflected by a drop in the mean IQ of military men in the 1950s, although, as we have seen, some data imply that some drop in IQ may have occurred among these men in the mid-1950s. In general, one feels that the post-World War II data cited are probably too sketchy and crude to reflect anything more than a band of IQ level over the years.

In any event, with the data at hand, it is difficult, except perhaps in the 1930s case, to associate long-term trends in academic achievement scores with trends in a changing mean IQ of men of military age. One could perhaps make the argument that IQ is only "raised" by superior education; that it works on a ratchet principle, so that the thrust of education can drive it up, but when this force is removed, IQ remains suspended at that point until another spurt in education peaks to a new high and boosts it again. The drop in academic achievement in the late 1940s may have indicated that IQ can remain relatively high while achievement falls. The drop in the California mean IQ and perhaps in other states as well, if it continues, may belie this theory, however.

A likely series of speculations derived from the preceding data may be that: (a) the IQ level of the country's young adults, if it changed at all between 1943 and the late 1960s, varied to a much lesser extent than between 1917 and World War II; (b) overall high school student IQ probably did not fluctuate very significantly between the mid-1930s and early 1960s; (c) young adult IQ may have risen somewhat by 1970 and high school pupil IQ by the mid-1960s; (d) the high school pupil IQ may have begun to fall off somewhat in the 1970s; but (e) it would be difficult to prove that the drop in achievement in the 1940s, when there apparently was no great drop in IQ, was due to IQ deficiencies; and (f) there are insufficient data to substantiate or disprove the premise that the current achievement slump that began in the mid-1960s was triggered by an IQ slump. (All upper grades seemed to drop in achievement together, while lower grades maintained their standing. A group of less gifted children moving through the system should cause the lower grades to drop first, and then the upper grades to fall one at a time, with the bottom of the upper grades—say fifth grade—falling first, then the next highest, and so on. In fact, as we have seen, peer groups of children moving through the system go up *or* down in achievement from one year to the next, apparently according to the achievement tracks of the *grades* they enter, not their inherent IQs.) And (g), the level of students' IQ has probably been adequate at all times to cope with learning the fundamentals in primary school and many of those in secondary school.

What we are asking these children to learn is normally not that demanding—reading, basic mathematics, and the other usual subjects. Even the majority of pupils in the twenty-fifth percentile IQ bracket, except perhaps for some of the handicapped, apparently should be able to handle most of the traditional primary school requirements. They should also be able to cope with some of the old high school material—and much of the mandatory high school material as we now know it in many of our large city school systems.

Above and beyond these speculations, however, is the question as to why IQ is falling in states where it seems likely that it is (and why the drop is more severe in the higher percentile brackets), as in California and apparently in New Mexico in the fifth grade. Of course, if the many states with records of continuing achievement decline in the upper grades should turn out to be having the same experience as California, that is, if a national drop in IQ is being experienced, particularly if it is among the higher percentiles as with the achievement drop, this question becomes very important.

The home environment of the ninetieth percentile achievement children, who demonstrated the largest drop in national ITBS scores in 1964–71, and the seventy-fifth percentile IQ children, who had the largest drop in California IQ scores in 1969–70 to 1972–73, is normally thought to be ideal by educators. Their parents are most likely to have high IQs, college degrees, and interest in education. These children are most likely to attend schools in the affluent suburbs, small cities, and better parts of large cities, normally considered the best endowed areas by educators. Such data raise some very important questions as to why *these* children should be dropping so rapidly in achievement, and perhaps also in IQ. What goes on inside their schools must also be scrutinized in our effort to determine what are the most important variables affecting these trends.

7

THE EDUCATIONAL PROCESS

A LONGITUDINAL STUDY

Apparently, the need for longitudinal studies is understood by educators and educational administrators. It is easy to see the value of such studies for planning purposes. One only hopes, however, that the greatest "longitudinal study" of them all is not overlooked. That study, of course, is the record of schooling in the two hundred years of America's existence. One can get the disturbing impression that such a broad study may be receiving insufficient attention, despite the fact that the dramatic changes that are going on today may benefit from it. We say this despite or perhaps because of the fact that over the decades there have been vast changes in the socioeconomic, ethnic, physical, and political backgrounds of the children involved.

In the early days, according to V. T. Thayer and Martin Levit, ". . . the importance of acquainting young people with the nature and operations of our political institutions and, as the guardians of the status quo saw it, with the principles of both private and public morality without which a stable society cannot endure"[1] was fully accepted by those in charge of our educational processes. When large groups of children from rural areas, or with parents from rural areas, both here and in Europe, vast numbers knowing little or no English, entered school,[2] they had to be taught the standards of behavior and requirements of the society, the country, and the city in which they now resided. Thayer and Levit observe:

> "Civics" no longer concerned itself with matters exclusively political, but undertook as well to acquaint young people with the agencies and institutions and the problems of the community. Thus, "community civics" came into being. Similarly, in the elementary school, particularly the need for health education was obvious, education that would safeguard the health of children even when this involved correcting the erroneous practices and ideas of parents.[3]

Because of the increase in adult female and child labor, schools began to teach home economics and shop.[4]

In this time period, however, the schools probably still reflected to some degree the attitude "that the child should fit himself to the curriculum, not the curriculum to the child,"[5] at least in the primary grades. Those children who went to junior high school were confronted with a somewhat different philosophy; ". . . genetic psychology was emphasizing the dynamic and instinctive potentialities of the young person, with the clear implication that nature was to be followed . . ." in contrast to ". . . life outside the school, in home and community, in business and industry, which stressed the importance of education for adjustment, one that would give specific and detailed attention to the formation of desirable habits and skills and techniques."[6] Confronted with this necessity of choice, their educators turned to a psychology that would further education for adjustment.[7]

Obviously, the "principles of both private and public morality" and the desirable habits taught in the schools in those days reflected the value system of the American society. This was basically an Anglo-Saxon society, with a value system adjusted generally to that societal idea. It was a country that, compared to any other great nation in history, provided more opportunity for more people than ever before. It apparently was understood that to take advantage of these opportunities, one would largely have to "adjust" to the society that prevailed in this land. Obviously, one of the places for immigrant children to learn about the value systems and the strange society in their newly adopted country was in the schools. In the case of these children, the schools did, indeed, seem to have a "strong independent effect,"[8] which apparently did much to make up for the "societal deprivation" they experienced in the truly foreign atmosphere of their homes and neighborhoods.

Of particular interest in a study of our public school system is the vast influx of immigrants between 1890 and 1910. By the late 1800s the public school system was well established. The "hump" of increased student population suddenly injected into the system about the turn of the century exceeded that of the 1930s or the 1960s, and the percentage of underprivileged amid this group probably was only exceeded by those of the Great Depression years of the 1930s, if then.

This school system, however, provided education for children of peasant immigrant parents who not only could not speak English but could not read or write the language of their country of origin.[9] Even if parents could read, they often read a language whose alphabet or symbols made it impossible, or at least very difficult, for them to help their children, such as Chinese, Arabic, Hebrew, Yiddish, and to a lesser extent, Russian, Greek, and German. Furthermore, this educational process functioned throughout wars, riots, rebellions, panics, and extended depressions the likes of which would be hard to imagine today.

The author attended grade and high schools in the anthracite coal regions of northeastern Pennsylvania during the Great Depression of the 1930s.

Even the "dumbest" kids in the vast classes of second- and third-generation immigrant pupils from neighborhoods sunk in poverty could read, knew the multiplication tables, and could handle straightforward arithmetic problems. They had much trouble with the tougher "thought" problems, but one suspects that these problems would be even more difficult for the "slow learners" among underprivileged children in our schools today. Both parochial and public grade schools were sometimes quite unpleasant places for a child, and one is glad that some aspects have changed, but the schools also had their good points. "Remedial reading classes" were unknown in those days because everyone could read adequately by the fourth grade. Furthermore, the immigrant and second-generation parents of the native pupils, who had themselves attended these schools for a few years under even worse conditions in the 1890s, could all read, write, and solve arithmetic problems.

After deploring the situation of twelve-year-old boys working in coal breakers, Charles Spahr, a student of the American social scene, wrote of the primary school system in the hard coal fields of eastern Pennsylvania in 1899, a period of a prolonged and rather severe recession in the area:

> . . . most serious of all was the appalling number of little children thrust upon the care of a single teacher. It seemed to me that one of the primary teachers had nearly seventy in her care, and most of these knew hardly a word of English when they came to her. . . .[10]

Later, when he had lost his way in the town and was surrounded by "uncouth and alien faces" of recent adult immigrants (Hungarians and Italians), a product of this school system, "a neatly dressed young married woman" came to this author's assistance. "I turned toward her to ask my question. She answered it pleasantly in the best of English. . . ." Taken aback, our visitor asked how long she had been in America.

> She said that she had come over a child of seven and had lived here ever since, getting her education in the district schools that had seemed to me so inadequate. Apparently her opportunities had been in no way exceptional save her American education, yet in manner as well as face, she seemed a different order from the women about her.[11]

Big city schools hit by the influx of immigrants in this time period had the same problems, "with more than 80 children per teacher in the primary grades" in New York City in the early 1890s. A New York *Times* article reports, "Many buildings were dark, dank and decrepit; in some, the only play space was a fetid, rat-ridden basement" and "thousands of children were denied admission because of lack of accommodations."[12] In 1893 an observer of big city schools, Peter Binzen, was also shocked by conditions, but did not like the achievement either. He wrote of a "typical New York primary school":

> Its characteristic feature lies in the severity of its discipline . . . of enforced
> silence, immobility and mental passivity. The primary reading is, as a rule,
> so poor that the children are scarcely able to recognize new words at sight
> at the end of the second year. Even the third year reading is miserable.

Such harsh discipline apparently was not universal. He later found in
Philadelphia that "the curriculum was narrow and the teachers were unpre-
pared," but also that ". . . the children at times amused themselves by
walking around the room, or by talking so loudly . . . that the teacher could
scarcely communicate with the other pupils. . . ." The reading was "very
bad," the arithmetic "not very much better," and not much else was "attempted."[13]

By 1900 things were still felt to be unsatisfactory. "Despite its compulsory school law, New York City estimated in 1900 that 40,000 children of
school age were not enrolled in school." The total enrollment in elementary
schools was 500,000 and "there were not enough truant officers to round
up the truants and put them in school."[14] This represents a nonenrollment
and/or truancy rate of 8 percent. Today, about 16.5 percent of New York
City's enrolled students are absent on any given day because of illness,
truancy, or other causes.[15]

Nonetheless, some observers felt that the students' behavior was exem-
plary and that these schools, too, seemed to be effective. According to Allon
Schoener, an *Evening Post* (New York) article of January 10, 1903, states:

> Visitors who are taken to lowly primary classes first and then immediately
> afterwards to the highest grammar grades are astonished at the difference.
> While in the lowest grades a glance shows how necessary is the eternal
> vigilance of the teacher, in the higher grades one can see the effect of
> training and habit.

The article noted that outside the school pupils were exposed to foreign
tongues and that these

> . . . often join with the latest slang to form the ordinary language of the
> youngest pupils. Upstairs in the classrooms, all day long, the teachers are
> struggling to overcome these habits of expression, and, considering that
> the child hears English only five hours out of the twenty-four, the results
> at the end of the fifth and sixth years of school life are wonderful.

Furthermore, many of the children

> whose mothers and fathers possibly went out daily to work as the young-
> sters were getting up for the day, acquired their habits through compulsion
> and insistence [of the teachers].[16]

According to a New York *Tribune* article of September 16, 1906 (in Schoener), one New York school had 5,000 students for 96 classrooms. Entire classes of children who couldn't speak a word of English were taught by teachers who used only English.[17] By the 1908–09 school year, however, the pupil/teacher ratio for New York had fallen to 36.9 to 1, which meant an average class size somewhat larger than that but less than 40. In Philadelphia the ratio was 36.5.[18]

These schools were not only inadequate, according to the contemporary observers quoted earlier, in terms of staff members, books (there were no libraries in elementary schools), floor space, and other such requirements, but there was, according to Oscar Handlin, an utter lack of respect for, or identity with, the students on the part of most teachers:

> From the desk the teacher looked down, a challenge they dared not meet. It was foolhardy of course to question her rightness. What an arsenal was at her command to destroy them! The steel-edged ruler across the knuckles was the least of her weapons. Casually she could twist the knife of ridicule in the soreness of their sensibilities; there was so much in their accent, appearance, and manners that was open to mockery. Without effort she could make them doubt themselves; the contrast of positions was too great. . . . There was visible evidence of her correctness in her speech and in her bearing, in her dress, and in the frequent intimations of the quality of her upbringing.[19]

In thirty cities examined during the 1908–09 school year, when schools in our cities were crammed with lately arrived Italian, Polish, Lithuanian, and Russian immigrant families, the makeup of the teaching staff was:

Native-born White	49.8%
Native-born Negro	1.5
English	4.7
Irish	17.8
Scotch	2.3
German	8.0
Other	16.0

NOTE: Reprinted from U.S. Immigration Commission's *Reports,* Vol. 29, p. 137.

A 1909 twelve-city survey showed that 52.8 percent of students in the sample who were children with fathers of non-English-speaking races lived in homes where English was not spoken.[20] In 1909, 57.8 percent of the pupils in thirty-seven of our largest cities were immigrants or the children of immigrants. In New York City such children made up 71.5 percent of the pupil population, in Chicago 67.3 percent, and in Boston 63.5 percent.[21] As we have seen, even when the teachers were "foreign-born," they were not of the "lower class" later East European and Italian immigrant stock, but primarily of "superior" English-speaking (including Scots and Irish) and earlier German immigrant stock. A comparison of national origins—that is, the place of the father's birth—of pupils and teachers in some major cities in the 1908–09 school year is interesting:

1908-09 COMPARISON OF 4 LARGE CITIES: RACIAL COMPOSITION RANKINGS OF STUDENTS AND TEACHERS (PUBLIC SCHOOLS)

	Students		Teachers	
	First Rank	Second Rank	First Rank	Second Rank
Baltimore	Hebrew 13.5%	German 8.7%	German 7.5%	Irish 5.9%
Boston	Irish 16.5	Hebrew 15.7	Irish 23.2	Canadian 4.5
New York City	Hebrew 33.6	German 11.9	Irish 20.7	German 8.0
Philadelphia	Hebrew 16.9	German 9.4	Irish 10.1	Scotch-Irish 5.7

SOURCE: U.S. Immigration Commission, *Reports,* Vol. 29, pp. 21, 140.

NEW YORK CITY RACIAL COMPOSITION, K-12, 1908-09

	Students	Teachers
Native-born White	27.4%	44.6%
Native-born Negro	1.1	.3
English	2.3	4.5
German	11.9	8.0
Greek	.1	--
Hebrew German	3.8	3.7
Hebrew Polish	2.8	--
Hebrew Russian	19.2	3.7
Irish	5.1	20.7
Italian North	3.1	--
Italian South	7.4	--
Swedish	1.2	.4

SOURCE: U.S. Immigration Commission, *Reports,* Vol. 32, p. 615.

CHICAGO RACIAL COMPOSITION, K-12, 1908-09

	Students	Teachers
Native-born White	31.0%	40.0%
Native-born Negro and Indian	1.7	.3 (exclusive of Indian)
Bohemian and Moravian	6.9	.7
Dutch	1.1	.5
English	2.7	5.6
French	.4	.70
German	16.2	10.4
Hebrew German	1.9	1.4
Hebrew Polish	.9	.2
Hebrew Roumanian	.4	n/a
Hebrew Russian	6.8	.2
Irish	4.5	25.2
Italian North	1.1	less than .05
Italian South	3.2	less than .05
Norwegian	2.7	1.7
Polish	3.2	less than .05
Swedish	7.5	2.4

SOURCE: U.S. Immigration Commission, *Reports,* Vol. 30, pp. 546, 678.

PHILADELPHIA RACIAL COMPOSITION, K-12, 1908-09

	Students	Teachers
Native-born White	50.6%	65.4%
Native-born Negro and Indian	5.0	2.5 (exclusive of Indian)
Danish	.2	.1
English	4.4	5.3
French	.4	.4
German	9.4	4.0
Hebrew German	1.9	.8
Hebrew Russian	12.3	.4
Irish	4.4	10.4
Italian North	1.1	.3
Italian South	3.5	.1
Scotch	1.2	2.3

SOURCE: U.S. Immigration Commission, *Reports,* Vol. 29, pp. 21, 140.

BOSTON RACIAL COMPOSITION, K-12, 1908-09

	Students	Teachers
Native-born White	34.9%	58.3%
Native-born Negro and Indian	1.6	.2 (exclusive of Indian)
Canadian (non-French)	7.7	6.3
English	4.1	4.0
French	.3	.1
German	3.0	1.9
Hebrew German	1.1	.5
Hebrew Polish	1.1	.3
Hebrew Russian	12.4	n/a
Irish	16.5	23.8
Italian North	2.2	.2
Italian South	5.9	.1
Scotch	1.8	3.1
Swedish	1.9	.4
Syrian	.3	0.0

SOURCE: U.S. Immigration Commission, *Reports,* Vol. 29, pp. 178, 266.

Nor do the conditions in the smaller cities in the hinterland seem to have been significantly different where large groups of recent immigrants existed. In Shenandoah, Pennsylvania, in the anthracite coal mining region, the national origins of the pupil and teacher population were:

Father's General Nativity	Students	Teachers
Native-born, White	32.9%	29.5%
Foreign-born		
Lithuanian	20.3	2.0
Polish	17.7	1.0
Irish	19.1	56.8
All others		10.2

Source: U.S. Immigration Commission, *Reports,* Vol. 33, pp. 477, 479.

The later immigrants' children were obviously vastly underrepresented on teaching staffs. By modern standards, these were teachers who very likely would have been considered alien to the majority of pupils in many core-city and industrial-area schools.

Nonetheless, though specific data such as modern scholastic achievement scores are rare for these years, one gets the impression that these students did learn to read and write a new language. They also learned fundamental grammar, mathematics, geography, civics, and history—American history. In Chapter 3, we noted some comparative data on reading ability from the second through eighth grades in St. Louis for 1916 and 1938—itself a period of high achievement—and in all cases the 1916 students were superior, except for third graders, who were equal. Even the harshest critics of schools in the depths of New York slums in 1893—schools with eighty children to a class—obviously expected much of the wretchedly deprived foreign-born and children of the foreign-born in these institutions. They complained when these expectations were not realized. The critic cited earlier who condemned these schools stated that *second* graders "are scarcely able to recognize new words at sight" and that "*even* the third year reading is miserable." (Author's emphasis.) He did not voice the same criticism of fourth and fifth grade reading; one feels that today critics of our vastly more expensive, relatively uncrowded core city schools might often expect less from second and third graders.

What general hard data there are seem to substantiate the impression that the children of immigrants were being educated. The World War I achievement levels of foreign-born draftees who had completed significant amounts of schooling in America, cited earlier, seem to bear this out. There is other evidence. For example, according to the Census Bureau, illiteracy among native-born whites dropped from 6.2 percent in 1890 to 1.6 percent in 1930, when out of a native-born white population of 96.2 million, 25.9 million were children of at least one foreign-born parent.[22] Furthermore, they and their children adapted to this unique culture and as a whole, within two generations, made the American dream come true.

In 1909, of the major immigrant groups in thirty cities studied, those with the most pupils "retarded"—that is, more than two years below the grade in which they should be enrolled, for example, twelve instead of nine years old in the fourth grade—were the Italians, Poles, and Russians (almost entirely Russian Jews).

A glance at the charts on pages 88–89 and 90 indicates part of the reason many of these students were "retarded" when they entered school. Obviously, the foreign-born pupils, particularly those who had never been inside a school in their native land, who entered the country "over age in grade," would be the hardest hit. A pupil who did not know English would almost have to start in first or second grade even if he were ten years old. Those few who risked starting in the higher grades apparently did worse than those starting in the lower grades.

Whatever the reasons, however, the large identifiable groups of children of immigrants, the children of Italians, Poles, and Russians, were on the bottom of the heap. Two generations later, the 25- to 34-year-old descendants of these groups, those who left high school in or prior to the early 1960s, before almost automatic promotion and graduation had become quite so prevalent (see last section of Chap. 8), came out above the median educational level of that age group of the population as a whole for that year: between 12.5 and 12.6 years of schooling.[23] Some were also above earlier immigrant groups and the Russian Jews surpassed all groups. (See the table on page 91 for this information.)

GRADE ENTERED BY PUPILS 8 YEARS OF AGE OR OVER (1909)*

General Nativity and Race of Pupil's Father	Percent Who Entered:			Percent Retarded Who Entered:	
	First Grade	Second Grade	Third Grade or Above	First Grade	Second Grade or Above
Native-born:					
White (primary grades)	98.2	1.3	0.5	33.6	49.1
White (grammar grades and high school)	93.0	3.0	3.9	24.3	33.0
Total white	95.7	2.1	2.2	27.9	36.1
Negro	96.2	3.1	.7	66.2	70.8
Indian	90.0	6.7	3.3	54.5	**
Total native-born	95.7	2.2	2.1	30.1	37.9
Foreign-born:					
English-speaking races	92.3	3.1	4.6	25.8	38.0
Non-English-speaking races	94.5	2.5	3.0	41.4	64.7
Total foreign-born	94.1	2.6	3.3	38.6	58.6
Grand Total	94.7	2.5	2.8	35.3	52.4
Foreign-born pupils				60.7	64.0
PRINCIPAL FOREIGN RACES					
English-speaking races:					
Canadian (other than French)	94.7	2.5	2.8	24.3	43.6
English	92.5	3.4	4.1	24.9	33.2
Irish	87.4	3.6	9.1	27.0	35.9
Scotch	88.4	5.3	6.3	28.3	45.9
Welsh	95.1	1.2	3.7	33.3	**

Non-English-speaking races:					
Bohemian and Moravian	96.7	1.9	1.4	34.6	54.7
Canadian, French	84.7	4.0	11.3	40.4	75.7
Dutch	78.2	5.5	16.2	11.9	23.9
German	94.8	2.1	3.1	31.0	60.7
Hebrew, German	97.7	1.1	1.1	36.3	**
Hebrew, Polish	95.1	2.0	2.9	64.7	**
Hebrew, Roumanian	95.0	3.3	1.7	50.5	**
Hebrew, Russian	96.2	2.4	1.4	40.4	55.3
Italian, North	93.6	3.7	2.7	51.3	51.1
Italian, South	96.4	2.5	1.2	62.9	76.9
Italian (not specified)	95.6	2.8	1.6	55.4	73.9
Lithuanian	96.2	1.6	2.2	45.0	**
Magyar	91.5	4.4	4.1	55.0	76.0
Polish	82.0	4.6	13.4	51.1	80.1
Portuguese	97.8	1.5	.7	45.2	53.8
Ruthenian	100.0	--	--	44.1	--
Slovak	90.8	3.9	5.3	53.4	62.5
Swedish	98.1	1.7	.2	15.3	9.7

*Data refer to grade entered in public school; kindergarten excluded.

**Not computed due to small number.

SOURCE: U.S. Immigration Commission, *Reports,* Vol. 29, pp. 69, 70.

PUPILS' AGES AT TIME OF ENTERING PUBLIC SCHOOL IN THE UNITED STATES
BY GENERAL NATIVITY AND RACE OF PUPIL'S FATHER, 1908-09*

General Nativity and Race of Pupil's Father	Total Reporting Complete Data	Number						Percent					
		5 Years or Under	6 Years	7 Years	8 Years	9 Years	10 Years or Over	5 Years or Under	6 Years	7 Years	8 Years	9 Years	10 Years or Over
Native-born:													
White (primary grades)	11,162	3,449	6,052	1,295	256	61	49	30.9	54.2	11.6	2.3	0.5	0.4
White (grammar grades and high school)	10,407	2,956	4,979	1,700	443	83	246	28.4	47.8	16.3	4.3	.8	2.4
Total White	21,569	6,405	11,031	2,995	699	144	295	29.7	51.1	13.9	3.2	.7	1.4
Negro	1,268	206	673	230	102	36	21	16.2	53.1	18.1	8.0	2.8	1.7
Indian	30	7	14	4	3	1	1	23.3	46.7	13.3	10.0	3.3	3.3
Total native-born	22,867	6,618	11,718	3,229	804	181	317	28.9	51.2	14.1	3.5	.8	1.4
Foreign-born:													
English-speaking races	6,728	2,748	2,599	852	226	84	219	40.8	38.6	12.7	3.4	1.2	3.3
Non-English-speaking races	31,140	6,424	15,140	5,104	1,806	818	1,848	20.6	48.6	16.4	5.8	2.6	5.9
Total foreign-born	37,868	9,172	17,739	5,956	2,032	902	2,067	24.2	46.8	15.7	5.4	2.4	5.5
Grand Total	60,735	15,790	29,457	9,185	2,836	1,083	2,384	26.0	48.5	15.1	4.7	1.8	3.9

PRINCIPAL FOREIGN RACES												
English-speaking races:												
Canadian (other than French)	1,807	717	697	282	58	12	41	39.7	38.6	15.6	3.2	.7	2.3
English	2,714	1,236	1,000	283	83	43	69	45.5	36.8	10.4	3.1	1.6	2.5
Irish	1,187	499	409	136	45	19	79	42.0	34.5	11.5	3.8	1.6	6.7
Scotch	321	137	94	48	19	6	17	42.7	29.3	15.0	5.9	1.9	5.3
Welsh	83	--	70	8	2	1	2	.0	84.3	9.6	2.4	1.2	2.4
Non-English-speaking races:												
Bohemian and Moravian	1,614	232	1,047	207	53	25	50	14.4	64.9	12.8	3.3	1.5	3.1
Canadian, French	1,255	534	337	154	62	20	148	42.5	26.9	12.3	4.9	1.6	11.8
Dutch	308	12	186	34	23	19	34	3.9	60.4	11.0	7.5	6.2	11.0
German	5,136	826	3,104	797	186	59	164	16.1	60.4	15.5	3.6	1.1	3.2
Hebrew, German	264	54	134	52	14	2	8	20.5	50.8	19.7	5.3	.8	3.0
Hebrew, Polish	209	29	99	33	18	9	21	13.9	47.4	15.8	8.6	4.3	10.0
Hebrew, Roumanian	300	49	125	60	31	8	27	16.3	41.7	20.0	10.3	2.7	9.0
Hebrew, Russian	7,263	1,534	3,308	1,156	481	256	528	21.1	45.5	15.9	6.6	3.5	7.3
Italian, North	741	138	345	126	56	33	43	18.6	46.6	17.0	7.6	4.5	5.8
Italian, South	4,062	621	1,950	823	338	132	198	15.3	48.0	20.3	8.3	3.2	4.9
Italian (not specified)	1,029	175	501	187	66	34	66	17.0	48.7	18.2	6.4	3.3	6.4
Lithuanian	185	40	82	39	15	4	5	21.6	44.3	21.1	8.1	2.2	2.7
Magyar	312	20	148	63	26	20	35	6.4	47.4	20.2	8.3	6.4	11.2
Polish	1,609	351	514	302	138	64	240	21.8	31.9	18.8	8.6	4.0	14.9
Portuguese	1,835	828	542	245	105	40	75	45.1	29.5	13.4	5.7	2.2	4.1
Ruthenian	81	2	51	19	7	1	1	2.5	63.0	23.5	8.6		1.2
Slovak	353	13	216	67	19	10	28	3.7	61.2	19.0	5.4	2.8	7.9
Swedish	1,647	342	1,029	235	27	9	5	20.8	62.5	14.3	1.6	.5	.3

*Data refer to age at entering grades excluding kindergarten.

SOURCE: U.S. Immigration Commission, Reports, Vol. 29, p. 61.

GRADE ENTERED BY FOREIGN-BORN PUPILS 8 YEARS OF AGE OR OVER
WITH RESPECT TO RETARDATION, BY RACE OF PUPIL'S FATHER (1909)*

Race of Pupil's Father	Pupils Who Entered First Grade			Pupils Who Entered Second Grade or Above		
	Number Reporting Complete Data	Retarded		Number Reporting Complete Data	Retarded	
		Number	Percent		Number	Perce
English-speaking races:						
Canadian (other than French)	48	17,	35.4	27	12	44.4
English	188	48	25.5	111	36	32.4
Irish	1	--	**	--	--	--
Non-English-speaking races:						
Bohemian and Moravian	160	85	53.1	23	15	65.2
Canadian, French	55	38	69.1	37	36	97.3
Dutch	18	3	**	20	9	45.0
German	157	77	49.0	29	20	69.0
Hebrew, Polish	42	33	78.6	10	9	**
Hebrew, Roumanian	67	47	70.1	6	5	**
Hebrew, Russian	1,994	1,177	59.0	203	128	63.1
Italian, North	109	84	77.1	10	9	**
Italian, South	929	713	76.7	55	47	85.5
Italian (not specified)	211	151	71.6	20	19	95.0
Magyar	81	56	69.1	14	10	**
Polish	37	26	70.3	25	22	88.0
Portuguese	341	242	71.0	15	13	**
Ruthenian	4	4	**	--	--	--
Slovak	28	18	64.3	6	5	**
Swedish	1	--	**	--	--	--
Total***	5,674	3,444	60.7	933	597	64.0

*Data refer to grade entered in public school; kindergarten excluded.

**Not computed due to small number.

***Including pupils of races not enumerated above and also pupils of above-enumerated races in cities where less than 50 pupils (native-born and foreign-born) of the races were reported.

SOURCE: U.S. Immigration Commission, *Reports,* Vol. 29, p. 71.

YEARS OF SCHOOL COMPLETED BY PERSONS 25 TO 34 YEARS OF AGE
BY ETHNIC ORIGIN, MARCH 1971

| | Total | Percent Distribution of Years of School Completed | | | | | | | Median School Years Completed |
| | | Elementary | | | High School | | College | | |
		0 to 4 Years	5 to 7 Years	8 Years	1 to 3 Years	4 Years	1 to 3 Years	4 Years or More	
German	100	0.3	1.1	3.2	11.8	48.8	15.0	19.8	12.7
Italian	100	0.9	4.3	3.1	12.3	51.3	12.1	16.0	12.6
Irish	100	0.5	2.2	3.9	15.7	46.4	16.0	15.5	12.6
Polish	100	0.6	0.6	2.8	12.5	46.5	20.1	16.8	12.7
Russian	100	0.0	0.0	0.0	2.7	27.9	18.2	51.6	16.0
English, Welsh, Scotch	100	0.5	1.2	2.9	11.4	41.2	18.7	24.1	12.8

SOURCE: U.S. Census Bureau, *Current Population Reports,* "Characteristics of the Population by Ethnic Origin: March 1972 and 1971," p. 31.

These same immigrants climbed the economic ladder, too, right past earlier immigrants and natives to the top.[24] There is evidence that today 49 percent of blue collar workers' sons between the ages of 18 and 19 are "entering college" and 20 percent of those between 20 and 24 are "continuing college,"[25] so the process of ever higher levels of education obviously continues.

One is always disappointed that there apparently are few, if any, publicized, thorough, scientific studies of past underprivileged children who have bettered themselves and gone to schools of higher education. For example, it might be valuable to see a study of the current status of World War II GI bill students who came from lower socioeconomic backgrounds; many were from first- or second-generation immigrant families. These students generally did not come from scholastically-oriented homes and during their high school years there was no family pressure for children to go to college. On the contrary, there was no expectation of going to college, and the money these boys could earn after leaving high school in the 1930s and early 1940s was eagerly anticipated as family income. There may have been some encouragement from the family to do their best, behave properly in grade and high school and obey the teacher, but this was enforced primarily by teachers, not parents. Many of these students were forced by law to stay in school until the age of sixteen.

In short, they were work oriented and many took vocational courses in high school during the 1930s Great Depression. Nonetheless, when the opportunity presented itself, these "common" but competent young men went on to college and attained what was perhaps the most spectacular scholastic achievement record of any large student group in university history. One observer, Peter Drucker, says about GI bill students who surged onto American campuses after World War II, "Every educator then 'knew' that the large masses of students would inevitably 'debase' academic standards. Instead every teacher found out that the real problem was that these students were so incredibly superior that they made demands the faculty could not satisfy."[26]

A study of these students' grades showed that they surpassed non-GI bill students in *every* discipline.[27] It should be noted that their success has been attributed to everything from their deprived background, which was said perhaps correctly to have motivated them to seize the opportunity for advancement through study (interestingly, some of the same people say current, much less severe deprivation kills learning incentive and even ability), to their relatively advanced age as students. What is overlooked is that, as we have seen, in the mid- and late 1930s, when these boys were the correct grade age, they showed very high academic achievement scores, and in World War II, as normal-age soldiers, caused that spectacular increase in mean mental competence score. The GI bill achievements were attained by this same group. Their GI bill record may have been partly due to their age, but their overall scholastic and intellectual record may also have been partly attributable to the curriculum and work habits forced on them in schools of the 1930s. In Pennsylvania, probably a typical industrial state, even the vocational curricula had strict requirements, including two years of foreign language, one year of algebra and one year of geometry, one year of science, three years of history, and four years of English composition and literature.

Thayer and Levit claim that in the latter part of the nineteenth century:

> The school was envisaged as a means for bettering one's station in life. This gave to learning the appearance of an instrument for purposes practical and ornamental and to culture an external aspect. It was something one might acquire more or less as he buys a new suit of clothes with which to improve his appearance and to gain status, rather than the cultivation of interests and talents genuinely one's own.[28]

Some of this attitude about bettering one's station in life through education seems to have persisted, particularly in the less affluent areas of the country, right up to World War II, and indeed seems to persist today.[29] One is prompted to ask, also, whether this motivation necessarily sees fewer children ending up with "interests and talents genuinely one's own." It would be hard to prove conclusively that people could never end up with their own interests and talents if motivated by the belief in upward mobility through education. It is less difficult to prove that a child with no motivation or one who will not remain in or attend school is highly unlikely to acquire much in the way of academic "interests and talents." The question is probably whether this materialistic approach is more or less likely to motivate children than some higher goal, and, more important, whether the schools will endeavor to equate achievement in academic subjects with success, materialistic or otherwise.

We are not yearning for "the good old days" in education, about which some people say Will Rogers commented, "Schools ain't what they used to be—and never were." There was much wrong with the old schools and the period in which they flourished; yet they never doubted that their primary responsibility was to educate children to "middle-class" standards—a position they would not abdicate regardless of the circumstances or the socioeconomic level of their charges. The system was complicated and quite sophisticated, but it was possible for the teachers turned out by our colleges, by following the system's tenets, to educate all kinds of children. Changes in fundamentals were apparently few and probably long considered before being implemented.

In the late 1930s or the early 1940s, however, apparently a change in attitude took hold in primary and secondary school systems and grew through the mid- and late 1940s. There is evidence that the progressive education movement probably reached new heights in this country just prior to World War II and that its influence began to penetrate the system.[30] The reason for the rather sudden success in the 1940s, in Lawrence Cremin's words, of "a movement that had for more than a half-century commanded the loyalty of influential segments of the American public"[31] is a more interesting issue.

Perhaps the increasing influence of the "progressives" on the school system was the result of a combination of several factors that together weakened the normal leavening influences on such innovative activity. First, the extension of secondary schooling to all had been reinforced by a desire to keep the dropout out of the job market during the Depression. Second, the new politics struck the schools. It was said, for example, that in New York City, "The atmosphere of social tinkering and experimentation, embodied by the New Deal in Washington and Fiorello LaGuardia in City Hall, reached into the office of the superintendent of schools. . . ." Initially a limited experiment that "shifted emphasis from subject matter to the child" was successful, but in 1941 the progressive method was extended throughout the city. As is the case so often, the educators' assumption that "a program which succeeded in a *selective* situation would also succeed in a *universal* situation" was wrong. The top students did well but for the slower students, who were retained in high school almost to adulthood, different "programs" were developed. Diane Ravitch writes:

> Vocational education was one route; a diluted academic curriculum was another. Nonpromotion was frowned on, since it might impair a student's personality development.[32]

In fact, Frederick Breed points out, subject matter, as a whole, and the measurement of pupils' academic achievement was rejected by some:

> The attack on the outmoded subject curriculum first degenerated, in certain activist quarters, into an attack on subject matter as a negligible factor in education and, in its more recent emphasis, on educational measurement as an effete support of subject matter.[33]

Third, the war had a drastic effect on the teaching staffs of our elementary and secondary schools. During World War II, it was estimated that "more than a third (350,000) of the competent teachers employed in 1940–41 had left teaching," most "to accept higher paying positions in business, industry, and government services." Not only were many of the new teachers ill-equipped to teach—almost one-third worked with only emergency one-year teaching certificates—[34] but most of them were probably less well-qualified than their predecessors to evaluate proposed new teaching techniques and programs or moderate them, and/or defend what was good about the old system.

Finally, the old system came under attack from all quarters because it failed to teach what was now felt necessary for the war effort. Ever since the coming of the immigrants there had been recommendations to the schools by various commissions, including those of the American Council on Education and the National Education Association, "to place an emphasis on practical and vocational education." Since 1917 this trend had been encouraged by federal aid,[35] and no doubt the Depression further encouraged it. I. L. Kandel reports:

> There had thus developed a conflict at the secondary level between academic and vocational education. The urgent demands of the war for increased production, industrial and agricultural, and the unrest of youth threw the balance in favor of vocational education. . . . The trend toward the provision of instruction that appeared to be more practical in character and more contributory to the war effort, as well as to the maintenance of student morale, was hastened by the war training program of the U.S. Office of Education and the introduction of preinduction courses encouraged by the armed forces.[36]

"Work-study" programs sprang up in the larger centers, such as the "four-four plan," under which a student went to school four hours a day and worked four hours, for which he also received credit toward graduation.[37] The 1940 report, *What the High Schools Ought to Teach*, written by a special committee for the American Youth Commission and other cooperating organizations, and published by the American Council on Education, had recommended some such program,[38] but it had also recommended a drastic watering down of high school academic subjects. The authors of the report recognized the probability that "teachers of mathematics and parents, wedded to the tradition," would ignorantly or narrow-mindedly insist on retaining such teaching as that of "specialized methods of mathematical manipulation which now confuse pupils. . . ." Foreign languages were said to "consume too much time, much of which could be better spent on newer courses." Natural science courses were said to be:

> ". . . often mere encyclopedic lists of the findings of scientific research. They often fill the memory with facts rather than stimulate pupils to scientific thinking." The separation of facts from thinking is itself interesting. . . . The Committee clearly considered the traditional curriculum to be bookish, nasty, and long.[39]

The whole mobilization of education for the war effort[40] seems to have had a somewhat disrupting effect on education, and though the recognition of the long-range cost of losing pupils and the back-to-school drive of 1943[41] may have been successful in keeping more children in school, the morale of many traditionalist teachers must have been low. They probably felt people were clearly not satisfied with their efforts, and, consequently, their ability to oppose the progressive forces must have been weakened. Even their own faith in the traditional approach to teaching may have wavered under the assault. In any event, the way was now apparently opened for progressives to move in.

In New York City, Ravitch observes, "The schools fulfilled the progressives' demand that they take on the problem of 'the whole child' by enlisting an army of psychologists and social workers."[42] By 1947, "life-adjustment programs," with work experience as an integral part of them, were promoted nationally at local and state school administration levels.[43]

By the late 1940s, however, the "progressives" were under attack from many quarters—parents, taxpayers, and a growing number of intellegentsia.[44] A prime example of the logic behind the criticism from the more thoughtful intellectuals is Cremin's description of the position Arthur Bestor took in his books and articles in the early 1950s:

> . . . intellectual training may not be the only function of the schools, but in the last analysis it is their *raison d'être*. . . . True education, then, is the deliberate cultivation of the ability to think through training in the basic academic disciplines: history, English, science, mathematics and foreign languages.
>
> . . . Democratic education differs from aristocratic education only in the number of persons with whom it deals, not in the values it seeks to impart. To convert the education of the common man into something other than systematic intellectual training is to rob him of his birthright; it is to vulgarize culture under the guise of democratizing it. By training all in the ability to think, the schools distribute intellectual power widely among the people. This and this alone is their distinctive way of contributing to social progress.[45]

Under "the assault of the fifties," Cremin goes on to say, the progressive movement is said to have "collapsed."[46]

In any event, the "silent fifties" seem to have seen a reduction of the influence of the progressives, and things apparently settled down somewhat in primary and secondary schools, as well as on college campuses. These events coincided, as we have seen, with an apparent rise in academic achievement throughout this period in primary and secondary schools.

The respite for the "traditionalists," however, was short lived. In the mid-fifties a policy decision was made in Washington that the Navy, which had no operational long-range missiles and was relatively deficient in space-oriented organization or experienced senior personnel, would be responsible for Project Vanguard, the program to put a small satellite in orbit around earth. The Army, which had the operational Jupiter missile, a top-notch team of space-oriented rocket experts under Wernher von Braun, and an excellent organization and facilities at Huntsville, Alabama, was specifically ordered *not* to attempt to launch a satellite. (The men at Huntsville apparently had designed a satellite.) Meanwhile, the Navy had been singularly unsuccessful in building a satellite launching missile from scratch, and the Vanguard program dragged on through a series of launch and other failures. Eventually the Russians, using a standard military rocket, managed to launch a small satellite into orbit in 1957. At this juncture Washington took the ban off von Braun and his team and within four months the United States, too, had a satellite in orbit. The damage had already been done, however. Few people looked on this progression of events as what it really was: a failure in policy. With such an important event at stake, the government should never have allowed bureaucratic competition and self-interest to divert the project from the group with the operational launch vehicle. Instead, the media began to paint a picture of a Russia that was ahead of us in science, and the inevitable followed: our schools were seen as inadequate in the scientific fields. Furthermore, not only were our universities seen as requiring overhauling, but so were our primary and secondary schools.

Some worthwhile, as well as some ill-advised, programs resulted from the subsequent renovation efforts, but one cannot help feeling that here again was a factor that may have helped to weaken educators' morale and faith in the primary and secondary school system. Even the morale of traditionalists and moderates who otherwise might have leavened the reforms that were to be pressed on the system in the sixties could have been affected. In fact, of course, we were far ahead of the Russians in scientific competence, and twelve years later, in 1969, Americans trained in the old primary and secondary schools put a man on the moon, a feat that the Soviets, by abandoning the race, tacitly admitted was beyond them.

As in the 1940s, coalescing events may have affected the public school system in the 1960s. These events appear somewhat similar, but their sequence is reversed. This time, the late 1950s challenge to the schools' competence on the narrow front of what the schools traditionally have taught came first, in the form of accusations that they were not teaching science well enough. The second attack came during the Kennedy era and the "Great Society" years of President Johnson. During this period the schools were also told that they had a broader social mission that they were not performing. Then, with the rise of the youth and counter-culture movements of the sixties, the "relevance" of all standard education came under attack.

With this bombardment, traditionalists and even moderates found themselves under a pressure somewhat similar to the one their predecessors had experienced twenty years before. The innovators apparently gained strength and, as in the 1940s, we again heard the recommendations emphasizing education of the "whole child." In this case, however, there seemed to be a stronger emphasis by many in the educational field on the theme which implied that the schools could not perform the required educational job. By the mid-1960s a report by Alan Wilson and others stated:

> ... for many years teacher training institutions have taken a fairly uniform stance on the environmentalistic side of the old nature-nurture controversy, and almost all writers in the blossoming literature on the "culturally deprived" have done so. . . .[47]

A principal finding of a 1973 *Study of the Achievement of our Nation's Students* by HEW's Office of Education was:

> Although the role of home and family background factors in achievement greatly outweighs that of school factors, virtually all the differences in achievement associated with racial-ethnic group membership could be

accounted for by considerations that were primarily social in nature and origin.

Furthermore:

It was concluded that, at present, there does not appear to be any single approach by which the achievement levels of large portions of poor children can be transformed so that they can catch up with their more advantaged counterparts in a few years. The problem is one that affects every aspect of society and cannot be solved by the schools alone.

The difficulty with the foregoing statement is that it is perhaps true that "large portions of poor children" would never be able to match the competence level of most of their more affluent fellow students. This, however, may reflect the possibility that the "large portions of poor children" under normal economic conditions in our society, are generally likely to be of a lower average IQ level than children of more highly skilled, better educated, more affluent parents.[48]

The important question is, what happens to the vast majority of poor children with adequate learning ability, or even to the sizable minority of poor children who normally equal or exceed the IQ level of most of the more affluent students? Certainly those students should do just as well in achievement as their counterparts in the more affluent group. The usual argument is that the societal influences mentioned earlier prevent the poor children with adequate IQs from being able to utilize them. For example, the "fading" achievement phenomenon noticeable in the early grades among underprivileged children who have had intensive preschool training (IQs hold up better than cognitive tests) has been explained by the statement by Gray and Klaus that the training was not sufficient "to offset the massive effects of a low income home in which the child had lived since birth onward."[49] That a similar drop in average achievement level as pupils move to higher grades is almost a universal phenomenon affecting pupils at all socioeconomic levels, state- and countrywide, seems to suggest the possibility of other causes. (See Chapter 4.)

The HEW study mentioned just before also seems to say, however, that the socioeconomic level of the family is not nearly as relevant to the child's achievement in school as the family's expectations that he do well. Parental interest in the child's achievement reinforces the idea that he is expected to do well. As one would anticipate, the HEW study shows a relationship between children with high IQ scores and the degree of family interest in their scholastic activity. The most important things to find out, however, are whether parental interest among any and/or all socioeconomic groups is less now than in the past (as we have seen, academic achievement among affluent and high IQ students is apparently falling rapidly, too), and whether, if there is the absence of parental interest and incentives, the school can provide this, that is, give the child the idea that he is expected to learn, work hard, measure up. The statement in the HEW achievement study, ". . . if learning styles and needs are a function of family background, and the schools are able to match individual student learning styles with school resources in such a way that the outcomes of schooling are more nearly equal to the poor children, then we would not be unhappy with this result,"[50] could mean, for example, a greater stress on retentive ability in teaching poor children. But one also fears an interpretation that could mean further questionable tampering with a functioning system. In light of the longitudinal study of the history of our school system, what may be called for here is not a change in teaching style to match poor children, but an insistence on the part of someone, either the parents or teachers, that the students measure up to the standards as they are.

One becomes concerned when the study discusses learning styles. Apparently, what is required is motivation, and one of the proven motivations seems to be that people expect children to do something. It is better if the family expects them to, and, as we shall see in Chapter 8, the degree of expectation does seem to be considerable among the majority of parents, but one feels "surrogate fathers and mothers," that is, the teachers *in loco parentis,* should try to give the impression that they, too, expect these children to work hard to achieve the difficult in the traditional way. But many educators fail in this regard. For example, according to George Kohn, a former English teacher, "Some teachers say flatly that the grammar, the speech pattern, of any individual is all right. . . . Each group has a correct grammar; there is no one correct way."[51]

There are indications, such as the following from Alan Wilson, that schools maintaining high academic standards serve a good purpose, particularly for underprivileged students:

> Students in schools where teachers have stronger educational backgrounds, and higher levels of verbal achievement themselves, benefit by this exposure. This is especially true of minority group children. (It is generally true that disadvantaged youths are more sensitive to extrafamilial environmental influences, while middle-class children are not so strongly affected.)[52]

In fact, in one experiment, reported by Wilson and others, teachers were given fictitious "intellectual potentialities" for their students and by the end of the year pupils' IQ test scores "showed changes commensurate with the false information that had previously been given to the teacher."[53] A worldwide study, described by the New York *Times,* indicated that, in areas where everyone was "deprived" as far as help from parents was concerned, such as foreign languages and science, "school conditions were generally more important." The speculation that this effect might result from the fact that "reading is very closely related to language acquisition which starts at home, while science and foreign languages are more school oriented"[54] is quite important. If true, this may mean that the more things that can be maintained as "school oriented," that is, demanding something desirable for the child to aspire to that may be different from what he is accustomed to at home, the more likely we are to be successful in raising him from his disadvantaged position. Mathematics with its meticulous work can be "school oriented"—even behavior and correct grammar might become school oriented if they are demanded of children. And one feels that a Puerto Rican, Mexican, or other non-English-speaking child, if we treat him as we did immigrant children of old and insist he learn in English-language classrooms, may do better than his home life would indicate, for English is a "foreign language" that is school oriented, with no relation to his home life. The statement in The Coleman Report that "equality of educational opportunity through the schools must imply a strong effect of schools that is independent of the child's immediate social environment . . ." is very pertinent. The report adds, however, "that strong independent effect is not present in American schools."[55]

Such findings would seem to imply that one of the steps needed in this direction is to maintain school requirements and standards. Instead, as we shall see, many school systems have lowered standards in the very schools where underprivileged children are in the majority.

The question that naturally follows is *why* that "strong independent effect" is not now present in our schools.

Some educators feel that we are unfairly penalizing underprivileged children by slanting the education toward areas in which they are less competent. In fact, there is an argument, described in Thayer and Levit's book, that the whole process has always been biased against those less verbally inclined.

> Since, moreover, teachers have tended to be verbal-minded, it was natural that they should favor the verbally inclined over other types of mind and find them easier to instruct. Likewise, with the advent of intelligence tests —instruments which have consistently been skewed in favor of the verbally intelligent—educators as well as laymen have been prone to infer that the verbally intelligent are over all the more intelligent.[56]

Perhaps one cannot dispute this position on teachers' preference, but on the same standardized verbal achievement tests the underprivileged pupils of ten years ago, with the same disadvantages, scored higher than those of today. The IQ test argument may be even less convincing, but overall one feels that we must guard against downgrading the other skills. Certainly we want the underprivileged to strive to become more like those who have been successes in this society, and apparently, among others, adequate *written*— as much as or more than spoken—verbal skills are important to success in our system. At the same time, other skills are also important in our system, those that allow a person to *do* things, to discover things, to find solutions to problems, and to make decisions, even though that person may not be able to write or speak eloquently on the subject. Before one goes too far down this verbal preference road, one must hasten to point out, first, that demands on students to acquire verbal skills were never that excessive and, as we have seen, verbal achievement and—according to considerable evidence—demands, have apparently decreased in recent years among pupils in all socioeconomic levels, and second, that the skills held in such high esteem in our schools are by no means all verbal. There is and has been over the years a great emphasis on deductive reasoning, whether in mathematics or in matching comparable geometric figures and lines.

In fact, this emphasis has increased to a point that might, at least for some children, be counterproductive to the learning process—many current educators do not like rote learning. According to Andrew Mayes, ". . . a heavy amount of memorising is [fashionably] thought to kill spontaneity and curiosity; by generating a passive outlook, it is believed to decrease creativity."[57]

Some facts ". . . can be logically organised—but no one has discovered how." In such cases, Mayes continues, ". . . there is good evidence that creative problem solving only occurs if all possible relevant data are so well remembered that they can be recalled very rapidly. It seems then that, paradoxically, rote memorisation is required as the first stage for achieving creative insight."[58] This is surely true in the fundamentals of many things children must learn. We do not teach children the complexities of the equinox before they learn that there are seven days in a week and twelve months in a year, which in the last analysis is to some degree arbitrary: why not eight months, why "thirty days has September . . . twenty-eight for February . . ."? It is also very difficult to explain such things as why "table" is masculine and "chair" feminine in a foreign language, and in English why "i before e except after c," and why the silent letters.

Part of the opposition to rote learning seems to stem from the fact that some educators identify it with the discipline and structure of the old school system, which they are likely to call a lock-step system and to compare to a "minimum-security prison." Unfortunately, in this way, some of those who were most vocal about helping the underprivileged were, by their refusal to consider the use of rote learning, perhaps also likely to be those who were reducing many underprivileged children's opportunities for learning.

In the past decade and a half, a "multiplying number of curriculum projects" have been fostered by "public and private funds." It has been noted by such observers as Thayer and Levit that "associated with the curriculum-reform movement is the idea that students should be taught not an encyclopedic collection of facts, but the basic principles and concepts and methodology which impart meaning and organization to the details and data of a subject."[59] Deductive reasoning may have been understressed in the past, but in the effort *not* to teach "an encyclopedic collection of facts" and to stress deductive reasoning, there often appears to have been a virtual all-out attack on the use of retentive ability in schooling. In fact, the extent of the apparent downgrading of the teaching of facts is disturbing. We are familiar with the displeasure that many modern educators display when they talk of "just learning facts" in history. Names, dates, and chronology in history have lost much of their importance in many educators' minds. Even in mathematics, children often are no longer required to memorize as they used to.

One could make a persuasive argument that the child with retentive ability is a second-class citizen in school and that this is made clear to him every day. Unfortunately, among children at the lower end of the IQ scale, greater numbers of underprivileged children display high retentive ability and may normally be more likely to be able to compete with, or even surpass, intellectually similar middle- and upper-middle-class children. Underprivileged children of average or above average IQ are said to show no such difference from the higher socioeconomic group children of similar IQ.[60] At least one psychologist, Andrew Mayes, states that ". . . it may pay educationalists to exploit the fact that many children with low IQs have superior rote learning capacity."[61]

Whether these children come from higher or lower socioeconomic groups is unimportant, however, because all we need worry about in the school system is whether they learn to the best of their ability. Because the child does not have a high IQ does not mean he hasn't the right to learn to read and write and do basic mathematics. He is no less a citizen than the high IQ child and has the same right as anybody else to achieve to the best of his ability. This raises the possibility that in one respect our *schools* as well as, or rather than, the family or neighborhoods, may have become "suppressive environments" for many children because people refuse to teach by the rote method and insist on using others that require a rather high degree of deductive reasoning. This may be one of the reasons why large segments of our population are not able to achieve to the best of their ability and are deprived of the basic skills required in our society for the pursuit of happiness. One is forced to ask whether, prior to the days when their ability was wasted, these children did not perform better than they do now. Certainly one had the impression in those days that less gifted and/or economically and culturally deprived children who completed school had learned to read and write, learned some basic geography, history, grammar, some science and civics, and generally were prepared to be productive citizens. Furthermore, achievement scores of grade and junior high school children of the mid-1930s seem to bear this out (see Chapter 2). In that time period not only were there opportunities to use retentive ability, but there were minimum requirements that students had to meet to move from one grade to another. For better or worse, through the innovations in our schools over the past decade these factors seem to have lost much influence.

In specific subjects, the most publicized innovation has no doubt been in mathematics instruction in primary schools. The "new math" stresses an emphasis on logic that may have a very debatable effect on small children. Certainly one can question the wisdom of introducing into lower primary grades a whole new jargon of cumulative, associative, and distributive laws and extensive and convoluted "proofs," when children are trying to learn whether 3 plus 2 is the same as 2 plus 3. Even describing which numbers come between 6 and 9 is likely to emerge as a complex speech on sets and set intersections rather than 7 and 8.[62] The possibility of confusing even the brighter children on issues of just how mathematics develops is perhaps also increased by this method. ". . . it was intuitive evidence," writes Morris Kline, "that induced mathematicians to accept [less intuitive numbers and concepts]. The logic always came long after the creations and evidently was harder to come by."[63] Quoting Henri Lebesgue, Kline records, "No discovery has been made in mathematics, or anywhere else for that matter, by an effort of deductive logic; . . . its role therefore, though considerable, is only secondary."[64]

It quickly became obvious, as indicated by *The Fleischmann Report,* that no matter what the level of the "new math," within our great states' school systems, children were having difficulty in mathematics:

> One of the most striking phenomena in the PEP [Pupil Evaluation Program, New York's own standardized achievement test program] score data is that over time more and more children throughout the state are falling below the minimum competence in both reading and mathematics.[65]

Similar evidence, as we have seen and as the Appendix illustrates, exists nationally and in most of our sample states. Furthermore, there seemed to be very well qualified people, such as Morris Kline, questioning the effect of the "new math" on students: ". . . the concentration on the deductive approach omits the vital work. It destroys the life and spirit of mathematics."[66] By the end of 1964, Max Beberman, one of the chief proponents of the new math, had integrity enough to admit that "we're in danger of raising a generation of kids who can't do computational arithmetic."[67] But if this was obvious to primary and secondary school teachers, it did not prevent them from plowing on. For a decade in classrooms where this math was really taught (many new math classes were heavily salted with traditional teaching), children were subjected to stressing of the deductive process of education while their retentive abilities, traditionally developed through drill in this area, were largely untapped.

The burgeoning of the new math coincided with an awesome innovation —the educators' fashionable new attitude toward pupils themselves. They were declared to be simply small adults and treated as having an approach to issues differing very little from that of adults. The attitude may have been reflected in the development of new mathematics instruction in our schools —the deductive approach to mathematics was made extremely rigorous. Pupils were confused by complicated proofs and demonstrations meant to prove what was otherwise obvious.[68] In 1962, Kline reports, Dr. Beberman had emerged as an outspoken critic of his own program:

> I think in some cases we have tried to answer questions that children never raise and resolve doubts they never had, but in effect we have answered our own questions and resolved our own doubts as adults and teachers, but these were not the doubts and questions of the children.[69]

By 1973 the New York *Times* was reporting that in New York State, "Ten years after a fundamental revision of the teaching of mathematics with its emphasis on sets. . . . The swing is back to a stress on computational skills, including old-fashioned arithmetic drills."[70] Interestingly enough, though, according to Kline, "most of the groups [advocating the new math in the late 1950s and early 1960s] undertook almost no experimental work,"[71] the swing back to a time-tested method was "to be tried in the schools on an experimental basis" starting September 1973.[72]

As always with a deductive approach to teaching, the underprivileged children, who coincidentally increased in our large northern cities during this time period, were hardest hit. Their parents, products of a primary education in "vastly inferior" (sometimes southern) schools, were often better grounded in math than their children who finished twelve years of fabulously expensive education. One problem indeed seemed to stem from one of the most obvious innovations in the new approach just mentioned before—children had not been forced to "drill" as of old. For example, they did not learn the multiplication ("times") tables. Since they could not readily multiply, they could not do long division. They had difficulty adding columns of figures because they were not given enough practice. Once a concept was taught, drill or rote memorization of salient facts, necessary to grasping a concept, and scholarly, meticulous work in employing it, were not stressed.

Here again, one fears that despite many dedicated teachers' anguish, the easy road for the teacher was often followed—that is, the difficult was avoided. For example, teachers apparently are often reluctant to correct pupils' homework or insist on additional work—which again would require correction—from those pupils who need it. When assigned, homework is often corrected by pupils themselves by exchanging papers, which takes time away from the already short class period, and is far less likely to provide teachers with a detailed knowledge of each pupil's needs.

One teacher, Paul Lissandrello, writes about this issue:

> Let's abolish homework. . . . Let's stop impeding the natural spontaneous after-school learning of children. . . . Let teachers use classroom time constructively so that students have opportunities to try out new ideas and new skills with teacher guidance.

Parents are thought by this educator to be behind the times with their ideas that school, like medicine, to be effective must be unpleasant.[73] Apparently such teachers give little thought to the possibility that parents may be asking for the kind of practice they empirically know children—in this case high school adolescents—must have to acquire a skill. They are to be dissuaded from such requests. "Let parents know that 200 minutes per week [time spent per subject in the classroom] is of any subject, or discipline, enough to learn that discipline." School administrators are also asked to ignore this possibly legitimate parental motivation. "Let school administrators do their part by trying to realize that parental approval of homework cannot be considered sound justification for making the educational decision to keep it."[74] We are increasingly witnessing a new phenomenon in households across the country: family problems resulting from, on the one hand, parents trying to halt their children's sinking scholastic achievement levels by demanding more effort on their studies (homework), and on the other, the *teachers* in league with children in resisting this parental demand. Many dedicated teachers may also be reluctant to bring pressure on the pupils, as well as make more work for themselves, by demanding significant amounts of difficult work, in school or out, from pupils not accustomed to it. As reported by the Los Angeles *Times,* one social science teacher said, "I abandoned requiring a lot of outside work (of students) because the kids won't do it. . . . The quality of work is so low that it's not worth it for them or me. If I give a 10-page paper in sociology, I get a three-page paper (back). I have," he added, "caved in to the pressure."[75]

Teachers who place demands on the kids, and/or refuse to inflate grades beyond what pupils deserve for the work they turn in, may find they no longer fit in so well in some schools. The author knows of one instance when a New York City high school teacher made the effort to teach a tenth grade business mathematics class to convert fractions to percent (it is not uncommon for such pupils not to know this process), only to have questions on the subject omitted from a departmental test because the other teachers had not made a similar effort. In some areas—the Los Angeles *Times* quotes the teacher again—"principals keep grade charts on teachers. . . . It is very subtle. You don't get talked to if you give a lot of high grades. You do get talked to if too many are low. You are asked, 'Are you sure you understand the nature of our students and their needs?' "[76]

Nor, as we have seen borne out in achievement score data, does this process of lowering standards affect only, or, in some cases at least, even primarily, the disadvantaged pupil. The very top category of students is supposedly taught high school courses in junior high school and college courses in high school, but since there is only a finite amount of time in school each day, and since some evidence indicates that their achievement scores are likely to be falling even faster than those of less gifted children,[77] adding new material may actually have meant inadequate time for the old, fundamental courses for the brightest children as well. Regarding the ability of pupils in this area, William Blanton, a reading specialist, states: "I think we are teaching a broader range of study skills, so that while the students are learning more skills, they are not learning each specific skill as well. It might well be that a child has learned 30 more skills than he would have four years ago, but has not learned each individual skill as well."[78] Furthermore, one is forced to ask whether, during a time when there was evidence of less teacher interest and dedication as well as some evidence of a drop in competence, we should allow educators to tamper with a functioning system, to say nothing of adding complicated, difficult-to-teach courses to the curriculum. The validity of this advancement in high school to college course level is not unconditionally accepted by all educators; some, like Karl Shapiro, definitely denied it:

> As far as I can tell, the high school has now reached the level of the grade school; the college is at high school level; the graduate school at college level; and whatever reading and writing is being done is being done by professors. . . .[79]

Along with the statistical data noted earlier and the evidence in the Appendix, there is much anecdotal evidence that the more gifted children, too, are not necessarily taught what does not come easily, nor are they necessarily indoctrinated with correct study habits. For example, a father asking a few questions of his child, who was in the advanced senior math program in one of the finest high schools in one of the most affluent communities in New York State, found that the youngster did not really understand sine or cosine. At the time, the pupil was supposedly taking calculus and had had "trigonometry" the preceding year. On entering college the following year, the work demanded simply overwhelmed this intelligent youngster; the result was another college dropout.

Perhaps, however, the greatest "innovation" in mathematics in large industrial-state high schools in recent years is that a child can graduate without having had either algebra or geometry. This is in contrast to pre-World War II mathematics curriculum requirements. Today a child need only take "pre-algebra" or high school arithmetic in order to graduate.

In foreign languages, advanced courses are offered along with basic language courses in some high schools. Foreign language courses can sometimes be started in the lower grades of junior high school as electives. Here again, however, the greatest change, compared to pre-World War II high schools, is that students can, if they so choose, get a high school diploma without ever having been required to take a single class in a foreign language.

In chemistry and science today, much more equipment is available to students, but again these subjects are more often not likely to be required.

Geography is no longer taught as a subject in many primary schools, and a type of social science curriculum is often offered as a substitute for geography and history. Reflecting the emerging theory of teaching history, the method for teaching American history is often thematic rather than chronological. For example, students learn about immigration and reaction to immigrants from the earliest times to today for a few weeks; then another theme is taken up. One fears that this system lays inadequate emphasis on interrelationships or the general sweep of history. Furthermore, courses superficially covering vast areas and time spans—such as Afro-Asian Studies: from Dakar to Tokyo, from 3000 B.C. to 1976 A.D.—beyond the competence of almost any high school teacher or even college professor to teach in depth, are now taught instead of such traditional courses as Ancient History. "Relevancy" has become a key word, and it too often is interpreted by educators from the simplistic viewpoint of mid-adolescence, instead of the deeper view of history's relevance, the story of our civilization, to everything we do. "Some educators believe mini-courses on themes like 'Women in American History' have too often achieved 'relevance' at the cost of any serious content," a New York *Times* article reveals.[80]

In English, too, there are courses for advanced students, but the old standard literature courses are often no longer required. Electives are available because of "enrichment" programs, which allow students to take courses of less academic value requiring little effort. A report by HEW states that ". . . many of the new courses are intended to offer pupils a choice of studies and answer their contention that the school curriculum is not relevant to their daily lives and concerns;" and their sampling indicates a "trend toward substitution of specific courses for traditional combination offerings, particularly at the upper high school levels."[81] As the following table shows, the percentage of pupils receiving much of the traditional standard instruction apparently has declined nationally.

	Enrollment (%)	
	1960-61	1970-71
World History	12.5	9.2
American Literature	16.7 (all 11th graders--part of 11th grade English)	6.7

NOTE: Reprinted from the HEW publication, *Patterns of Course Offerings and Enrollments, 1970–71*, p. 5.

The number of pupils in basic English classes in California dropped 19 percent between 1971–72 and 1974–75, and there was a 77 percent drop in pupils taking English composition. Algebra, geometry, and trigonometry classes also shrank.[82] In Los Angeles, the Los Angeles *Times* found, "enrollment in basic seventh, eighth, ninth and tenth grade English classes has dropped, and the number of eleventh grade students in the district's standard American Literature and composition class has fallen 28% during the last three years."[83]

Across the country, pupils now take vaguer courses such as classes on world cultures. English language arts include such courses as mass communications and radio/television/film. Courses such as Environmental Problems and Environmental Sciences have been on the rise.[84]

A closer look at some of the electives in English in one downstate New York suburban school district shows such "mini course" offerings for ½ credit as "I Love a Mystery," "Sports Communication," "Responding to Media," and "Art of Film." In another district, in Colorado, 57 English ("Language Arts") courses are offered in senior high school. One high school in Connecticut had 125 electives for a high school of one thousand students. Between 1968–69 and 1975–76, the English electives in Sacramento rose from 26 to 80, those in social studies from 16 to 53.[85] Between 1971–72 and 1975–76 in California the number of pupils taking "Children's Theater," "Mystery and Detective Story," "Executive English," as contemporary literature electives, had almost doubled while ethnic literature classes increased five times, with the exception of Afro-American literature classes, which are down. "Business English" classes are up.[86] Edward

White, special consultant on new program development and evaluation at California State University, said: "The elective curriculum . . . has been a powerful degenerative force for the curriculum [this] whole idea that everything is about as good as everything else. Kids are kids, after all. Why [should] they sweat over writing, which is so damn hard to do, when they could act in a play?"[87]

Mothers find that their youngsters have been watching films like *Butch Cassidy and the Sundance Kid* in school for English credit. Though their verbal skill test results continued to plummet, apparently the requirement to read the great authors was shrinking. In some affluent, and some not-so-affluent, school districts, the ultimate in this type of "innovative" curriculum seemed to have been accomplished: students even attended such courses as a study of Witchcraft and "witches" were brought in to lecture to them.[88] As noted earlier, we must consider the possibility that all this elective activity detracts from traditional learning, for it is carried out within the few hours of the regular school day. After-hours work with pupils—with the exception of paid jobs such as sports coaching—has become much less common for teachers.

One cannot but get the impression that though there are at least nominally some good courses for the better college-bound students from homes where school issues are well understood, the *required* courses have declined since the older parents of recent high school students attended school. Underprivileged students are likely to emerge even more unfavorably influenced under these circumstances. With parents who are unfamiliar with educational jargon, and who feel that since their children are going to high school things must be all right, students are free to take the easy way out. Some actually are encouraged to do so by educators and guidance counselors. One mother in an affluent community told the author that when she suggested that her child could do better than B work in foreign language, the child discussed the situation with the guidance counselor, who recommended that the student drop the course.

Furthermore, the recent well-meaning attempt to intervene, in Professor Ron Edmonds' words, "in the life of the school so as to compel a more effective instructional response to those who profit least from prevailing arrangements"[89] can apparently also be a dangerous process. Reaching for deprived children too often today seems to be taken to mean lowering standards. There are those who dispute the premise that pupils should be taught to emulate the traditional, standard grammar, vocabulary, and reading habits of the middle class. As mentioned earlier in this chapter, according to George Kohn, "Some teachers say flatly that the grammar, the speech pattern, of any individual is all right. No one should be made to feel 'inferior' because of his way of speaking and writing."[90] Nonetheless, the traditional idea has been to try to help the children meet certain standards, which is difficult. It is much easier to allow a slum child to use street grammar, with or without the assumption that somehow he eventually will learn the correct grammar. Kohn writes: "Teachers and many adults have felt that the old grammar was too rigid and irrelevant. . . . Besides the old grammar is too hard to teach to the masses."[91] It is also difficult to make a child behave himself; many things are difficult and distasteful for young children. While that may be unfortunate, it does not mean that these things are necessarily wrong.

The tendency to put more emphasis on vocational training in schools, again—possibly with certain exceptions such as office skills like typing and shorthand—may, in many cases, be a questionable policy. Strong evidence over the recent past reveals that children in these programs are often neglected as far as the basic skills are concerned. It is much more important that a school teach a child to read and do basic mathematics than to run a lathe, which he can learn on the job. If he reads well and knows mathematics, he can supplement any on-the-job training he needs by reading. The biracial Rodgers Committee, investigating charges of discrimination against Negroes and Puerto Ricans in construction unions in New York City in 1963, reported:

> One of the greatest eye openers to this Committee was the apparent abandoning of many youths in our school system. Most of the Committee was shocked that boys who were graduates of our vocational high schools . . . could not spell such words as "brick," "carpenter," "building," etc., or could not add inches and feet. . . . It is quite apparent that they are the product of a social system that pushed them through the earlier grades of school without insuring that they had the basic tools necessary for a minimal academic education. . . .
>
> We call attention to this problem because the apprentice in any trade must come equipped with these tools.[92]

It is very clear that the abilities to read, write, and solve arithmetic problems are much more important for those who wish to enter apprenticeship programs than shop courses alone. In fact, some unions were asking for apprentices with at least a "C" average in high school; they apparently did not necessarily stress the requirement for having had shop courses. Obviously an "A" student in the standard high school subjects who also had had shop courses would be a great find. But it is wrong to downgrade standard skills in schools, even for those who think they are going to spend their lives in a trade. Children in high school do not know, nor do their parents, what they will be doing in later life. If an opportunity should arise for them to go higher by means of advanced education, or positions that require better education of the classical type, these children should not be denied that right because of the failure of schools to insist that they learn the fundamentals in the traditional academic areas in primary and secondary school.

In fact, the more one looks at the evidence, the more one gains the impression that the current educational process, in large cities with their large numbers of underprivileged children as well as elsewhere, should be viewed with considerable skepticism. The reason for this growing feeling is that though there are differences in our current society, many of its "insurmountable" problems seem similar to problems that apparently were surmounted in the past. The difference appears to be in the way the current school system is attempting to overcome the problems. The arguments so prevalent today intimate that it is virtually hopeless to attempt to educate children to the traditional level of competence unless they come to school endowed with the correct social attitude, behavior, grammatical knowledge, and IQ. Interestingly, however, as we have seen, the better endowed children are also slipping academically, often faster than the less well endowed.

There have always been schoolchildren at the lower end of the socioeconomic and IQ scales, as we have seen; it has always been more difficult to teach them subjects that require deductive reasoning in the higher grades. Yet just prior to World War II, over 45 percent of children starting school finished high school[93] with the high academic achievement record mentioned earlier. Clearly these high school graduates included many with far less than top percentile IQ scores, but all students, including dropouts, could read and do math problems. At this juncture, one might begin to wonder whether educators are begging the question.[94] The idea is to teach children to read and solve math problems. Those who already know how to read when they come to school, or who have parents who spend time teaching them arithmetic at home, are in less need of the schools than deprived children. But that is what universal public education has traditionally been all about. One can't help noticing that in the 1950s and 1960s, as in earlier periods of heavy immigration, an influx of rural, disadvantaged children penetrated our big city school systems. In these latter instances, however, only a tiny minority did not speak English, and southern cities as well as northern cities experienced the influx.

At the same time, the standards of behavior, grammar, and effort have apparently been continually lowered. In effect, one fears the schools may no longer be trying to raise students' achievement to the level traditionally required for success in this country. Indeed, we may now have a reverse situation with some of our lower-class non-English-speaking immigrants from underdeveloped countries. According to a New York *Times* article, a small sample of Vietnamese children in California, "the sons and daughters of fishermen, farmers, clerks," the products of Vietnamese public schools, generally with classes of 60 to 90 pupils, averaged in the 95th percentile on arithmetic concepts and the 91st percentile on application.

Their middle-class, predominantly white, fellow-American students averaged in the 24th and 35th percentiles, respectively, on the same standardized achievement tests.[95]

This lowering of standards is possibly the worst course of action. Children are very sensitive to the degree of adults' resolve when they make demands of them. Elementary and secondary school pupils are deluged with many kinds of requests; the only way they can determine priorities for meeting them is by gauging the adults' sincerity on each specific issue. The fact that many adults involved in our educational process have not firmly and consistently demanded that underprivileged children strive to meet middle-class standards may well indicate to students a general lack of sincerity in all requests. Perhaps more important, bringing children out of their deprived status is *difficult,* as already mentioned, and too often in the past decade the difficult has tended to be avoided in our schools.

A large body of anecdotal evidence, as well as the comparative statistical evidence over the past decade cited earlier and that contained in the Appendix, indicates an apparent drop in student competence at all levels of intelligence, as measured by standard achievement and aptitude tests. This evidence seems to be strong enough to give pause to the prudent parent when it comes to supporting the whole new approach to educating children.

The emphasis on "teaching students to think" and stressing "immediate pupil response and constant exchange between pupils and teachers" (rather than lecture preceding discussion, if any), through such procedures as "inquiry" learning, should perhaps be reevaluated in light of how these approaches might influence children's learning activities. According to Fred Hechinger:

> The schools have adjusted to the new style by sacrificing much of the analytical part of learning to mere spontaneity. Under the onslaught of critics who consider all drill autocratic, teachers have moved away from parsing sentences, analyzing ideas, and preparing outlines. Modern language enrollment has declined sharply.[96]

Apparently, one of the most critical rocks upon which modern education has foundered is the inability of many educators bent on encouraging individualized education to recognize the degree to which this could be accomplished within the existing school system. In their rush toward individualized education, these educators were seemingly unaware of the inherent benefits of the old system that they were actually discarding.[97]

To the extent that the "new style" increases pupil tendency to feel everything is relative—so facts are not particularly important and, consequently, one person knows as much as anybody else about almost any subject—the process tends to downgrade the value of being well-informed, and the structured existence of the child could be adversely affected. Hazel Hertzberg, of Teachers College, Columbia University, says of history instruction: "There is no longer an agreed-upon body of knowledge that is thought to be necessary for everyone to have."[98] In fact, we have seen children who have been told in recent years that they had the only true grasp of things, that adults should learn from them. This could be a bad situation, especially from the viewpoint of underprivileged children. After attending a class in which a teacher told high school pupils that she learned more from them than she learned in college, one pupil commented incredulously about the quality of that teacher's alma mater. Children's learning is likely to be affected by adults who seem to lack the courage of their own convictions and who are uncommitted and uncertain in the educational milieu. A book by Lester Crow and others provides some evidence, for example, that, "it is the old-style, strict, highly structured teacher who appears to be the most popular and effective with underprivileged children." "The progressive approach . . . does not catch on," it continues. "It has too many features that are essentially alien to the culture of the deprived: the permissiveness; the accent on self—the internal—the introspective; creativity and growth as central goals of education; the stress on play; the underestimation of discipline and authority."[99]

In no way do we endorse the teacher as martinet, but even with brighter students, the structured existence of the school is probably very important and the new approach may endanger it. The teacher's authority must and does come from the school's administrative structure, but finally his stature derives, particularly when dealing with older children, from the fact that he is an authority: he has a superior knowledge of the subject matter he is teaching. His superior knowledge must, by definition, be based on a greater fund of concepts and facts, if he is to impress the child. Younger children will think that adults are smarter than they, but as they mature, their acceptance of adults' superior knowledge becomes conditionally based. According to one educator, Clara Dobay, "In the school, students grant initial respect to the authority of the teacher but continue it only as long as teachers earn and deserve it. Teachers are respected when they know their subject . . . are excited by the challenge of ideas . . . are sincerely interested in the students' welfare . . . and set high standards for themselves and their classes."[100]

No adult who has ever had any association with children has failed to hear early adolescents talk, usually unfairly, about their teachers as "stupid," "silly," or worse. This is typical of a situation in which young people deal with an adult. Their experience is so limited that, for example, they are likely to be unaware of restraints that rule out many ideas they feel are realistic. A teacher's duty is to impart the knowledge he possesses to the children so that their growing store of knowledge will eventually allow them to take such factors into consideration for future learning and/or decision making. As indicated earlier, the unavoidable truth is that oftentimes the teacher *has* a lower IQ than some students in the class, and although some teachers like to bolster their egos by "winning" arguments with their students, unless they do so by relying on their superior knowledge of facts, *usually restricted to their own fields,* many are going to find themselves outwitted by their adolescent students. Furthermore, if they have impressed these children with the idea that facts are not particularly relevant, then the only way less intelligent teachers can maintain control or authority is by stressing what appears to the children to be the teacher's position in the arbitrary administrative school structure.

There may even be more far-reaching effects in this situation. The only formal, structured environment with which all children have close contact outside the family is the school. This school organization might begin to look insecure, and children might begin to see it as having nothing more to back it up than an organization chart. They might not perceive its right to exist, based on its superior capability to impart knowledge to others, and might develop an unhealthy skepticism, not only about the structural environment and authority of the school, but about other governmental and nongovernmental organizations. Interestingly enough, from 1967 to 1971 educators often encouraged a kind of alienation from the government among students, apparently without seeing its connection to a similar response to schools and educators.

In general, discipline has slipped, in many schools to a degree that is a very significant factor in determining educational policy. Obviously, if the classroom is so disrupted that the teacher cannot make herself heard, she cannot teach. If it takes five minutes of a forty- or fifty-minute period for pupils to "settle down" (many teachers wait for them to do so), another five minutes to maintain order during class, and a few minutes at the end of class for children to gather belongings and get ready to leave, then pupils are actually taught for only thirty minutes or so. If children are only receiving so few minutes daily—and often, particularly in junior and senior high school, every other day—of sporadic instruction in difficult subjects like mathematics, reading, or grammar, it is highly unlikely that even well-qualified pupils will achieve up to their maximum potential. Nor is this situation confined to the worst schools; in varying degrees it is not uncommon in many areas. The big open classrooms, as well as many standard classrooms, in upper-middle-class neighborhoods can be chaotic. In cross-bused, lower-middle-class, and slum districts, the classroom atmosphere can range from hectic to dangerous; of course, in the last case, education can diminish in importance to both students and teachers. The halls and restrooms, and sometimes classrooms, can become gauntlets of danger to be avoided or run through, with first priority given to the preservation of one's property and physical well-being.

According to the chairman of the National Commission on the Reform of Secondary Education, B. Frank Brown, 66 percent of our school systems have police on the payroll today.[101] In New York City, teachers were issued self-defense handbooks by the United Federation of Teachers to help them learn to protect themselves and their students from menacing students and outsiders on school premises. Among other recommendations in the handbook is the one that teachers "talk politely to wandering older students when challenging them in hallways"; there is advice on how to deal with attacks by elementary school students, that is, first to sixth graders. Another section deals with the danger of rape: teachers are advised not to be alone in classrooms or faculty rooms, for example.[102] Experience tells us this includes being alone with a few students before or after class, for such groups have raped teachers in New York City.

The danger of assault against teachers had definitely increased; according to the New York *Times,* in 1972 there were 634 "reported assaults against teachers, their aides, custodians and other personnel"; in 1973 there were 717.[103] In order to protect the students, teachers, and buildings against violence by outsiders and other students, the number of security guards was increased from 732 in January 1972 to 1,815 in January 1974; 970 were for high schools and 845 for elementary and junior high schools. These guards arrested 420 suspects "in connection with crimes committed in or near the schools," compared with 305 arrested in 1972.[104] Jeremiah McEnna, the general counsel of the New York State Legislature's Select Committee on Crime, said "brokerages" were functioning in the New York City schools: "guns, narcotics or the services of youthful male and female prostitutes" were the merchandise. Nor, according to Mr. McEnna, were these deals particularly covert; the student dealers had the faculty intimidated. Teachers wouldn't talk about what they often knew. Furthermore, school officials often refused to aid police in infiltrating these operations.[105] Nor is New York that atypical of large cities with significant numbers of slum schools; as we have noted, two-thirds of the nation's school districts now employ police, and large numbers of them are there for functions other than guarding property at night.

Even excluding crime, any objective observer could not help being amazed at the change that has occurred in schools, particularly those with a majority of less affluent students, during the 1960s and early 1970s. The noise alone in schools in all neighborhoods today is often bewildering, and not just in the halls. The author knows of a suburban school board that wanted to soundproof schoolrooms because of noise from adjacent rooms. When asked how the children in the room from which the noise originated were supposed to learn, the superintendent indicated that these were art rooms, and the like, intimating that order in such areas was not expected.

The gutter language used by pupils, and even some teachers, in today's schools would have been considered a great disgrace in past decades. Apparently, filthy language in mixed company and other disreputable habits, indulged in by the dregs of all societies, are no longer considered by our school systems to be behavior that schools are designed to correct and to strive to eliminate. Today, such behavior is condoned and too often held up as a legitimate sign of another, far from disgraceful, "subculture" in our society. It is hard to deny the charge that during the 1960s and early 1970s many of the worst traits of the slums were introduced into our school systems, and not just ghetto school systems. The milieu thus created is hard to defend as one more likely to foster scholastic achievement, good deportment, or even pupils', particularly girls', self-respect, including children from working-class and middle-class homes.

The schools must bear the major responsibility for this recent development, but they were aided and abetted by many perhaps well-meaning, but also, from a broader viewpoint, perhaps sometimes ill-advised, outside groups during the period of the glorification of the "student activist." According to a Report to the State Commissioner of Education in 1969, as quoted in the Student Rights Project *Handbook* of New York City:

> High school students are asking for greater participation in the operation and management of institutions affecting their lives and this should be welcomed.
>
> Educational leaders must take the initiative in convincing their profession and their community that student activism is potentially a constructive force compatible with basic democratic principles.[106]

Some educators and outside forces also made efforts to convince students that they had less to fear from school officials than some may have thought. In 1970, the Student Rights Project of the New York Civil Liberties Union produced, and the New York City school system distributed to high school children, the *Student Rights Handbook.*

This handbook lists the legal rights of law-abiding students and explains that teachers dare not harass or punish students for exercising these rights. It points out to students that they can take the Fifth Amendment with the principal: "You do not have to speak to school officials when charged with offenses."[107] There is also the advice: "Don't put anything in your locker or carry anything in your possession that you would not want the police to know about for any reason."[108] Parents of the majority of students might question the advisability of dispensing this kind of information to adolescents, particularly in light of the already difficult job of coping with malefactors in the New York schools.

As pointed out earlier, however, the late 1960s and early 1970s was the awesome period when high school as well as college students often were assumed to have as much knowledge, stability, and judgment as parents and professional adults two or three times their age, even with regard to issues so vital as the kind of education they would need in later life. We all know parents and professionals who have exercised bad judgment, but, overall, they are normally superior to children in this area. In any event, the evidence to date seems to indicate that the educators over the past decade who were wrong were probably those who subscribed to this "youth cult" attitude.

GIMMICKRY, SOCIAL ENGINEERING AND DEMOGRAPHY

Permissiveness has probably been responsible for as many changes in our school systems as other factors. Discipline has deteriorated so far that instruction often becomes difficult and sometimes impossible; brutal violence stalks a sizable minority of our schools. It is also largely responsible for the very low student/teacher ratio in core-city schools. The more adults present, the better chance a teacher has of maintaining order, or at least of having help at hand if menaced or attacked by students.

But teachers like the idea of low student/teacher ratio, and safety in the minority of rough schools is not the sole reason. A greater number of burly guards would be much more effective and much less expensive security, and teachers abound in many of the nonviolent majority of schools, too. The rationale for this recent increase is not as clear as it should be, though we do know that, despite all the contradictory evidence cited earlier, teachers have continually blamed the failure of schools on too few teachers, too small salaries, too old buildings, and so on. In any event, in an effort to get quality education, school systems have made changes that at least coincidentally make life easier for teachers. This approach to improving education still predominates in many school districts, and whole states as well, though for years everyone who has looked at these "improvements" has realized both their questionable value, if not futility, in regard to pupils' academic achievement, and the crippling costs they impose on harried taxpayers.

In 1971 Irving Kristol wrote:

> Whether a class has 20 pupils or 30 or even 40 simply doesn't matter. Students who do well in small classes will do well in large ones. . . . This subject has been studied to death by generations of educational researchers, and the results are conclusive.[109]

Data from Arizona (see the Appendix) again show no correlation between reading skills and class size per se. In fact in this case, generally, the larger the class, the higher the reading achievement, with classes of forty to forty-five children doing best. It is possible, however, that these last are largely parochial school classes.

Not only do the extensive samples available for years in the Coleman Report bear this out, but such local studies as the *New York School Factbook* (2nd ed., 1972), prepared by the Institute for Community Studies of Queens College, City University of New York, also show similar results:

> We have recorded traditional variables that supposedly affect the quality of learning: class size, instructional costs, pupil/teacher ratio, condition of building, teacher experience and the like. Yet, there seems to be no direct relationship between these school measurements and performance. Schools that have exceptionally small class registers, staffed with experienced teachers, spend more money per pupil, and possess modern facilities do not reflect exceptional academic competence.

And, further:

> Nor has the More Effective Schools program—a saturation services compensatory education program of high cost—[as early as the 1967–68 school year this program had some schools with a student-teacher ratio as low as 7.5 to 1 and an expenditure of $2,152 per student per year] shown any noteworthy results in this year's tabulations. Of twenty schools measured in the MES program, nineteen schools reported reading scores for 1971. All of these schools reported reading scores below grade level.

And there is the observation: ". . . we are faced with the question that the variables we have been accustomed to measure are not the ones that should be studied." It should be noted again that the continuing emphasis on low student/teacher ratios is one of the chief reasons for the current extremely high school budgets and burdensome school taxes across the country. Furthermore, a lower student/teacher ratio often does not mean smaller classes in academic subjects even in the first through sixth grades. It often means additional teachers take over many of the classroom teachers' traditional chores in the nonacademic areas while the classroom teachers get one period a day away from pupils. Full-time music, art, gym teachers, and librarians—who read stories to each class one hour per week—for kindergarten through fourth grade are examples.

On another currently fashionable, often expensive, and sometimes, from the students' viewpoint, disruptive practice, Robert Biehler writes:

> Team teaching has now been used in enough places for long enough periods of time to have been given a fair trial. The results of studies on its effectiveness (Ginther and Strayer, 1962; R. W. White, 1964) reflect Stephens's spontaneous schooling theory; they indicate that academic per-

formance of students who learn under team teaching circumstances is about the same as those who learn under other circumstances.[110]

Yet student/teacher ratios have continued to be cut, team teaching continues to be installed, and old, proven methods discarded for new, questionable ones; the resultant taxes have continued to soar to amazing levels.

Despite such expenditures, as we have seen, much evidence points to schools proving less than adequate as places where children, including underprivileged children, could receive the traditional benefits of public education. The extent to which this deterioration has progressed becomes evident when we realize that, according to A. Harry Passow of Columbia Teachers College of Columbia University, one of the main themes of various reports is that "compulsory attendance laws should be eased to prevent youngsters from having to remain in school against their will."[111] This apparently means dropping the fifty-year-old policy of keeping children in school until they are sixteen (the public opposes reducing the compulsory age of school attendance by 2 to 1—see next chapter). Another "theme," according to Dr. Passow, is that "students must have more opportunities to benefit from actual job experience."[112] We seem to have come full circle again, for this is similar to the reasoning that led to the previously cited "four and four" work/study program implemented during the last academic achievement slump in the 1940s. *The National Observer* points out one competence of high schools, however, on which all can agree:

> That brings us to what some teachers bluntly call the high schools' "baby-sitting function." It sounds crass, but at roughly $1 per hour per child, the public schools are a baby-sitting bargain, with a gymnasium and a classroom education thrown in for free.[113]

Unfortunately, it is hard to avoid the impression that in too many cases schools have deteriorated to this level under the 1960s innovative school programs.

One rather unconvincing yet fashionable implication, however, is that in our disorderly but less than dangerous schools it is too much to ask an educator to teach today's supposedly more "adult," but ill-behaved, teenagers in the classroom, and handle them in the hallways, cafeteria, or elsewhere in the school. This is particularly unconvincing to those of us who came from big pre-World War II high schools in large cities, or even not-so-large industrial and mining cities, where teachers were few and far between and parents were likely to have only sixth grade educations. In those mill and coal-town high schools, football teams had lines averaging two hundred pounds per player, and boys left home in summer to search for and take jobs, when they could find them.[114] Some of these jobs were more complicated and demanding than the ones most of the current troublemaking minority of adolescents seem able to handle, even after they have graduated from high school.

Those schools of yesteryear were orderly. Improper behavior, including illegitimate sex, is not the unique discovery of today's high schoolers. Premarital sexual relations, along with many other illicit activities on and off school property, and all aspects of the many consequences to those engaging in them, were also well-known by the really "streetwise" kids of yesteryear. There was very little adult supervision of the normal scholastic, athletic, and social activities. In towns and suburbs, kids organized hikes themselves—there weren't enough bikes for the currently fashionable "bike hikes"; in all areas they organized their own "sandlot" baseball, stickball, and basketball teams. They ran big high school dances with only one or two teachers present. They also printed the tickets, collected the money, and did everything else necessary, all with very few adults around. Today, such functions are swarming with paid and unpaid adults, teachers, coaches, counselors, advisors, and aides.

As pointed out, there have been changes in the student body and the areas served by schools in some districts, which will be discussed in the next chapter, but such changes are not an adequate explanation for the discipline and teaching conditions in our schools. The emphasis on these changes, particularly those outside our core cities, may be more of a self-serving rationale than a reason for poor instructional staff performance.

This recent phenomenon of school boards more readily accepting excuses by administrators and teachers in lieu of doing what they are paid to do— teach children academic subjects and see that each pupil performs to the best of his ability—may constitute a large part of our current problems. If teachers and administrators are told to teach children to read, write, and solve math problems, or to give a reason why they cannot do so, we should perhaps not be surprised if we create a generation of teachers and administrators that includes many with a distorted sense of priorities. It is much easier to eliminate the student requirement to take difficult, though important, subjects, or to offer excuses why children cannot be taught, than it is to teach them—or to relax rules of conduct than to make children behave. In days gone by, except in the case of the small fraction of pupils who are always incorrigible and must be placed in special schools or correctional institutions, teachers were not allowed this luxury. They had to teach children, even if they had to stay after hours to help some of them keep up with the class; in essence, nobody told them that administrators or school boards would accept excuses for not teaching children. And, as indicated earlier, they were successful with all kinds of children, from diverse backgrounds, at all IQ levels, many or most of whom spoke up to a half dozen different languages in a single classroom. Indeed, to repeat, teachers and administrators of equal dedication can still be found in our schools today, but there seem to be far fewer of them, and the milieu is apparently much less conducive to this type of teaching.

What is disturbing, furthermore, is the apparent low opinion that many "innovative" educators have of the pupil as an individual. Schools now seem to operate on the premise that current students are somehow less competent than those of old and that if we give these young people information, they will not see analogies or know how to apply it in making evaluations and decisions.

As indicated before, we are told that students are being taught to think, a skill past educators would have been reluctant to say their charges lacked and had to be taught. And the ingenuity, creativity, inventiveness, and frequent brilliance their charges showed in later life, as they forged the modern era, seem to bear out their faith. One is also prompted to ask how one person teaches another to think, and how he knows when he has succeeded in such a task. Above all, how do we know that primary and secondary school teachers, who need only be able to transfer acquired knowledge to pupils to qualify for teaching positions, have the skills to teach someone to think, even if we can define such a skill?

Even granting that there may be satisfactory explanations for all these observations, the evident lack of emphasis on information is still disturbing. It is difficult to see how children are supposed to make judgments without the benefit of the wisdom of the ages and basic skills to help them. Nor, as we have seen, do these remarks apply only to the poorer products of our high schools. The greatest problems we have had with college students in recent years seem to have stemmed from their lack of information and basic skills. In attempting to follow the advice of "identity crusader" educators and involving themselves in "relevant" issues, either these students were led unknowingly to try to reinvent the wheel or to reach conclusions about our current society, country, and system with little, if any, knowledge about other eras, societies, countries, and systems with which to make comparisons.

The point has been constantly stressed that revolutionary changes in the educational process are required because the learning a child receives in primary and secondary schools now must serve him in an unpredictable technological future. (One is constantly amazed at the inability of current educators with this attitude to empathize with educators of the 1930s and 1950s. These teachers saw the same unpredictable technological future before them, but, without undermining the fundamental educational process, apparently successfully prepared people to cope with it.) This strongly implies, first, that people do not learn after leaving school, so that school must predict and provide for all possible future student requirements; and second, that the old system, which during the jalopy and biplane era of the late 1920s and 1930s taught the fundamentals to students who put a man on the moon in the late 1960s, was somehow inadequate for preparing people for the future. Yet, as we have seen, the ability to teach even the basics to large numbers of pupils in recent years seems coincidentally to be inadequate.

During the sixties, at the same time that many innovations, including drastic curriculum changes, were introduced into the schools, we began to expect results from schools in areas that we had never thought they were particularly competent to affect before. They were looked on as "magnets" of social engineering whereby "community action" could be developed for a range of adult responsibility all the way from correction of drug abuse to improvement in housing. Referring to the Anacostia Project in Washington, D.C., Mark Arnold writes:

> Using the schools as magnets to bring the community together, it was hoped that local residents would go on to tackle other community problems, such as crime, drug addiction, dilapidated housing, and shortage of community services.[115]

Nationally the schools were looked on as an engine for racial integration.

Clearly, the standards for measuring the success of a school system had changed radically in the minds of many. Perhaps we should not have been too surprised, therefore, when schools were considered by educational administrators and other policy makers to be continually improving, although by traditional standards of student achievement in the fundamentals of reading, writing, arithmetic, grammar, history, and geography, they evidently were not. These traditional standards seem to have been lost in the vast smoke, din, and confusion of the "war on poverty," "the equal rights movement," and even the "anti-war movement." At the very least, many schools viewed their role in terms of solving an identity crisis for children. "We made them feel a part of their community for the first time, a part of their school."[116] Alongside such objectives, teaching children to read, write, and solve math problems may seem insignificant, and worst of all, demanding, difficult, and dull. (Perhaps a question Karl Shapiro asked about universities is applicable here: "whether the university [read school] is a place where the student seeks his identity or studies his lessons, the lessons of experts and professionals."[117]) Moreover, shifting away from measurable criteria of achievement and indications of teacher competence obviously had a strong appeal for many of the less than highly dedicated educators.

Another new aspect of our school systems is the downgrading of the neighborhood school. Mandatory cross-busing outside the south, where it was long in use but declared unconstitutional for segregation purposes, because of new grade-grouping arrangements—involving such changes as neighborhood kindergarten-through-sixth-or-eighth-grade schools being eliminated and the buildings used for "k through fourth" grade schools and "middle schools," that is, fifth and sixth grades, and so on—takes children past their former neighborhood school, now housing the wrong grades for them, and deposits them miles away in some other child's former neighborhood school. Economy drives and the decline in pupils due to the plummeting birth rate have closed down some schools and brought on new mandatory busing too, as usual with considerable parental objection.

A heated controversy persists on the effectiveness of busing for purposes of raising academic achievement of the underprivileged, or for improving pupils' attitudes toward racial integration.[118] In any event, busing for racial balance continues on a massive scale and is expanding daily. *The Fleischmann Report* describes a vast racial desegregation program, with the target districts indicated for New York State. Long-haul busing has been envisioned from the centers of large cities such as Detroit and even New York to the suburbs and vice versa, to achieve racial balance. Noting the Supreme Court decision pending at that time on the busing plan for Detroit and its suburbs, a New York *Times* article on February 27, 1974, said of a recent New York City Board of Education report to the State Board of Regents, "... the implication is that an exchange of pupils between city and suburban school districts emerges as a key way of continuing to provide the city with enough white pupils to carry out its integration program." The neighborhood school district, and other larger regional administrative arrangements, also could be affected by such plans. They could have a singularly disruptive and worrisome effect, if suburban children were to be bused into the permissive, lawless, dangerous, drug-ridden "core" areas of large cities from which many parents worked so hard to remove them. The recent Supreme Court decision that outlawed the Detroit-suburbia busing scheme has eliminated some momentum, but it remains to be seen whether the long-haul busing movement has actually been halted. The premise, as expressed by David Armor, that "the burden must fall upon those who support a given school integration program [and, one should add, any other 'innovative' school program] to demonstrate that it has the intended effects (with no unintended, negative side effects)"[119] is, however, an idea whose time has evidently not yet come.

One harsh but perhaps not completely unfair way to describe the 1960s and early 1970s might be as the era of gimmickry in education. Many of the innovations that were supposed to accomplish with little scholastic effort what previously had taken considerable self-discipline and hard, sometimes tedious work seemed to fall into this category. Perhaps it was inevitable that shortcuts were also substituted for extremely complex social processes. And perhaps the most surprising fact is that their implementation was eagerly accepted by many educators who viewed themselves and the schools as the logical engines for such processes.

Another new factor in education is that school systems seem to be preoccupied with demographic data to a degree unusual since the first decades of this century.[120] This apparently is primarily for purposes of attempting to balance the ethnic and racial groups—the reason for some busing—but there may be other implications, since they are stressed so often in connection with low achievement. In 1948, before such groups became so vulnerable to the charge of racism, the Strayer study group, commissioned by Congress, stated in relation to District of Columbia schools what might preoccupy many educators today:

> The survey committee would suggest that there must be some factor other than instruction which may account in part for the downward trend of achievement in reading, numbers, language, and spelling as shown by these tests. It is perhaps the movement of a large number of underprivileged children into the District from areas where public education is very inefficient in the development of the fundamental tool skills.[121]

Present educators would be wise to use this reasoning cautiously, however, for most underprivileged children of families from the South—including Negro boys and girls—now in the schools of these northern cities are native northerners. There is still considerable difference in the achievement levels of southern-born Negro children attending schools in the north and west and Negro children native to these areas, but, when comparing skills of children by age, part of that may be due to the practice of starting children later in southern schools. Another factor cited is the lower level of education of in-migrating children's parents.[122] But more important is not only the large percentage of the native-born majority who are below modal (appropriate) grade, but the large numbers who are promoted through the grades without learning. In the following table, the figures on children below modal grade today are considerably smaller than those on "retarded" immigrant children—those two years or more behind modal grade—in the 1908–09 school year given earlier in this chapter, and, as we saw in Chapter 4, the drop in numbers of all children "kept back" in recent years has been sharp.

Despite this bad academic record, no educational system in the country pleads the innate inability of these children to learn the basics, though some very liberal educators come disturbingly close to it at times, and it certainly is not the argument educators from the large sophisticated urban school districts used in the past, when they criticized the "hick" schools that parents and older brothers and sisters of these pupils attended.[123] They blamed pupils' poor academic achievement on the unqualified teachers

[PE]RCENT OF BLACK CHILDREN LIVING IN THE NORTH AND WEST IN 1970
BY ENROLLMENT STATUS, AGE, ENROLLMENT BELOW MODAL GRADE
AND REGION OF BIRTH AND RESIDENCE IN 1965

Residence and Age	Born in North	Born in West	Born in South		Moved out of South since 1965		
			Total*	Moved out of South before 1965	Total**	Moved from metropolitan areas	Moved from nonmetropolitan areas
Living in North in 1970			Percent not enrolled				
Children 6 to 8 years	4.3	3.6	5.0	5.4	3.9	3.7	3.7
Children 9 to 12 years	3.7	2.3	4.6	4.8	3.6	3.0	3.9
Children 13 to 17 years	10.8	9.8	16.2	14.9	20.4	15.7	22.7
			Percent enrolled below modal grade				
Children 9 to 12 years	21.7	19.6	28.2	26.9	31.0	26.4	33.7
Children 13 to 17 years	30.9	28.9	37.0	36.0	40.1	34.9	42.8
Living in West in 1970			Percent not enrolled				
Children 6 to 8 years	3.1	3.4	3.6	3.6	2.0	1.7	1.4
Children 9 to 12 years	3.1	2.7	3.0	2.7	2.8	2.4	3.2
Children 13 to 17 years	11.1	7.8	11.6	9.2	18.4	18.4	17.8
			Percent enrolled below modal grade				
Children 9 to 12 years	13.5	13.2	16.9	16.0	18.9	18.7	19.8
Children 13 to 17 years	17.4	18.2	22.0	19.6	32.2	29.7	36.0

*Includes persons not reporting state of residence in 1965.

**Includes persons reporting state but not county or city of residence in 1965.

NOTE: Reprinted from the *Manpower Report of the President,* Apr. 1974 (Wash.: GPO), p. 96.

without college degrees, the antiquated methods, the "open classroom"—
the little red schoolhouse, with six or eight grades ("tracks"?) in the one
room—and so on. Are we now saying that we cannot teach these children
the fundamental-tool skills in our multibillion dollar school program with
its many very highly "qualified" (and paid) instructors, modern physical

plants and methods, audiovisual aids, school psychologists, and family programs? This is the message that often seems to be conveyed. Furthermore, there seems to be evidence that traditionally Negro city schools in Harlem, Detroit, Washington, D.C., and elsewhere in the country did a far better job in bygone years than they are doing today. Is it because of "changing" *Negro* neighborhoods? Is it that these children's IQs are so low they cannot learn even the simplest, most fundamental skills? Or is it lower standards in the schools?

One fears the last factor must bear much of the blame. As we have repeatedly shown, declining academic achievement over the last decade is not confined to the poor, the immigrants, the Negroes, or to school districts where these children are found; it is nationwide. The achievement of high average IQ students in solidly native, affluent districts is falling rapidly. And, as we have seen, the children of immigrants, in-migrant Negroes and other minorities simply are not numerous enough, and have not increased rapidly enough, to account for the decline in most states. For example, we noted earlier in Chapter 6 the academic achievement decline in California, and even a drop in average IQ over the school years from 1969–70 through 1972–73 (see also the Appendix). Yet the change in ethnic composition of the school population over this time period in this state was negligible:

MEAN PERCENTAGE OF SCHOOL ENROLLMENT
BY ETHNIC BACKGROUND, CALIFORNIA

	1969-70	1970-71	1971-72	1972-73
Negro	2.31%	2.36%	2.45%	2.45%
Oriental	.96	.94	.95	.95
Spanish	14.76	15.14	15.35	15.35

SOURCE: *California State Testing Program 1971–72 & 1972–73.*

One also doubts that California was inundated with unintelligent, underprivileged children of other ethnic backgrounds during this time.

As has been stressed before, underprivileged children have always been with us, and the ethnic group that included the largest number of them was often easily identified by accent, skin color, stature, and surname, but seldom have our northern city school systems made such an issue of identity as they do now. We have seen that there may be reasons for the unusual school environment of today's underprivileged children, but the most important differences may have little to do with ethnic origins. As we shall see, the same might be said about their neighborhood and home environments.

With the start of the 1970s, there were signs that disappointment with the primary and secondary education trends of the 1960s—particularly education of the underprivileged—so obvious among many parents and a growing number of school administrators, might affect school policies. By fall 1971 it could be reported by George Gallup that "there is evidence that discipline has been tightened in public schools just as it has been in colleges and universities."[124] In December 1973, Irving Anker, chancellor of New York City schools, announced an end to the "automatic promotion" policy. Henceforth, in order "to improve reading levels, pupils in the fourth through eighth grades will as a general rule not be promoted if they are more than a year behind grade level in reading."[125] If enforced, the new rules will, by definition, raise average reading achievement scores for these grades. For example, if students may no longer enter the ninth grade reading at the sixth or fifth grade level, but now must read at least at eighth grade level, the *average* reading score for the ninth grade must go up. As yet, however, apparently no great improvement has occurred.[126]

As will be documented later, the majority of parents have long favored "tightening up" in our school system, with emphasis on greater discipline and traditional academic achievement. Some teachers have also favored the traditional approach throughout the era of innovation.[127] Now educators seem to be slowly beginning to consider such tried and true methods as drill in multiplication tables,[128] particularly to teach the less fortunate children. As reported by the New York *Times,* the movement seems to go beyond the back-to-basics in academic subjects: "A number of . . . educational agencies" that include the New York State and Tacoma, Washington, school systems are stressing "moral development" in their curricula.[129] One hopes the discussion of these new/old programs indicates that we may soon reach a bottoming out of our downward slide in the country's educational process. It remains to be seen whether there are enough current educators with the will and talent to halt the decline.[130] Because of the decreasing student population, fewer new educators will be added and the attrition will be chiefly among retirees, so the current younger group of teachers and administrators will be the material with which the school system will have to work for some time to come. If success in educating children depends on a sincere group of well-wishers and supporters among parents and the public as a whole, as educators so often claim, one feels these teachers and administrators could hardly be better endowed for this endeavor.

8
PARENTS, THE HOME
ENVIRONMENT, AND EDUCATION

In the recent past there has been an increased emphasis on the important effect of parents, the family, and the home and neighborhood environment on students' scholastic achievement and even their future economic status. According to an HEW study:

> In sum, what many of these analyses have shown, we believe, is that the schools reflect a deep-seated social problem that permeates almost every aspect of our society. This problem, in the main, is that a child's birth into a particular stratum of our social structure largely determines where he will and will not end up in the scheme of things. The problem is more than one of birth, however, because one's skin color and language habits tend to be associated with one's position in this social structure. It does not seem that the schools alone can rectify this problem, although they may play an ameliorative role. It seems more likely that the problem warrants a concerted attack in many different sectors of society (viz. jobs, housing, schooling, etc.).[1]

Statistically, one may be able to justify the contention that the "stratum of our society" into which we are born "largely determines" where we will end up "in the scheme of things," particularly if that stratum is large enough. For example, the "working class" has always been larger than the "professional class," which means: a) more children were born into the working class than the professional class; b) more jobs were available in the working class categories than in the professional categories. Therefore, it would not be surprising if traditionally most people born into the working class remained in it. In addition, because of normal parental instincts, people who can afford to send their children to college tend to do so, even if they are not brighter than some children from other families. This "nepotism" applies to careers; a father who is a lawyer is likely to take his son into practice rather than advertise for a junior partner, for example. These factors tend to inhibit downward mobility as well as restrict upward mobility. Nor is this practice confined to the upper class. Skilled artisans are quite likely to pass on their knowledge of the trade, and support for union membership, to their interested offspring; entrepreneurs of all types take their sons into the business, and so on.

When one acknowledges all these factors; however, one finds that much of the blame for shortchanging the intelligent, less fortunate child may still lie with the school. The already-mentioned facts alone—that the "upper class" is smaller, its birth rate lower, and the growing demand in a modern, expanding economy for a growing upper class—seem to indicate a continuing opportunity for upward mobility. The role of the school system is to equip those who are qualified among the lower strata to use the opportunities for upward mobility that become available. The fact that all cannot move up is hardly relevant. Furthermore, in recent decades, professions have been expanding rapidly, and higher paid, more prestigious technical work is becoming available at a rate that makes even the old restrictions less inhibiting.

From the viewpoint of immigrant parents (today we still have approximately 10 million foreign-born residents) and even parents who are sons or daughters of at least one immigrant (about 23 million), a paragraph like the one quoted on the previous page, written without qualifications about the United States, with its unparalleled record of upward mobility for all classes and people, may express one of the most confusing aspects of education studies done in this country today. Of all the countries in the world, most foreign-born people and their offspring look on the United States as the nation where it is *least* likely that "a child's birth into a particular stratum of our social structure largely determines where he will and will not end up in the scheme of things." Heretofore, one felt the public school system was relied on, to the degree a child's ability permitted it, largely to reduce the probability that he would fail to proceed upward socially and economically. Both native-born and immigrant parents believed instinctively what the *Statistical Abstract of the United States: 1975* seems to confirm: schooling means upward mobility.[2]

MEAN INCOME OF MALES 25 YEARS OLD AND OVER
BY YEARS OF SCHOOL COMPLETED, 1968

Elementary		High School		College	
0-7	8 Years	1-3	4 Years	1-3	4 Years or More
$3,981	$5,467	$6,769	$8,148	$9,397	$12,938

SOURCE: U.S. Census Bureau, *U.S. Stat. Abst.: 1975*, p. 123.

PERSONAL AND FAMILY INCOME BY GENERAL NATIVITY AND
RACE OF INDIVIDUAL FOR NEW YORK CITY, CHICAGO, BOSTON,
PHILADELPHIA, CLEVELAND, BUFFALO AND MILWAUKEE FOR 1909

General Nativity and Race of Individual	Males 18 yrs. and older	Females 18 yrs. and older	Male Heads of Families*	Percent of Families Having Income From		
				Wife	Children	Border
Native-born of native father:						
White	$595	$278	657	16.0	21.9	14.4
Negro	441	207	465	64.2	9.5	32.4
Native-born of foreign father by race of father:						
Bohemian and Moravian	518	315	632	45.5	6.1	6.1
German	581	317	674	16.0	25.4	11.8
Hebrew	541	327	-	-	-	-
Irish	535	294	601	20.3	24.8	12.6
Italian South	413	270	-	-	-	-
Polish	403	211	-	-	-	-
Swedish	516	327	-	-	-	-
Foreign-born:						
Bohemian and Moravian	538	300	552	34.7	33.5	15.3
German	613	204	630	20.2	42.0	10.7
Greek	352	-	-	-	-	-
Hebrew, Russian	461	259	463	7.8	35.6	43.0
Hebrew, Other	465	230	484	12.1	34.2	31.5
Irish	535	213	557	19.6	41.9	17.5
Italian, North**	425	232	449	13.2	28.3	56.6
Italian, South	368	179	390	16.8	21.6	27.0
Lithuanian	410	191	419	6.5	8.8	77.3
Magyar	346	198	390	22.5	9.3	52.7
Negro	385	121	369	67.6	5.4	51.4
Polish	365	168	379	10.7	21.9	38.1
Servian	325	-	-	-	-	-
Slovak	384	208	402	14.6	14.9	44.8
Slovenian	398	-	433	.0	11.0	36.0
Swedish	692	221	703	20.4	36.3	42.5
Syrian	321	218	356	11.8	8.8	2.9
Grand Total	413	239	475	17.7	26.0	30.3
Total native-born of foreign father	526	292	625	20.6	23.1	11.8
Total native-born	533	275	612	26.8	20.2	16.5
Total foreign-born	385	219	452	16.1	27.0	32.7

*In 13% of the families, the husband contributed nothing to the family income.

**Northern Italians make up less than 4% of Italians in the sample.

SOURCE: U.S. Immigration Commission, *Reports*, Vol. 26, pp. 136–40.

Of course, realistically, parents know we can't all be chiefs, that there must be more Indians than chiefs. But without simultaneously curing all the ills in many different sectors of society, the question is, can the Indian become a chief? In this country, the answer traditionally has been yes. And he did, as current income and social levels of previously underprivileged, blatantly defamed, exploited minorities attest. In 1909, in seven large sample northern cities, Polish, Russian—primarily Russian Jews—and southern Italian immigrant male heads of families made less money than family heads of any of the other white or nonwhite large identifiable groups of citizens in our society. Second-generation male southern Italians and Poles were also the lowest-paid men of all such identified groups.

Not only did these immigrants achieve within two generations education levels equal to or higher than those of earlier immigrants and native Americans, as shown in Chapter 7, but in the same time period, the offspring of those of Russian origin raised themselves economically to the very top of the income ladder, and those of the lowest groups in 1909, the Poles and Italians, held second and third place in 1970.

INCOME BY PERSONS 14 YEARS OLD AND OVER, 1970,
BY ETHNIC ORIGIN AND SEX, AND FAMILY INCOME
BY ETHNIC ORIGIN OF HEAD

	Total	German	Italian	Irish	French	Polish	Russian	English Scotch Welsh	Spanish	Other	Not Reported
ian Income											
Males	$6,665	$ 7,467	$ 7,883	$6,881	$6,775	$ 8,154	$ 9,160	$ 7,414	$5,477	$5,972	$6,013
emales	2,278	2,316	2,667	2,422	2,248	3,052	2,959	2,428	2,167	2,141	2,045
ily Median Income											
Ethnic Origin Head	9,891	10,402	11,089	9,964	9,558	11,619	13,895	10,727	7,379	9,630	8,676

SOURCE: U.S. Census Bureau, *Current Population Reports*, April 1973, "Characteristics of the Population by Ethnic Origin: March 1972 and 1971," pp. 33, 34.

In 1962, one-third of United States workers saw their children enter nonworking-class jobs—including entrepreneurial jobs—and white-collar jobs, and though only about 30 percent of these, constituting 10 percent of all workers' children, entered what Andrew Levison calls the "professional and technical 'elite,' "[3] the process of upward mobility apparently continued. The rate of progress, though likely to be greater now than in 1962, Levison indicates should still not be deemed satisfactory; however, the percentage of *children* of that 10 percent of manual laborers' children who enter the "elite" will follow in their parents' footsteps at a far greater rate than 10 percent—probably closer to 80 or 90 percent.

Today the need for basic schooling among the underprivileged is as great as it was in the last major immigrant era. The overwhelming majority of the children of these new arrivals in our large, and even smaller, cities speak English and are in a far less alien environment than were former immigrants from foreign shores. But unless they are able to *read* the language and do basic math problems, they are often virtually unemployable. Unlike the era of the last great immigration, there is less call for pick-and-shovel work in our society. The percentage of manual labor construction and industrial production jobs has been declining for years, and in our growing service-industry oriented economy, the gap between types of available jobs is great, and is directly related to education. Service-type jobs for the uneducated are not only fewer and generally ill-paid, but often very menial—garbage men, floor swabbers, septic tank cleaners are a few examples. For the educated, however, service-type jobs can range from such fields as communications and transportation to computer operation. Ditch diggers no longer are required; backhoe operators are, but they must be able to read the operator's manual and often pass operator's tests. That kind of service job requires a knowledge of the fundamentals—reading, writing, and arithmetic.

As stated earlier, the underlying philosophy of the American public school system is to smooth the path upward, and it is in this area that parents seem to fear the school system has been failing recently.

In recent years, parental concern for children's welfare and achievement in school, which educators seem to feel is so important for students' progress,[4] was quite evident in public opinion polls. Of the choices given, the choices of those surveyed are ranked by order of the number of times each was mentioned.

> QUESTION (1972):   "Which three of these educational programs would you like your local elementary schools (grades 1–6) to give *more attention* to?":

1. Teaching students the skills of reading, writing and arithmetic.
2. Teaching students how to solve problems and think for themselves.
3. Teaching students to respect law and authority.
4. Teaching students how to get along with others.
5. Teaching students the skills of speaking and listening.
6. Teaching students vocational skills.
7. Teaching students health and physical education.
8. Teaching students about the world of today and yesterday (that is, history, geography and civics).
9. Teaching students how to compete with others.

NOTE: Reprinted from *Gallup Opinion Index,* No. 87, Sept. 1972, p. 18.

Respondents were then asked the same question in relation to junior and senior high schools (grades 7–12). In order of mentions:

1. Teaching students to respect law and authority.
2. Teaching students how to solve problems and think for themselves.
3. Teaching students vocational skills.
4. Teaching students how to get along with others.
5. Teaching students the skills of speaking and listening.
6. Teaching students about the world of today and yesterday (that is, history, geography, and civics).
7. Teaching students the skills of reading, writing, and arithmetic.
8. Teaching students health and physical education.
9. Teaching students how to compete with others.

NOTE: Reprinted from *Gallup Opinion Index,* No. 87, Sept. 1972, p. 18.

In addition to such survey data, much anecdotal evidence indicates that parents want children taught the basics rather than the generalities of progressive education. One primary schoolteacher, Kim Marshal, reported in 1970:

> . . . I was well aware of the legitimate demands in the black community for *results* in the three Rs. I knew that the suspicion of white liberals "experimenting" with black children was such that I could not afford to be accused of dillydallying around with a "permissive" classroom that did not have very visible and effective effort to teach the basic skills needed to get kids into high school and college. I simply couldn't tell a parent that the development of her child's soul in an idealistic "open classroom" was more important. . . .[5]

Traditionally, adults seem to emphasize teaching the basic skills and, as mentioned in Chapter 7, are also in favor of orderly schools; poll data over the past twenty years have borne this out.[6] Feelings remain basically unchanged.

Looking at the table on page 134, one should note that more adult Negroes (62 percent) than whites (52 percent) felt discipline in local public schools was not strict enough, while those who thought it too strict were statistically insignificant (4 and 2 percent respectively).

Furthermore, though these parents and other adults were, and certainly still are, very interested in achievement, they were unwilling to accept the local educators' opinion of their children's achievement. High school juniors and seniors concurred with their parents.

Parents and the rest of the public, including high school juniors and seniors, were so concerned with progress that they wanted to hold school staffs responsible.

DISCIPLINE IN THE LOCAL PUBLIC SCHOOLS

QUESTION: "How do you feel about the discipline in the
             local public schools--is it too strict, not
             strict enough, or just about right?"

National	Too Strict	Not Strict Enough	Just About Right	Don't Know/ No Answer
Sex				
Men	2%	54%	31%	13%
Women	2	52	31	15
Race				
White	2	52	32	14
Nonwhite	4	62	21	13

NOTE: Reprinted from *Gallup Opinion Index,* No. 66, Dec. 1970, p. 17.

NATIONAL TESTS IN LOCAL SCHOOLS?

QUESTION: "Would you like to see the students in the local schools be
             given National Tests so that their educational achievement
             could be compared with students in other communities?"

	National Totals	No Children In School	Public School Parents	Parochial School Parents	High School Juniors and Seniors
Yes	75%	74%	75%	80%	76%
No	16	14	19	15	23
No Opinion	9	12	6	5	1
	100	100	100	100	100

Note: Reprinted from *Gallup Opinion Index,* No. 66,
Dec. 1970, p. 18.

THE ACCOUNTABILITY OF THE SCHOOL FOR
STUDENTS' PROGRESS

QUESTION: "Would you favor or oppose a system that would held
teachers and administrators more accountable for the
progress of students?"

	No National Totals	No Children In School	Public School Parents	Parochial School Parents	High School Juniors and Seniors
Favor	67	66	68	71	65
Oppose	21	21	21	19	29
No Opinion	12	13	11	10	6

NOTE: Reprinted from *Gallup Opinion Index,* No. 66, Dec. 1970, p. 18.

HOW SHOULD TEACHERS BE PAID?

QUESTION: "Should each teacher be paid on the basis of the quality of
his work or should all teachers be paid on a standard scale
basis?"

	National Totals	No Children In School	Public School Parents	Parochial School Parents	High School Juniors and Seniors
Quality of Work	58%	57%	61%	52%	59%
Standard Scale Basis	36	36	35	43	39
No Opinion	6	7	4	5	2
	100	100	100	100	100

NOTE: Reprinted from *Gallup Opinion Index,* No. 66, Dec. 1970, p. 18.

TENURE FOR TEACHERS?

QUESTION: "Many states have "Tenure" laws which mean that a teacher
           cannot be fired except by some sort of court procedure.
           Are you for giving teachers tenure or are you against
           tenure?"

	National Totals	No Children In School*	Public School Parents	Parochial School Parents	High School Juniors and Seniors
For	35%	38%	29%	28%	30%
Against	53	48	60	62	61
No Opinion	12	14	11	10	9
	100	100	100	100	100

NOTE: Reprinted from *Gallup Opinion Index,* No. 66, Dec. 1970, p. 18.

TEACHER TENURE

QUESTION: "Most public school teachers have tenure; that is, after a
          two- or three-year trial period, they receive what amounts
          to a lifetime contract. Do you approve or disapprove of
          this policy?"

	National Totals	No Children In School	Public School Parents	Private School Parents	Professional Educators
N =	1,790	996	698	144	270
Approve	28%	28%	27%	28%	53%
Disapprove	61	59	64	63	42
No Opinion	11	13	9	9	5
	100	100	100	100	100

NOTE: Reprinted from *Gallup Opinion Index,* No. 87, Sept. 1972, p. 23.

Apparently, many teachers were unlikely to be amenable to an achievement testing and evaluation approach. A New York *Times* article reports, "In practice, the growing movement has often provoked teachers' fears that they will be held accountable if their pupils fail to progress." A spokesman for New Jersey teachers cited, among others, the fear that test results would be used as a club with which to intimidate nonconformist teachers.[7]

Parents and students also frown on a tenure system that largely puts the teacher out of reach of administrators' and school boards' dismissal power; professional educators, by only a modest margin, approve of it.

Of the choices given, there has been some change over the years in what are mentioned most often as the problems facing schools, but lack of discipline was "named the number one problem in five out of six years" between 1960 and 1974.[8]

MAJOR PROBLEMS CONFRONTING THE PUBLIC SCHOOLS IN 1972

QUESTION: What do you think are the biggest problems with which the public schools in this community must deal?

1. Lack of discipline
2. Lack of proper financial support
3. Integration-segregation problems
4. Difficulty of getting "good" teachers
5. Large school, too large classes
6. Parents' lack of interest
7. Lack of proper facilities
8. Poor curriculum
9. Use of dope, drugs

. . . The professional educators interviewed in this same [Gallup Opinion] survey regard school finances as the number one problem, followed in order by integration/segregation, discipline, parents' lack of interest, quality of teaching, curriculum, use of dope and drugs, and lack of proper school facilities.

. . . The question of "student rights" was probed in the present survey. The question:

Generally speaking, do the local public school students in this community have too many rights and privileges, or not enough?

The general public replied:

Too Many   41%
Not Enough   11
Just Right   33
No Opinion   15

Since 18-year-olds now have the right to vote, the question has arisen as to whether, as full-fledged citizens, they should not have more rights than other students. The public says "No" in resounding fashion. The question:

Should students who are 18 years of age, and now have the right to vote, have more rights and privileges than other students?

Yes   21%
No   73
No Opinion   6

NOTE: Reprinted from *Gallup Opinion Index,* No. 87, Sept. 1972, p. 17.

In 1974 integration/segregation problems appeared in second place on the list of problems and use of drugs moved from ninth to fourth place, but poor curriculum remained second from last, in ninth place.[9] By 1976 a Gallup survey showed that poor curriculum had moved up from ninth to fourth place, with use of drugs right behind it.

1. Lack of discipline
2. Integration/segregation/busing
3. Lack of proper financial support
4. Poor curriculum
5. Use of drugs
6. Difficulty of getting "good" teachers
7. Parents' lack of interest
8. Size of school/classes
9. School board policies
10. Pupils' lack of interest

Note: Reprinted from *Gallup Opinion Index,* No. 135, Oct. 1976, p. 15.

This same Gallup survey showed that more emphasis on the "basic skills" was first choice of ways for improving our schools. Also, 65 percent of the public would like to see a requirement that all high school students pass a standard nationwide examination to get a diploma. This figure is up from 50 percent who said they favored such a test in 1958. Sixty-six percent were against lowering the compulsory age of school attendance and by a ratio of 59 to 31 percent (10 percent had no opinion), those surveyed felt that declining test scores meant that the quality of education is declining. A New York *Times* article spoke of "rising disenchantment with the public schools."[10]

There is also much evidence that people prefer that their children attend schools close to home. After closing five schools ranging in size from one to four rooms in favor of a new, centrally located school, due to a dip in enrollment, a Pennsylvania hinterland school superintendent encountered heated parental opposition: "All those coal miners want a school near their homes."[11] Nor is this merely the attitude of people with "a small town mentality"; the school board in East Ramapo, to a significant degree a "bedroom" area for New York City, experienced parental opposition when two neighborhood schools were to be closed for the same reason.[12] Parents have been known, however, to support voluntary busing to what they feel are superior schools away from local neighborhoods. As David Armor writes: ". . . black parents stressed quality of education as the most important benefit of such programs [busing of core-city Negro pupils to suburban schools]. . . ."[13]

Of course, as mentioned earlier, the effort to achieve racial balance has affected neighborhood schools, too, and caused mandatory busing and cross-busing in areas where it was unknown previously, again with continuing opposition from parents. A National Opinion Research Center survey in spring 1974 showed 72.9 percent opposing busing: 82.2 percent of whites and 36.9 percent of Negroes. The same survey showed that 73 percent of whites had no objections to sending their children to integrated schools—presumably neighborhood schools.

Surveys showed the following results over the years on the question of busing for racial balance:

BUSING OF SCHOOL CHILDREN

QUESTION: "In general, do you favor or oppose the busing of Negro and white children from one school district to another?"

	Favor		Oppose		No Opinion	
	8/71	10/71	8/71	10/71	8/71	10/71
National	19%	17%	73%	77%	8%	6%
Sex						
Men	20	16	73	78	7	6
Women	17	17	74	77	9	6
Race						
White	16	14	76	80	8	6
Non-white	43	45	46	47	11	8
Education						
College	23	22	72	75	5	3
High School	17	15	75	79	8	6
Grade School	17	17	70	75	13	8
Occupation						
Professional and						
Business	21	18	74	78	5	4
White Collar	19	18	74	76	7	6
Farmers	11	15	78	75	11	10
Manual	19	17	74	77	7	6

Age					
18-20 years	32	28	64	63	4
21-29 years	25	23	69	73	6
30-49 years	17	17	76	78	7
50 and over	15	12	74	81	11
Religion					
Protestant	15	15	78	80	7
Catholic	18	19	71	74	11
Jewish	x	x	x	x	x
Politics					
Republican	11	10	81	83	8
Democrat	23	12	70	74	7
Independent	17	17	74	77	9
Region					
East	22	18	68	76	10
Midwest	17	17	74	75	9
South	15	10	79	87	6
West	22	25	69	68	9
Income					
$15,000 and over	21	16	73	79	6
$10,000-$14,999	18	19	75	75	7
$ 7,000-$ 9,999	21	15	72	81	7
$ 5,000-$ 6,999	15	17	76	76	9
$ 3,000-$ 4,999	19	15	66	77	15
Under $3,000	17	23	73	72	10
Community Size					
1,000,000 and over	23	25	71	69	6
500,000-999,999	17	17	74	79	9
50,000-499,999	21	15	71	81	8
2,500-49,999	18	15	71	78	11
Under 2,500, Rural	14	14	77	79	9

SOURCE: *Gallup Opinion Index,* No. 75, Sept. 1971, p. 20; No. 77, Nov. 1971, p. 24.

A 1972 survey by the National Opinion Research Center for the U.S. Commission on Civil Rights asked a somewhat more restricted question about busing where "courts have found unlawful segregation." For example, much busing these days is for "racial balance," involving neighborhood schools that have not even experienced de facto segregation, for they have some Negro children already in attendance. The term "unlawful" in the survey question may eliminate in many people's minds their own school district's procedures. The question and results were as follows:

In areas where the courts have found unlawful segregation of white and black schoolchildren the courts have ordered desegregation, including busing where necessary, so that whites and blacks will not be kept from attending school together. Do you favor or oppose such busing?

Favor	Oppose	No Opinion
21%	70%	9%

Note: Reprinted from U.S. Civil Rights Commission, *Public Knowledge and Busing Opposition: A Interpretation of a New National Survey,* March 1973, Appendix I, p. 1.

QUESTION: "Do you favor busing of school children for the purpose of racial integration or should busing for this purpose be prohibited through a constitutional amendment?"

	Favor %	Prohibit %	Don't Know No Answer %
National	18	72	10
Sex			
Men	19	73	8
Women	18	71	11
Race			
White	15	75	10
Nonwhite	40	47	13
Education			
Elementary	21	70	9
High School	15	75	10
College	22	67	11
Age			
18 to 29 years	22	67	11
30 to 49 years	16	74	10
50 years and over	18	72	10
Religion			
Protestant	16	75	9
Roman Catholic	19	70	11
Jewish	21	68	11
All others	30	55	15
Region			
East	17	70	13
Midwest	18	74	8
South	20	73	7
West	17	70	13
Political affiliation			
Republican	13	78	9
Democrat	22	69	9
Independent	16	72	12

NOTE: Reprinted from *Gallup Opinion Index,* No. 119, May 1975, p. 27.

It still seems as though busing for any reason, except perhaps to transport children to a religiously oriented or superior school, has not appealed to the population as a whole; according to one report, even many well-educated Negroes, formerly active proponents of busing, now doubt its advisability. They and Negro groups such as Atlanta's chapter of the NAACP have discontinued their support.[14]

There seems to be a vast amount of interest, however, among parents of every race, religion, income level, region, and occupation in the scholastic achievement of their children, as a result perhaps of increased opportunity for upward economic and social mobility.

QUESTION (1972):   People have different reasons why they want their children to get an education. What are the chief reasons that come to your mind?

1.	To get better jobs	44%
2.	To get along better with people at all levels of society	43
3.	To make more money—achieve financial success	38
4.	To attain self-satisfaction	21
5.	To stimulate their minds	15
6.	Miscellaneous reasons	11

NOTE: Reprinted from *Gallup Opinion Index,* No. 87, Sept. 1972, p. 18.

Jean Heinig reports that in a Roper Poll taken several years ago in Louisville, Kentucky, 79 percent of Negroes and 79 percent of whites felt "the favored way to Negro progress" was to "get more education."[15]

We find that, as indicated earlier, there seems to be some disapproval of the situation under the old school systems in which, from the parents' and students' viewpoints, education was something "practical and ornamental" to be used to better one's station in life.[16] Yet we see in the HEW study of national student achievement mentioned earlier that parents *are* interested in seeing their children advance:

> . . . under what conditions are parents likely to engage in educationally related child-rearing activities? A study by J. M. Garza (1969) suggests that when parents perceive opportunities for their child to obtain a better

life through education, then they will be more prone to engage in such activities. These, in turn, translate into motivation for achievement.[17]

Apparently, if a child appears smart, parents expect him to do well. If he does not seem to have the tools necessary to excel, parents may be reluctant to push him in areas he might not be able to deal with successfully. On the other hand, it is likely that many parents will help a child more if they think he needs it.[18]

But it seems that it was felt that this parental interest had to be coupled with a certain type of involvement:

> We concluded, then, that the crucial factor in achievement was not so much the presence or absence of parents or parental surrogates as the nature of their involvement in the educational process.

Furthermore, success in this specific type of involvement seemed to be related to skin color:

> However, economically depressed nonwhites find it harder to overcome the effects of their low status by such means than do economically depressed whites. In this sense, the outputs of schooling are the inputs of society.[19]

We are thus led to asking some basic questions regarding parents and home environment that may not be as relevant to education issues as some seem to think. Apparently it is not clear what determines the probability of children of greater talent being found in one socioeconomic group rather than another, environmentalists notwithstanding. As mentioned earlier, one should not be surprised if in an affluent society with an expanding economy, the probability of people with incentive and higher IQs remaining poor is relatively low. Certain elements, such as prejudice, can change the situation somewhat, but, generally speaking, in a booming economy and expanding job market, those with talent, particularly those willing to relocate in order to work, will not remain poor. In Oscar Handlin's words, "The ability to move upward in occupation or status, having narrowed during the depression of the 1930's, broadened dramatically after 1950. No one ever expected rags to riches; but the hope of a climb, step by step, increasingly was open to fulfillment by all."[20] As one would assume, the offspring of a group of relatively high IQ parents are more likely to be above average IQ and vice versa. There is a positive correlation between the levels of skill required by specific jobs and the mean IQ levels of children of fathers holding these various jobs.[21] This correlation probably reflects not only the father's IQ, but the fact that assortative mating in this country draws like

IQ men and women to each other to a degree that assures closer IQ ratings between husbands and wives than between siblings.[22] When we look at the IQ and/or achievement levels of lower-middle-class students as a group, the lower "competence" of this group is borne out.[23]

As natural as the selection of a wife of like IQ is the selection by the more highly skilled and more highly paid man of the best home in the best neighborhood he can afford. This is the reward for his skill and diligence in our society, and the incentive for his endeavors. It means that there is a filter system at work that tends to cluster people of higher skills, higher education, and higher average IQ in certain neighborhoods and certain school districts. It would not be surprising if pupils from such selected groups outscored pupils of lower average IQ—particularly if both have a basic curriculum, good discipline, and are given homework—regardless of such factors as the student/teacher ratio, availability of equipment, teachers' salaries, age of school buildings. Indeed, we have many examples of "selected" student bodies, from very modest homes, in parochial schools across the country with high academic achievement on very small amounts of money per pupil.

But the "selected" neighborhoods with high IQ people often, though not always, also happen to have posh schools with low student/teacher ratios, many "elective" courses, many audiovisual aids, large playing fields, and are located on tree-lined streets. Clearly, one should consider that perhaps the people in these schools—and in the lower-class parochial schools—also help to make the environment, rather than only the other way around. Yet many educators are likely to stress the physical and social home environment, rather than the differences in mean IQ amid groups of parents and pupils, when discussing the differences among pupils from differing socioeconomic groups and different school districts. As we quoted Alan Wilson et al, in 1966, in the last chapter, "for years . . . teacher training institutions . . . and almost all writers . . . on the 'culturally deprived' . . . have taken a fairly uniform stance on the environmentalistic side" of the discussion.[24] In the case of "middle-class white populations," we read in Theodore Dobzhansky's book, *Genetic Diversity and Human Equality,* "investigators have reached the conclusion that genetic variability accounts for about 75 percent of the total variance in IQ scores. . . ."[25] But among disadvantaged groups, "Carriers of genetic endowments who could unfold high IQs under favorable conditions will fare no better than genetically less well-endowed people in suppressive environments."[26]

It is difficult to determine exactly what underprivileged homes and neighborhoods have done, or not done, to or for these students so that they cannot be taught when they enter school, where incorrect influences traditionally were counteracted. And though it might be true that for some reason "economically depressed non-whites find it harder to overcome the effects of their low status by [involvement of parents in the educational process] than do economically depressed whites,"[27] it is not at all clear, for example, that Negro parents or neighborhoods have traditionally impressed their children with their inherent "low status" and hopeless position in school. Nor is it clear that their schools in the past have had this effect. In a study of tenth grade boys, Jerald Bachman writes, researchers found results ". . . surprising; black males score noticeably *higher* than whites on our self-esteem scale, and when adjustments are made for other background factors the difference becomes larger."[28]

Furthermore, as we have seen, adult Negroes, as much as or more than whites, indicate a desire for the schools to "take charge" of children and school them in the fundamentals. But if "involvement in the educational process" means that the Negro (or white) father should teach his child at night what a teacher failed to teach him during the day, this is a different problem. Lower-middle-class fathers often "moonlight" on a second job, work twelve-hour days, arrive home at 10:00 or 11:00 P.M.; most mothers of schoolchildren now also work. Many of those who do not work are busy with several children, frequently under six years old.[29] It seems wrong, somehow, that such a mother or father should have to do at night the job of a teacher, who, for as little as five hours' work, earned two or three times the father's daily income. It is doubly galling since the teacher is paid with the father's hard-earned money, taken from him in excessively high school taxes, which show up in rent costs as well. Clearly the reasoning behind expectations of this kind of parental "involvement" seems questionable.

Professional educators traditionally have considered homes, and parents in general—in particular those of the lower class and lower-middle-class, here and in other countries—to be grossly inadequate as teaching institutions. This is one big reason that tax-supported public education was introduced. It is strange, therefore, that a large part of the responsibility for teaching children to read, write, spell, and do mathematics is now thought to rest with the parents (whether rich or poor) and the home, rather than with our $75 billion-a-year primary and secondary public and private schools systems. Unfortunately, this is what educators too often imply, and equally unfortunate, too often it *is* the hard-working mothers and fathers, or tutors for those who can afford them, who teach their children at home what teachers fail to teach in school. This, however, does not necessarily prove these parents' adequacy in doing what educators have heretofore insisted they could not do; it could indicate only a relative ability to teach children measured against the present observable inability of many of our current public and private schools. Nor is this inability observable only as regards the slow learners; the experience of bright children is the same.

The author knows one rather affluent, well-educated father who, after complaining to the public school that his child could not read, and despairing of their teaching him, finally spent an hour a day for six weeks during one summer teaching the child himself. That September the school guidance counselor informed the parents that their fears were groundless—the child was now reading above grade level. Upon being informed that, after years of disappointment, the father had finally taught the child himself, the guidance counselor asked, "Why did you wait so long to teach him?" This home schooling is a particularly difficult task for parents with inferior education, particularly if a child is behind in high school subjects.

On the other hand, it is not so clear that all educators want parents to become involved in what the *schools* are doing academically for and to their children. As any interested parent can testify, there has been a growing tendency in recent years to dissuade adults—parents and nonparents—from interesting themselves in results of standardized pupil scholastic achievement tests. The author knows of one midwestern *school board trustee* who was said to have come under heavy fire from the educators when he forced the disclosure of the local ITBS scores—which, of course, were falling. When parents do evidence interest in—and sufficient dissatisfaction to contact teachers about—children's classroom progress, they are often told not to "put so much stress on pupils' grades." But since test scores and grades are the only indicators of how the children and the school are performing, parents cannot really become involved, at least not beyond rubber stamping what teachers decide, without this information.

In fact, as indicated earlier, a growing number of parents who are truly concerned about their children's education, and who know what children should learn, experience prolonged family unpleasantness, in part because teachers with ever-decreasing standards support the children's opposition to their parents' demands for greater efforts in schoolwork. Schools today commonly reinforce many a talented youngster's tendency to do as little as possible, instead of supporting the involved parents' wishes and urging the child to work to his full potential as they used to do. Although it is fashionable, moreover, for educators to stress constantly how much effort and money parents owe their children—and the school system—to further children's education, virtually no mention is made of what students owe parents for the unending, tension-filled, cardiac-causing labor and effort, on and off the job, to obtain for them the best education possible.

On the contrary, in the recent past educators have been more likely to convey the idea that these parents—including blue-collar workers, particularly if they are unionized—are members of the "establishment," and as such, are hypocrites—cold, even heartless, selfish, and anything but honest. The author knows a very hard-working man of exceptional talent who pulled himself up by his own efforts from being a person on relief during the Depression to a point where he can now raise his children in an area, and send them to the kind of school, he could only dream about previously.

A few years ago, he flew all night in order to get to his oldest child's high school graduation in time. He then heard the valedictorian speak about how rotten, heartless and evil was the "establishment," to which the parents in the audience, of course, belonged. This phenomenon was not confined to upper-middle-class schools; the widening myth of the "generation gap" was fostered in working class and "slum" schools as well.[30]

THE HOMES AND PARENTS OF THE UNDERPRIVILEGED, THEN AND NOW

As we have seen, there is no evidence that parents, in general, are significantly less concerned with their children's education these days than previously. Even amid the underprivileged of this country today, there is no irrefutable evidence that parents in the standard nuclear family are any less knowledgeable about the subtleties of the educational process, or are any less qualified by social and educational background to become involved, than were the newly arrived Polish and Italian peasants and Russian serfs whose children flooded the schools of the 1890s and early 1900s.

Between 1868 and 1910, 21.5 million immigrants came to America. By 1905 they were arriving at the rate of one million a year, and the percentage of immigrants from Northern and Western Europe had shrunk to 19.4 percent (from 92.5 percent in 1868), while those from Southern and Eastern Europe increased to 70.9 percent of the total (from 1.3 percent in 1868).[31] In 1920, 13.2 percent of our population was still made up of immigrants, 15 percent of sons and daughters of immigrant parents, and 6.5 percent of people with one immigrant parent.[32]

Though it is rarely mentioned, the general physical home environment of current schoolchildren is, on the whole, the best in our history. The affluence of our society compared to societies of the past extends to the lowest families in the land. As great as the contrast is today between the poor and the more affluent, and badly as improvement is needed, the circumstances today are nothing like that of the earlier underprivileged. Handlin writes:

> (In all, the 312,000 residents [of New York] of 1840 had become 3,437,000 in 1900.) Chicago's rise was even more precipitate; the 4000 inhabitants there in 1840 numbered 1,700,000 in 1900. Every ten-year interval saw two people struggling for the space formerly occupied by one.[33]

Such crowding led to conditions in which, in New York in 1853, five hundred people lived in one barrack building a hundred-fifty feet long and five stories high. In this building each family had a two-room "apartment":

one room nine by fourteen feet, one nine by six, "without interior plumbing or heat." Ten years later, when the building had "more than eight hundred dwellers," there was installed "for the service of the community, a row of privies in the basement, flushed occasionally by Croton water." This building "continued in use till the very end of the century."[34] Later tenements had common water closets on the upper floors, but "from one hundred and fifty to two hundred human beings" lived in a building twenty to twenty-five feet wide, ninety feet long, and six to eight stories high. One block of such tenements housed four thousand people.[35] Open sewers were common. (Chicago's "Bubbly Creek wended its noisome way aboveground until well into the twentieth century.") "Not till late was city water directly connected with the toilets; it was later still to reach the kitchen sink; and bathrooms had not yet put in an appearance in these quarters." Everything was in disrepair: ". . . the rain comes through the ceiling, the wind blows dirt through the cracks in the wall." People tried to divide their tiny crowded domains with calico sheets hung on ropes for some privacy.[36] According to The New York *Times* of January 18, 1895 (in Schoener), though "New York, including the thinly populated annexed district, ranks sixth [in population density] . . . New York below the Harlem has a greater density per acre than any other city in the world—143.2 per acre." The article further indicated that 39,138 tenement buildings housed 1,332,773 people. The estimated population of the city was 1,891,306. In these neighborhoods, up to "nearly 93 percent of the total area" was covered with buildings.[37] Nor, as indicated, were these the worst conditions. Even outside the big cities, dismal rows of coal and iron "company houses" set against culm and slag heaps on mud roads housed hundreds of thousands of non-English-speaking parents and their many children.

Such homes, in which were heard only Hungarian, Italian, Polish, Russian, or Yiddish, had no books, no writing paper, no pencils, no quiet—only endless toil, sickness, and malnutrition.

An article in the New York *Times* of January 18, 1895 (in Schoener), stated that as of June 1, 1890, New York City had 1,489,627 whites, of whom 42.8 percent, or 636,986, were foreign-born; and 76.2 percent had foreign-born mothers.[38] In 1909, 72 percent of New York City's population was first- or second-generation immigrant,[39] as was 72 percent of its school population,[40] and English was not spoken in 53 percent of its homes.[41] Over the years, there were drunkenness, roaring family arguments and fights, epidemics, wars and rumors of wars, and political graft and corruption on local, state, and federal levels, the like of which is almost inconceivable today. Finally, the 1930s Great Depression caused want and misery to reach a level, scale, and duration that makes the economic plight of our underprivileged today seem mild by comparison.

Yet the public school system did not seem to view these as reasons to abdicate its responsibility to educate children; it seemed to cope with the problem for which it was designed. As we have seen, there is no evidence of widespread illiteracy among the students who went through the system's primary schools during the Great Depression, nor is there any evidence that large numbers of these children could not handle simple mathematics. They were not all Rhodes scholars, though some were, but a standard of achievement was maintained that apparently prevented large numbers of illiterate children, or children who could not make change for a dollar, from existing among our primary school graduates. As mentioned earlier, in the 1930s the author was familiar with the chronically depressed coal-mining regions of what is known today as northern "Appalachia," where there were vast numbers of Eastern European immigrants. Here, during the Great Depression, men roamed from house to house begging for a meal, and in some areas the economic situation had almost deteriorated to a barter system. Immigrant parents, living in grinding poverty and *de facto* segregation, economically exploited, generally could be of little help to their children in schoolwork. Many still could not read or write the language they spoke—Polish, Italian, Magyar, Syrian, anything but English. In the United States in 1920, 13.1 percent of white foreign-born residents told the census takers they could read neither English nor their native tongue; the figure apparently had remained substantially the same since 1890.[42] However, there is some reason to think this figure is optimistic for the later immigrant groups; for example, the following table gives illiteracy rates for the southern provinces of Italy in 1901, the source of so many of our immigrants in the early 1900s.

	Percent of Illiterates					
	6 Years and Over			21 Years and Over		
	Male	Female	Total	Male	Female	Total
Abruzzi	58.5	79.8	69.8	59.5	85.2	73.4
Campania	56.9	72.6	65.1	57.3	76.5	67.5
Apulia	63.7	75.3	69.5	63.3	80.3	71.9
Basilicata	66.5	83.1	75.4	67.4	87.9	78.7
Calabria	69.2	87.0	78.7	67.7	89.5	79.8
Sicily	65.2	76.6	70.9	64.9	81.4	73.2

SOURCE: U.S. Immigration Commission, *Reports,* Vol. 4, p. 186.

Census data are not an accurate measure of literacy, for no proof of performance is required in a census survey, and only those with fewer than five years of school were even asked this question. Seventeen years ago, in 1959, the rate of illiteracy among Negroes was thought to be 7.5 percent, and in 1969, 3.5 percent, but since 1952 only people not having completed *six* grades of school were asked about literacy.[43] As we have seen, however, *functional illiteracy* runs to several times that number among Negroes—particularly young males—of all levels of primary and secondary education.[44]

These pre-World War II times were the "bad old days," and no one who spent most of his primary and secondary school years in one of the really deprived areas during the Depression could wish his or anyone else's children, even poor children, to exchange their situation for the economic conditions their counterparts endured then. It is important, however, to keep the environment of the "control group" of past students in mind when the stampede down the economic, or even sociological, environmentalist road, with its excuses for children's low scholastic achievements, tends to sweep us along. We have been there before, so these factors alone seem inadequate to explain why our current school system cannot do today what it did then for terribly disadvantaged "slum" children, at least up to age sixteen, the age of compulsory school attendance then as now. (See Chapter 3 for the high scholastic achievement test scores of 1937 students in the ninth grade, a year before most dropouts occurred.)

SLUM VIOLENCE, THEN AND NOW

There are some aspects of our current slum areas, however, that most likely do not compare favorably with early slums. The caveat that urban citizens are chronically concerned about crime and traditionally are apt to consider that "things are getting worse" should be remembered. It is to be found in every work on the subject, including those cited hereafter. Obviously, such concern can color the judgment of those attempting to describe the situation at any given point, today as well as before. On the other hand, for this very reason, in examining past works on large-city conditions, we should at least see a version that does not understate the situation. Documentation on the last period during which we had great numbers of underprivileged immigrants living in our slums cites the violence there. Oscar Handlin speaks of gangs of young toughs menacing a stranger "simply because his looks offended them." Still, ". . . the crime willfully planned and executed for gain rarely involved the immigrant. The lawbreakers often congregated in the districts in which the newcomers lived and sometimes recruited American-born children, but not the immigrants themselves."[45]

Nonetheless, in light of the anecdotal and statistical evidence today, even keeping in mind the important caveat regarding the urban citizen's tendency to exaggerate, the crime problem does seem worrisome. Random, violent crimes "against the person" of simple citizens, sexual promiscuity, and indigence are apparently tolerated in some of our largest cities to a greater extent than during the past immigrant era. One gets the impression that the slum-dwelling American of 1900 would have been surprised, by the frequency at least, of some commonplace happenings witnessed by the average law-abiding citizen in sections of Harlem, the south Bronx, Brooklyn, Chicago, Detroit, Washington, D.C., Boston, and many other U.S. "core-city" areas today. Roger Lane wrote in 1968:

> While public "attitudes" are slippery concepts to compare, it does seem that . . . [based on acceptable levels of violence which change over time] the State of Massachusetts, and the United States in general, had a criminal problem less worrisome in the 19th century than in the 1960's . . . As the sons and daughters of Massachusetts migrated to the metropolis Boston in the late 1800's the image conjured by the fearful was the rake or tempter, not the robber or rapist.[46]

Even earlier in the nineteenth century, in the low-class immigrant areas, the threat of random violence is said not to have been as high as some have implied. According to Maldwyn Jones:

> In 1859, for instance, 55 per cent of the persons arrested . . . in New York City were Irish-born, and a further 22 per cent had been born in other foreign countries. Yet these statistics are misleading in that few immigrant lawbreakers committed the more serious offenses. In most cases conflict with the law resulted either from petty thievery or, still more commonly, from drunkenness and disorderly conduct.[47]

Hard statistical evidence on the number of reported crimes in the early 1900s is also almost nonexistent. There are some records of such things as the number of arrests and the number of people charged in courts, but we have no way of knowing how accurate these were, or what the arrest rate was for a given number of offenses or for persons charged for a given number of offenses reported. These statistics, therefore, cannot be converted with any significant degree of reliability into something similar to the report of offenses per 100,000 population in today's uniform crime reports of the FBI. The following tables may still be of interest, however, despite these vast shortcomings. The first table indicates the approximate number of arrests per 100,000 people in the city of Chicago between 1905 and 1908 for homicide, robbery, rape, and violent assault. Using an assumed arrest rate lower than that experienced nationally today, although perhaps not much lower than that of our large cities, we derive an estimated reported number of offenses per 100,000 population. Obviously this number is highly questionable. But it is interesting to note that, using this approach, the average yearly homicide rate for the years 1905 through 1908 inclusive for the city of Chicago was considerably higher than it was for 1973. In the case of robbery, the opposite is true. For 1973, the rate is about twice as high as the average yearly rate for the 1905–08 period. Reported rapes for 1973 are over twice as high per 100,000 people and violent assault over three times as high.

CHICAGO

	1905-1908 Arrests Per 100,000 Population[*]	Assumed Arrest Rate Per 100 Offenses	Reported Offenses Per 100,000 Population	1971 Reported Offenses Per 100,000 Population[**]
Homicide	37	90	41	24.5
Robbery	60	25	360	715
Rape	11.5	50	23	46
Violent Assault	53	45	118	336

[*]U.S. Immigration Commission. Reports. V. 36: Immigration and Crime. (S. Doc. No. 750, 61st Cong., 3d sess.) (Wash.: G.P.O., 1911), p. 36.

[**]U.S. Bureau of the Census, Statistical Abstract of the United States 1973 (Wash.: G.P.O., 1973), p. 148.

The next table uses the same technique to convert the persons charged in magistrates' courts in New York City between 1901 and 1908. The magistrates' courts were police courts that probably handled the majority of cases resulting from arrests in the city. The numbers indicated were for people held for further trial or committed to institutions by those courts. By again assuming a rate of persons charged per 100 offenses, these figures can be converted into reported offenses per 100,000 population within these courts' jurisdiction. The assumed number of persons charged per 100 offenses is somewhat less than today on a nationwide basis but, again, probably not much less than in the city as a whole. In some cases, however, it is much higher than currently in New York City. For example, the 85 percent rate of persons charged compared to offenses for homicide is significantly higher than in New York City today, when only 71.6 percent in 1973 and 74.6 percent in 1974 were cleared by an arrest or charging of a person.[48]

This seems, however, generally to be considered low, indicating that at least in the recent past the actual rate used to be higher. A further problem with this list is that we do not know whether some of the cases came into courts through other channels, so that we may be undercounting considerably on the first column. Interestingly, even if we were to double all the numbers in column three, we would not begin to approach the rate of random crimes, in which the victim is less likely to be an acquaintance or relative of the perpetrator, that we note for 1973 in New York City—that is, robbery and rape and, to some extent, violent or aggravated assault.

NEW YORK

	Persons Charged Per 100,000 Population[*]	Assumed Rate of Persons Charged Per 100 Offenses	Reported Offenses Per 100,000 Population	Reported Offenses Per 100,000 Population	
	Magistrates (Police) Court, 1901-1908			1971[**]	1972[***]
Homicide	9.5	85	11.1	18.6	20.8
Robbery	8.5	20	42.5	1131	2400
Rape	2.7	40	6.7	31	46
Violent Assault	21	40	52.5	430	1100

[*]Computed from persons charged (U.S. Immigration Commission. Reports. V. 36: Immigration and Crime. [S. Doc. No. 750, 61st Cong., 3d sess.] [Wash.: G.P.O., 1911, p. 36) and average population of New York during this period.

[**]U.S. Bureau of the Census, Statistical Abstract of the United States: 1973 (Wash.: G.P.O., 1973), p. 148.

New York and Chicago are not the most violent of our large northern cities. Detroit, for example, has a murder rate of 45.8, a rape rate of 78.2, and a robbery rate of 1,107—all per 100,000 population. (See the U.S. Census Bureau, *U.S. Stat. Abst.: 1975*, p. 152.

Such numbers may or may not be of any value in getting some feel for the random street violence in our past immigrant slums, but there is another aspect of these statistics that, while again not that definitive, might be of more value in indicating the level of violence then. In Chicago, for example, less than 23 percent of those arrested for robbery—a crime more likely to be committed against a stranger—were foreign-born; the rest were native-born. Over 41 percent of those arrested for homicide, almost half those arrested for violent assault, and better than 38 percent of those arrested for rape were foreign-born. In New York City, a little over 37 percent of those charged with robbery, more than half of those charged with homicide, and over 60 percent of those charged with violent assault were foreign-born. Over 51 percent of those charged with rape were foreign-born. In a very definitive sample of the Court of General Sessions cases heard between October 1, 1908, and June 30, 1909, taken at the request of the U.S. Immigration Commission, native-born people outnumbered foreign-born by almost two to one among those charged with robbery, and among the native-born those with native father outnumbered those with foreign father by better than two to one.[49]

This last sample, though more definitive, is very small, and perhaps not too much emphasis should be placed on it. If we do consider it, we must remember that almost three-quarters of New York City's population was then composed of immigrants or their children,[50] and though their arrest rate was high, given how large this group was, its actual rate was relatively low compared to that of the city's minority, those of third-generation American status or more. Furthermore, in both Chicago and New York, the immigrants showed higher crime rates in the areas of homicide and violent assault, where the criminal and victim traditionally are more likely to be acquainted.[51] We do not know what the rape pattern was in those days, nor how and at what rate it was reported, nor whether rape criminals were more or less likely to be acquainted with their victims.

Despite the apparently rather high crime rate in our immigrant slum areas at the turn of the century, therefore, the implication that the streets were not as unsafe as today may still be valid. Though there were areas of certain cities where it was probably best not to become "involved"—sometimes because of native-born "sharpies" and an occasional "hard case"—by the 1900s a significant degree of law and order seems to have generally prevailed. Clearly, indulging in family quarrels, fights over gambling, or other kinds of disputes could be a dangerous pastime, particularly in Chicago, but for the citizen who was just walking in the vast "lower class" immigrant areas of our cities, there are some indications that life may have been safer then than now. By "late century" in nineteenth-century Boston, writes Roger Lane, "All of the city had been brought under more or less effective patrol, and the voters were demanding that the streets be cleared not only of arsonists but of drunks, peddlers, and truants. . . . uniformed men with revolvers were stationed not only in potentially dangerous areas but in the quiet confines of the public library."[52]

New York at the turn of the century had 4,156 policemen for its three and a half million population,[53] of whom over half who were over twenty-one were immigrants.[54] About three-quarters of the city was made up of first- or second-generation immigrants.[55] In 1933 there were 19,000 policemen in New York City,[56] which at that time had a population of over seven million. By 1973, with the city's population reaching 7.9 million,[57] the city, transit, and housing police had increased by better than an order of magnitude from 1900, and more than doubled since 1933 to well over 40,000. Furthermore, in 1900 police could go into at least some of the worst slum areas to enforce laws, the violation of which amounted only to a misdemeanor.[58]

Of course, the violence against strangers in slum areas today seems infinitely greater than during the Great Depression and the post-World War II period. At least up to the 1940s, people went "slumming" after dark in underprivileged areas, including Harlem. Does anyone do it now? It is hard to avoid the feeling that the current high rate of "crimes against the person" perpetrated against the *average citizen* is not only new in the annals of our large cities over the last forty years, but perhaps for some earlier periods as well. This even seems to be true compared to our last great immigrant slum period in the early part of this century. There was, to be sure, a dip in violence in the late 1930s and 1940s, but the rise was sharp between the late 1950s and early 1970s. In 1949, only 4 percent of the people in our largest cities rated crime as their city's worst problem, ranking it behind many others, including that of traffic congestion. In the 1960s and 1970s crime became a major concern of city dwellers.[59]

There is also evidence that the crimes are increasingly finding their way into middle- and upper-middle-class neighborhoods. To the extent that criminal behavior is apparently tolerated on our streets, one is bound to ask whether it has a direct effect on the schools. In fact, the city's attitude toward our most recent "immigrants" from rural areas of the south seems new and unusual. It seems to fly in the face of much experience and acceptable social theory encountered since the Industrial Revolution.

When a rural area is urbanized, or when rural people come to live in the faceless city, the informal constraints on antisocial actions of the small rural community may break down or be left behind. Traditionally such breakdowns have been compensated for by the introduction or strengthening of formal constraints. As Elmer Johnson writes:

> With the rise of urban-industrial culture, formal control techniques have been employed in efforts to compensate for the declining effectiveness of informal controls of the family and neighborhood.[60]

Of virtually unpoliced, late-eighteenth-century London, with its "insufficient law enforcement," the National Commission on the Causes and Prevention of Violence found:

There was little if any security for law-abiding citizens who armed themselves and their servants and fortified their houses. Many people kept
pistols within reach while they slept. Similar conditions existed in other
English cities in the late 18th century as towns grew quickly in size and
environmental conditions deteriorated during the Industrial Revolution.

Crime in London began to decrease slowly in the late 18th century.
After 1829, the new police forces were very successful, and within 30 years
violent crime ceased to be a national problem.[61]

In the 1960s, our cities were experiencing the height of the influx of rural
southerners, who traditionally have a high record of violence; coincidentally, these were primarily Negroes with the highest record of lawless
violence.[62] In 1970, nationally, they committed the overwhelming majority
of murders, rapes, aggravated assaults and armed robberies. With the exception of the last offense, by far the majority of their victims were fellow
Negroes.[63] At the same time, however, a nationwide effort apparently
greatly weakened formal constraints against antisocial behavior. It may be
significant that the cities with large numbers of rural southern in-migrants
generally showed the highest levels of reported "crimes against the person."

The outlawing of the preventive approach to law enforcement (no clean-
ing up of neighborhoods by police "leaning" on known "bad actors" without trial-level evidence of criminal activity), the appearance of money and
lawyers to guarantee the new, vastly broadened interpretation of the rights
of the accused when he did commit a crime—all occurred during this
period. These approaches, as well as the very liberal "no questions asked"
welfare benefits, can be accepted as good ideas, yet from another viewpoint,
their implementation may have had some negative effects.

In any event, in our cities' worst areas, the most cowardly type of mug-
gers—preying primarily on children, women, the old, and the weak—
rapists, and pathologically vicious hoods practically own the streets after
dark, while honest citizens barricade themselves in their apartments until
daylight. Even then, hustlers, pimps, drug pushers, addicts, prostitute/ad-
dicts, "gigolo" loafers, some no doubt flitting from one "unwed mother" to
another as the former's child support and welfare monies dwindle, and
other unsavory characters roam the streets, evidently with impunity.
Homes are burgled of anything movable and police seem to have little time
for tracking down the thieves. Furthermore, as in days gone by, some police
are evidently on the take from those who prey on society, even occasionally
from drug pushers. In certain core-city areas the level of violence after dark
is so high that one fears, at least temporarily, that the fabric of society might
begin to come apart. It becomes obvious in studies of the subject—whether
they are based on a Vietnam town in the 1960s or on Cicero, Illinois, in the
1920s—that when violence directed against specific individuals reaches a

CRIME RATES BY TYPE--SELECTED CITIES: 1973[1]

	TOTAL[2]	Violent Crime					Property Crime			
		Total	Murder	Forcible Rape	Robbery	Aggravated Assault	Total	Burglary--Breaking or Entering	Larceny--Theft (Except Auto Theft)	Auto Theft
New York, N.Y.	6,067	1,483	21.4	47.6	928	486	4,585	1,904	1,626	1,055
Chicago, Ill.	6,433	1,168	25.9	48.6	725	368	5,265	1,342	2,809	1,114
Los Angeles, Calif.	7,453	1,065	17.2	75.6	483	489	6,389	2,420	2,894	1,075
Philadelphia, Pa.	3,739	755	22.3	35.9	439	258	2,984	972	1,112	900
Detroit, Mich.	8,047	1,681	45.8	78.2	1,107	450	6,365	2,487	2,301	1,577
Houston, Tex.	6,283	687	20.0	42.5	478	146	5,596	2,169	2,510	917
Baltimore, Md.	7,332	1,771	31.4	55.9	965	719	5,561	1,748	2,890	923
Dallas, Tex.	7,916	998	26.1	65.2	358	549	6,918	2,511	3,754	653
Washington, D.C.	6,842	1,558	35.9	79.9	961	481	5,284	1,582	3,070	632
Cleveland, Ohio	5,817	1,009	38.2	60.7	638	272	4,809	1,257	1,803	1,749
Indianapolis, Ind.	3,895	339	9.3	38.3	178	113	3,557	1,209	1,873	475
Milwaukee, Wis.	4,371	295	9.5	25.1	155	105	4,076	804	2,525	747
San Francisco, Calif.	8,483	1,198	15.8	79.7	711	391	7,287	2,267	3,642	1,378
San Diego, Calif.	6,155	372	7.6	23.4	192	149	5,783	1,564	3,607	612
San Antonio, Tex.	6,381	588	18.9	37.6	233	298	5,794	2,185	2,959	650

[1]Offenses known to the police per 100,000 population. Population in 1973 as estimated by U. S. Federal Bureau of Investigation.

[2]Includes manslaughter by negligence, not shown separately.

SOURCE: U.S. Census Bureau, *U.S. Stat. Abst.: 1975*, p. 152, table 252.

certain level, the normal factors determining how a society functions no longer apply. Admittedly, societies and neighborhoods are amazingly resistant to brutality, but they all have limits. When these are reached, normal sociological theory is often irrelevant.[64]

Schools and universities are much more fragile institutions than societies, and their tolerance for violence is much lower. If higher levels of violence begin to spill over into them from the neighborhoods, they can be rather quickly turned into places where normal educational theory no longer applies. On the other hand, they are normally much more easily isolated from such violence if the administration insists its students leave undesirable habits outside—as they used to—and if they receive staff and city officials' support.

The current, often irresponsible, permissiveness encouraged in, and sometimes almost forced on, the more responsible underprivileged citizens indeed seems new, and may well color the attitude of the pupils from the slums. Traditionally people—even the underprivileged—have been held accountable, fairly or unfairly, for their acts in our cities. A New York *Times* article of March 6, 1893 (in Schoener), in complaining about the stacks of refuse cans in the streets due to lack of garbage collection during heavy snows, pointed out that tenement dwellers, including some named "unclean" ethnics, had neighborhoods in worse condition than "better parts" of the city where people "took steps" to alleviate conditions.[66] Traditionally the authorities and the newspapers "leaned" on the newcomers to measure up to community standards and to obey the laws. Today this kind of pressure is hard to find; sometimes there is not even the pressure to live up to the law.

Everybody in New York City slum areas knows that today virtually nobody serves time for most of the crimes on the books. For example, despite former Mayor John V. Lindsay's incessant cries in the media and before congressional committees for stronger federal gun laws, virtually nobody served time for carrying pistols in New York City, even though New York City and State have the harshest gun laws on the books and bushel baskets full of pistols are taken from "hoods" each week. New York is not unique in this respect. The U.S. Attorney General designate, in hearings on his confirmation before a Senate committee in 1974, stated:

> I live in the District of Columbia and I have lived here ever since I have been here. When I came, there was a registration law, a very stiff registration law which requires the registration of guns in the District. I hoped that this would be vigorously prosecuted. It is not. There are no cases brought under it.[66]

After listening to assistant district attorneys and others in the field, one gets the impression that the criminal justice system has almost broken down in some of our large cities, at least as far as nonfatal street crime is concerned. (Stringent new New York State drug laws may eventually change the picture for drug offenses in New York City.) Homicide rates increased in Chicago, Detroit, Washington, D.C., and Philadelphia between 1973 and 1974. In New York, they decreased from 1,669 in 1973 to 1,530 in 1974, but of the cases in which such facts could be ascertained—a difficult task because only about 74.6 percent of homicides are "cleared" by arrests in the city—stranger-murders, in which victim and perpetrator have no previously known relationship, rose from 28 to 34 percent.[67] Under these circumstances, city streets, particularly in poor neighborhoods, are dangerous for the ordinary peaceful pedestrian, quite a different murder victim from the barroom brawler, unfaithful wife or husband, suspiciously lucky gambler, or swindler.

Children living in big-city slums today *are* underprivileged and deprived, but not necessarily because of discrimination or economic conditions. They and their long-suffering parents are deprived of the protection necessary for raising a family, despite the heavy tax burden all citizens bear to support public services. There was always the danger that youngsters in rough areas would emulate a "hood"-hero; but when hoodlums and hustlers are the only ones who can walk the streets, children are more likely to be influenced.

Several years ago the author had some contact with a group of adult Negroes in the toughest section of Harlem who had an excellent record of accomplishments with young people. Their greatest desire was to develop a situation in which decent men could function in the area so the children would pick up their values, habits, and language rather than those of the hustlers. In this respect, on the evidence in the area, I felt that many city and other upper-middle-class white-instigated and -backed community and youth programs were failures. (A former official of a social agency of one of our largest cities indicated that such programs were often ineffective and sometimes counter-productive.)

In 1968, in New York City, 27 boys under 16 were arrested for murder. In 1972, 73 were arrested. Males under 16 arrested and charged with forcible rape numbered 77 in 1968; in 1972 the number was 152. In 1968, 2,487 juveniles were arrested for robbery; in 1972 the number was up to 4,086. The number of juveniles arrested for burglary remained about the same—3,884 and 3,703.[68] Between 1968 and 1973, nationally, the number of arrests of boys under 18 for murder and nonnegligent manslaughter rose from 718 to 1,140; for forcible rape from 1,959 to 2,972; and for robbery, from 17,450 to 27,683. For girls under 18, the number arrested for murder and nonnegligent manslaughter rose from 67 to 109, and for robbery from 1,032 to 2,035.[69]

One could also speculate that youngsters on the streets, especially "drop-outs," have been a concern for everybody, particularly in many poorer neighborhoods of larger cities. Responses to the following Gallup Opinion survey may have been influenced by this concern.

YOUTH CONSERVATION CAMPS

QUESTION: "Some people say that all young men between the ages of 16 and 22 who are out of school and out of work should be required to join a Youth Conservation Corps to carry on their education, learn a trade and earn a little money. Do you approve or disapprove of this plan?"

(Underlining author's emphasis)

	May 1971			August 1964		
	Approve	Dis-Approve	No Opinion	Approve	Dis-Approve	No Opinion
NATIONAL	66%	27%	7%	73%	21%	6%
SEX						
Male	62	33	5			
Female	71	21	8			
RACE						
White	64	29	7			
Nonwhite	86	10	4			
EDUCATION						
College	47	45	8			
High School	69	26	5			
Grade School	80	11	9			
OCCUPATION						
Professional and Business	58	35	7			
White Collar	60	33	7			
Farmers	64	30	6			
Manual	70	26	4			
AGE						
18-20 years	56	42	2			
21-29 years	59	38	3			
30-49 years	66	29	5			
50 and over	72	18	10			
RELIGION						
Protestant	65	28	7			
Catholic	72	22	6			
Jewish	x	x	x			
POLITICS						
Republican	67	25	8			
Democrat	72	22	6			
Independent	59	35	6			
REGION						
East	70	23	7			
Midwest	65	26	9			
South	69	26	5			
West	58	37	5			

INCOME			
$15,000 and over	56	37	7
$10,000-$14,999	62	31	7
$ 7,000-$ 9,999	64	32	4
$ 5,000-$ 6,999	75	21	4
$ 3,000-$ 4,999	64	26	10
Under $3,000	81	9	10
COMMUNITY SIZE			
1,000,000 and over	70	22	8
500,000-999,999	68	24	8
50,000-499,999	67	29	4
2,500- 49,999	60	33	7
Under 2,500, Rural	67	26	7

NOTE: Reproduced from *Gallup Opinion Index,* No. 73, July 1971, p. 25.

As indicated earlier, it is difficult to attribute the excessive crime, juvenile delinquency, sexual promiscuity, and vandalism in some urban areas solely to poverty or to rural people moving to urban areas,[70] not only because of comparisons with past conditions—including the low crime rate during the Great Depression and the "Okie" movement, when there was dire poverty and an obvious great gap between the haves and have-nots—but also because of comparisons with certain low-income and urban areas with heavy rural influx elsewhere in the United States today. Idaho, the thirty-second of the fifty states in personal income, and Maine, the forty-third, also have rising, but still relatively low, violent crime rates,[71] and when the poor farmers from Idaho and elsewhere went to Seattle, they failed to drive the murder and nonnegligent homicide rate for that standard metropolitan area (Seattle-Everett and all suburban fringe towns) above 6.4 per 100,000 people, while robbery stood at 180 in 1974.[72] Comparable figures for the standard metropolitan area of Chicago were 15.9 and 431, for SMA Detroit 20.2 and 576, and for SMA New York 16.3 and 812.[73] Evidence points to high urban crime in many cities of the South: New Orleans SMA had a murder and nonnegligent manslaughter rate of 22.7; Little Rock–North Little Rock, Arkansas SMA, a rate of 16.4; Atlanta SMA, 20.8; Columbus, Georgia SMA, 21.4, and so on.[74] In the core cities of the North at least, crime seems to have spilled over into the schools to a great degree.

At the same time, youngsters are now faced with other questionable environmental factors. At all socioeconomic levels and in almost all areas these days, they are exposed to motion pictures in which gutter language and illicit sex are treated as the norm, and illegal behavior and irresponsible, antisocial people are glamorized. Eventually these late-1960s and early-

1970s movies began to appear on television, and though obscenities and excessive nudity are cut out of them, adequate "editing for television" is not possible in many cases. Frontal male and female nudity has appeared in dance programs on public broadcasting television. Many recent television programs, particularly post-prime-time shows, have assumed an air of "sophisticated" sexual permissiveness and in their verbal material present highly questionable life-styles as glamorous. This is far from a normal state of affairs for families of most adolescents; the youngsters themselves can watch these shows when parents are out or when they are out baby-sitting.

Magazines, of course, are the worst offenders; since they are all over, there is no rating system to guide parents on the less obvious offenders, and their formats are slick and seemingly respectable. Even magazines for the early adolescent occasionally have run questionable and irresponsible articles. Articles supporting the smoking of pot or "documenting" such themes as the "generation gap," parents' inability to "understand" their children, and the "hypocrisy" of the older generation have abounded in recent years. The epitome of irresponsibility may have been reached when *Ingenue,* a magazine for early teen-age girls, ran an article, "After the First Kiss Where Do You Go?" (April 1973), that described mutual, extreme "petting," including initial stages of oral sex, as options. Intercourse had drawbacks —girls could get pregnant and venereal disease was a possibility—but curiously, at least from the layman's viewpoint, the article did not associate oral sex with the risk of infection.

Rock music lyrics also often stress illicit sex and drug use.

These environmental factors are new. Apparently never before have parents of the underprivileged youngster, and often not so underprivileged youngster, been forced to cope with such a widespread attack on authority, the home, morals, and values while at the same time trying to earn a living, to raise a family, and see to their children's education. When schools, too, began to back down, many parents were in despair.

Many a pupil from core-city sections of our large cities brings to school the feeling that he is highly unlikely to suffer any consequences for breaking rules or, for that matter, the law. Permissive schools merely reinforce this feeling and "prove" again that only the naive do things the hard way—by the rules. Very soon the cynical student is "hustling" and "shaking down" smaller and weaker students for whatever he can get. If he is cross-bused into a nonslum school, he is likely to feel like a bear dropped in a tub of honey—until the local children learn to stop bringing lunch money or valuables to school, stop using the rest rooms, and do anything else needed to stay out of his path. As important, he disrupts the classes; he uses unbelievably filthy language and gets away with it in the classroom just as he does in the streets, where he even addresses a policeman in the same foul way.

Indeed in city and suburban areas, policemen, youth club directors, school bus drivers, and even teachers are apt to accept language and behavior from youngsters that cannot be described as anything but delinquent. What is more, in addition to affecting the dress and other trappings of the youngsters, these adults all too often indulge in the offensive language themselves in the presence of the pupils, thinking it increases communication, by making them one of the "boys (or girls)." Children of the past were not deprived in this way—deprived of a structured existence and of the generally proper and civilized public behavior that was exhibited by adults in positions of authority over children. One can but consider the effects of such deprivation on the youngsters involved in the civilizing process of growing up in an advanced country and society.

9
FASHIONABLE EDUCATION ATTITUDES

It is somewhat troubling to examine education in the United States during the 1940s, and again in the late 1960s and early 1970s. As we have seen, because of the general milieu of the late Depression years and the momentum of the New Deal programs, the progressives gained influence in the 1940s. During World War II, the greatly depleted ranks of competent teachers were constantly told the standard curriculum was not relevant enough. Many educators began to talk of "educating the whole child" and to play down the traditional emphasis on academic achievement of all pupils.

In the late 1960s the same thing began to happen and, as indicated earlier, the relevance not only of the curriculum of the fifties but even the scope and priority of education goals came under attack. In the 1960s and early seventies, there was no reduction of experienced educators as there had been in the early forties. However, there was a great influx of new, younger teachers, which might have tended to weaken educators' ability to withstand the attack on the role and mission of our school systems. But this alone cannot explain why state departments of education, principals, and experienced teachers allowed proven teaching methods to be discontinued. Normally older, experienced educators had had the courage of their convictions and faith in the methods they used. (Young—and some old—radical innovators have always been around; principals usually told them to watch a teacher with thirty years' experience and learn the trade.) In the mid-1960s, however, under the assault of the fashionable "counter-culture," and even today when that assault has subsided, many educators and policy makers seem once again to have lost perspective.

Though there were many teachers dedicated to teaching children the fundamentals in the 1960s—and indeed they are present today, too—some of the most articulate educators and writers no longer seemed sure what the goal of the educational system was or should be. Having rediscovered the traditional plight of the underprivileged and, at the same time, discovering that one group in this category were Negroes who had additional disadvantages, many educators and writers on the subject, as we have seen, also seem to have doubted the entire unparalleled process of successful, upward mobility in this country, and therefore of course the part played by education in it.

These discoveries coincided with a period of change in the approach to teaching itself. Our primary- and secondary-school children were to be taught "truth" as opposed to "fantasy" with regard to such subjects as our government and the system's justice, and "relevance" to immediate headlines became a major influence on curricula. In the euphoria of the Kennedy years and the "War on Poverty" era, many proven fundamental processes of education were jettisoned in favor of insufficiently tested but supposedly more relevant practices and curricula. It is time to ask whether the current crisis in our schools is not in large part due to these new practices rather than to the inadequacies of the old system that was more or less abandoned.

There apparently were questions about the role of education in our present system reported by some writers and educators of the 1960s.

> In a society where the ballot box was not merely the symbol but the reality of access to power, democracy did seem to depend on a marching together of literacy and suffrage. In a society profoundly divided between a rich minority and a poor majority, education to promote social integration seemed necessary for social survival. It is hard for us to recapture either of these concerns. When we think of the importance of voting it is not of the well-informed newspaper reader who puts aside all demagoguery and votes, as a social atom, on the pure merits of the case; it is of the masses of disfranchised poor who can use the ballot to alleviate their exploitation, and we need effective demagogues and demagogic techniques to make it work.[1]

The above author, however, did not see the requirement for drastic changes in our school system, although he saw the need for *"relatively simple"* changes, "considering the effort and money which went into its creation originally" to accommodate Negroes' needs.[2] Even in the case of Negro requirements, one feels that along the way people should have been suspicious of a process that, as it developed, to a great extent threw away dirty water before we had clean. The Negro student's learning progress apparently has not improved under the new system. In fact, compared to an earlier period, it seems to have decreased. Furthermore, even if one accepts the description of changed requirements as just cited, the question whether there exists a system superior to the old one for teaching Negro or white students was not and has not been answered. (One must know how to read even to read the pamphlets of a demagogue.) Nonetheless, fashionable writers, administrators, and educators joined in an unseemly rush to eliminate many fundamental processes from the old system.

Much of what has been done to improve the school system seems to have little to do with improving education and may actually be a disrupting influence. As we have seen, the improvements include changes that often resulted in the removal of much of the discipline necessary for maintaining adequate order in a teaching and learning environment. Fashionable writers on education have also recommended curriculum changes involving the incorporation of slum attitudes and terminology into school systems; to the dismay of some well-known Negro educators, these included attempts to list ungrammatical slum speech as an initially acceptable, "indigenous language," with correct English as a "second language they need."[3] As we noted earlier, by the 1970s, such attitudes had not only begun to appear among teachers in the schools, but some (perhaps self-serving teachers—for grammar is hard to teach) asserted flatly that there is no correct grammar or speech pattern.[4] Slum children may sometimes even have been given to understand that their behavioral patterns are assets and that society has no right to expect them to accept the behaviorial norms of a respectable citizen. In fact, some educators have suggested that slum children be given school credits for "street skills."[5] That such practices are frequently dishonest and illegal is apparently overlooked, as is the difficult job of insisting that these children acquire the education they will need and which teachers are paid to impart.

Most disturbing, perhaps, was the apparent immunity that some educators seem to have developed to logical criticisms of the innovations in this period. The attitude of many conservatives on busing pupils for racial balance in northern cities has been described as follows:

> Racial integration, however desirable and necessary, is the concern of other institutions in the community and to disrupt the instructional process by attempts to provide integrated schools in a segregated metropolis is an overextension of the school's role, and takes its attention from the task which only it is set up to do. . . .

In the same work we find:

> . . . but, for the school as an institution to deny its involvement in those concerns, and its share of responsibility for the problem, can only further alienate it from those of its pupils with whom it fails most dramatically already in its instructional role.[6]

The question whether busing for "racial balance" in northern cities should be carried out at the cost of the "disruption of the instructional process," is a question at least worth considering. The implied answer of some seems to have been the affirmative, in which case one can accept the goal but still question its benefits compared to the costs of disrupting functions always before considered essential for any group's socioeconomic upward mobility: the vital teaching of reading, writing and arithmetic to primary- and secondary-school students, including Negro boys and girls.

This loss of perspective, in my opinion, was largely due to a crisis attitude fanned by the general long-term "revolution" of the young and rapid, deep-seated fundamental changes in general, presumed in the late 1960s by many writers, administrators, and educators. To some of them it apparently was clear that things were so different and a crisis of such proportions had descended on us that on this subject there was nothing left to discuss.

> This book is based on two assumptions of ours. One, it seems to us, is indisputable; the other, highly questionable. We refer to the beliefs that (a) in general, the survival of our society is threatened by an increasing number of unprecedented and, to date, insoluble problems; and (b) that something can be done to improve the situation. If you do not know which of these is indisputable and which questionable, you have just finished reading this book.[7]

The contention that, in two hundred years of our history, and possibly five thousand years of civilized history, there was no precedent for our current problems was, and to some degree still is, widely accepted among some writers and even some educators. Under these circumstances, it was quite difficult to suggest, among other solutions, that perhaps the old school process might indeed be adequate for the task. In point of fact, however, in a calmer milieu, it seems that the extremist arguments were far from formidable.

First of all, in the area of education, there seemed to be adequate precedents for solutions to many of the modern "insurmountable" problems. After all the old school system had been teaching children speaking all languages and of every color, creed, and socioeconomic level to read, write, and do math for two hundred years, and for close to a century a universal, compulsory educational system had apparently been functioning adequately through good and some very bad times.

By the early 1970s, however, the basic priorities of education were being questioned by state departments of education. One ad hoc committee on "Test Score Release" stated:

> For example, basic skills development in music, art, and interpersonal relations are almost always excluded from such testing, while arithmetical and punctuation skills are almost always included; thus, the tests embody assumptions about priorities in learning arithmetic and correct punctuation which may or may not reflect the needs and aspirations of given communities.[8]

(One is curious how one should test objectively for "development . . . in interpersonal relations" or even in music and art, rather subjective areas compared to arithmetic and reading.) It is interesting not only that the priority of these basics is being questioned, but that the traditional rate at which children have been learning over the decades was also being questioned. Thus another state department of education, in discussing multiplication and division in fourth grade, said, "There is some question by committee members as to whether the students are 'ready' for these items at this grade level."[9] One wonders what the committee's reaction was to the obvious rejoinder, that we know the children must be "ready" because children in that grade have *always* learned multiplication and division—for over half a century.

Departments of education now also use the "external factors" argument. Rhode Island's department says, "Persons who study school quality believe that there may be out-of-school factors that are very powerful in influencing how children perform on tests."[10] Other "authorities" blame downward trends in achievement tests on a list of causes ranging from irrelevancy of tests vis-à-vis the changed curriculum to social unrest. According to the Hawaii Department of Education:

> Several speculations may be ventured in explaining declines in test scores. Hawaii is not unique in showing a gradual decline in test averages since 1969. The situation appears to be nationwide. Some authorities in educational testing and measurements attribute the downward trends to curriculum changes, thereby implying that the content of the tests may not be as applicable as it once was. Changes in student characteristics are also cited as a possible cause of dropping test scores. Attitudes toward school, societal unrest, changing value systems have all been considered in formulating hypotheses for explaining the gradual decline in school achievement as measured by standardized tests. As further research is focused on these developments, specific causes may emerge in due time. On the other hand, in these rapidly changing times a reversal of present trends may occur.[11]

One wonders who authorized curriculum changes which had the effect of lowering pupil skills in the fundamentals measured by most of these tests. The striking feature in all these writings, however, is the absence of any reference to the possibility that some responsibility for pupils' falling academic achievement may rest with the educators.

A vaguer, but perhaps extremely important, "class" factor seemed also to be at play in recent years. In examining the attitudes of activists, writers, educators, and policy makers over the past decade, there are disturbing indications that guilt-ridden, upper-middle-class people were trying to cope with a serious issue for disadvantaged children. Running through their approach, also can be found, perhaps, an odd kind of unintentional "racism." Possibly because these upper-middle-class people do not really understand, or cannot empathize with, the successful struggles for upward mobility of the earlier disadvantaged, non-English-speaking (and nonwhite) ethnic groups, they seem to be saying that only the Negro can't make it under this system. This could be the case, of course, and even though so many of the Negroes' problems parallel those of other disadvantaged groups, they may have other difficulties that prevent them from succeeding in school or afterward. But guilt-ridden upper-middle-class whites are hardly the ones to judge. Prior to the 1960s, Negroes finished northern high schools and went to college, and, as we have seen, some all-Negro high schools turned out college-bound students superior to students in the best white high schools in their areas.[12] Even those Negroes who flunked or dropped out of high school in those days may have had a better grasp of the fundamentals than many of those who go through school today.

This is not to imply that the old system had no faults or needed no improvement. The education received by Negroes as well as immigrant children could have been better, and their chances for success greater. The immigrant children did become literate, however, and they did acquire enough mathematics to hold the journeyman positions they secured. As we saw, the children of the most deprived immigrants became our most affluent citizens, and their educational level equaled or surpassed that of the nation's other large identifiable groups. Today, one cannot say this about the children of the disadvantaged with the same confidence.[13] One must ask again, therefore, whether many of the current ills may not actually have been aggravated by the recent attempts at improvement.

In fact, perhaps we should not give educators such unqualified deference when it comes to teaching children. To an alarming degree we have seen educators seeming to imply, as mentioned before, that they believe children think like fully educated adults, which should give any parent pause. First, let us look at the debunking process popular among some writers on education in the last decade.

> . . . Hemingway replied, ". . . In order to be a great writer a person must have a built-in, shockproof crap detector."
>
> It seems to us that . . . Hemingway identified an essential survival strategy and the essential function of the schools in today's world. One way of looking at the history of the human group is that it has been a continuing struggle against the veneration of "crap". . . . The mileposts along the road of our intellectual development signal those points at which some person developed a new perspective, a new meaning, or a new metaphor. We have in mind a new education that would set out to cultivate just such people—experts at "crap detecting."[14]

What never seems to be understood by such people is that, in most cases, children, particularly young children, do not have the adult's strong feeling about things; their feelings are bound by what their parents deem fundamental to their safety and happiness. To take an oversimplified example, debunking the myth of George Washington's innate honesty is merely to tell the grade-school child that Washington was a liar, because, unlike an adult, he has no strong feelings about Washington's honesty to balance out the debunking. Telling the child Washington was just like anyone else is no good either. Furthermore, the image of Washington as a man of integrity and courage (note that the "myth" does not ascribe brilliance to him) is historically a correct one to implant in young minds, just as is the idea that this is a great and noble nation for, as nations go, it is.

A more insidious process, however, may be the one being tried on our Negro children. The debunkers' arguments that history texts do little to indicate the Negro's true role in the Civil War, are probably valid.[15] There are limits to this approach, however. The same lack of emphasis can be said to hold true for other ethnic groups. In fact, the many photos of Negro troops in Union blue document their sacrifices in the Civil War in a way not possible with, for example, people of Irish or German descent, for their ethnic identity is less obvious. This should come as no surprise, however, because the distinction was between Confederates and Unionists. The boys in blue were all thought to be of one group (the other group was in butternut or gray), just as the boys who went to Europe in World War I were all considered Americans, even though these "Yanks," including those from Georgia and Alabama, were of German, Polish, Irish, or other descent, or were Negroes, Indians, Whites, or Orientals. Textbooks are criticized for their coverage of the Revolutionary period, because though they mention that the first man to fall at the Boston Massacre was a Negro—Crispus Attucks—no mention is made of outstanding Negro personalities such as the poet Phillis Wheatley and the mathematician Benjamin Banneker.[16] But if the textbooks mention white poets or mathematicians of the Revolutionary period, the emphasis must be slight for no pupil seems to know of them. In any event, we question this whole procedure; it tends to be divisive and there is no adequate evidence of its value.

Even more divisive is the movement that directly or indirectly encouraged American schoolchildren to identify with foreign nationals. The development of the various Afro-American study programs is highly questionable from many points of view, yet because of activists' attitudes inside and outside the educational system, we have used our mandatory school systems to offer a segment of our citizens the opportunity to place themselves in this dubious position. Learning a foreign language is always advisable, but encouraging Americans to identify with a foreign group or country is another matter.

Traditionally, most underprivileged immigrants, including those most blatantly exploited, have striven to cut their ties quickly with the "old country" and to identify only with America, which "was better" than where they came from. They used the American heritage for identity in their successful movement up the socioeconomic ladder. It may be true that "the third generation is sufficiently American, but there is the problem of self-identification . . ." and Marcus L. Hansen's "What the son wishes to forget, the grandson wishes to remember"[17] may also be true. But such positions, despite the credentials of those who make them, are not conclusive. There is too much evidence of grandsons and great-grandsons who do not feel this way, to say nothing of the millions who do not know what their ethnicity is, and who are well-adjusted, successful people. In fact, with a few exceptions, most groups—including immigrants' offspring—do not seem to identify readily with foreign nationalities. They seem at least as likely, after saying they are American, to identify with a religion or a region—they are southerners, westerners, midwesterners, New Englanders—or a state—Texans, Missourians, Californians—or even cities—New Yorkers, Philadelphians, Bostonians. Some are obviously "hyphenated" Americans: Chinese-Americans, Japanese-Americans, Afro-Americans. Many others are less obviously so—only American Indians truly do not fit this category—but we are all the products of, and have all influenced, our unique society.

Yet we now help to place our young Negro citizens in the position not only perhaps of feeling more "segregated," but possibly of feeling they have to defend past and present actions of undemocratic, often savage groups on a foreign continent from which their great-great-great-grandfathers came. That is quite a burden to ask children of any identifiable ethnic group to bear, for far too many of us have forebears who can be traced to countries whose records are not always admirable. One thinks of several examples: the brutality of the Swedes in the Thirty Years War; the French during the Reign of Terror after 1789; the Germans in the 1930s and 1940s; the long record, including the current one, of similar actions by the Russians and the Chinese.

Again the haunting question arises why such programs foster the official backing they do. Obviously administrators and educators felt they were useful in forming the self-"identity" of Negro children. But why identify with a specific group and even a foreign source group or country? Why not identify with the American heritage? Many might answer that because the Negro was originally enslaved, alienated, and shamefully treated, he could not be expected to identify with this society. This could be true, but the education decisions were by and large not made by Negroes. The schools encouraged the movement, and the school system was predominantly white controlled. Are we seeing guilt-ridden upper-middle-class whites working out their own feelings again? (As we have seen, Negro parents, too, seem to be largely concerned with the teaching of basic academic skills and maintenance of discipline in the schools.)

As might have been expected, however, the constant official, tax-supported emphasis on ethnic studies for one or two groups through the 1960s may have finally led to an official, tax-supported "backlash" of white ethnic studies. Under the heading, "White Ethnic Groups in Nation are Encouraging Heritage Programs in a Trend Toward Self-Awareness," it was reported in the New York *Times* that "Contrary to the philosophy of assimilation, ethnic pride and ethnic identification are being stressed in the new programs." The Ethnic Heritage Studies Act will provide $2.5 million in federal funds for a program that elementary and secondary schools are investigating as well as colleges. One enthusiast of considerable influence is quoted as saying that, "The action marks the first time in American history that Congress has recognized that the melting pot was not the reigning theory of American society but that ethnic pluralism was much more the reality."[18]

Such talk must be regarded with caution. This country *is* a melting pot, current popular ideas to the contrary, probably to a greater degree than any other great nation in the world. (On considering other immigrants, one is reminded, for example, of the length of time that "Volga Germans" retained their identity inside Russia or the Chinese in Southeast Asia.) With some exceptions, a great and increasing difficulty about ethnic studies in this country is isolating white ethnic groups. As in the case of Negroes, one would have to set an arbitrary level of one-sixth German or Polish descent, for example, to identify a person with an arbitrarily selected dominant ethnicity. But the facts apparently are that white Americans, by and large, intermarry with something less than primary regard for their spouses' ethnic background.

One author, Andrew Greeley, however, claims that figures he compiled show that within their own religious group, ethnics still tended to marry similar ethnics and that, in the main, the largest group within which any one group was likely to marry was its own. On the other hand, the figures also showed that amid a sample of eight groups of Catholic "ethnics" in the United States in 1963, three showed a majority intermarrying with their "own kind," two showed 50 percent marrying their own kind, and three showed a majority marrying other ethnics. It should be noted that ethnicity was determined by the ethnicity of respondents' *fathers* and that 20 percent of the respondents were "half-breeds" already. Furthermore, about 11 percent of the original sample had married non-Catholics whose ethnicity was not listed, and about 7 percent had married people of unknown ethnicity. Both groups were dropped from the sample from which the cited percentages were derived.[19]

The important consideration, one would think, is the American heritage as the melting pot. Rejecting that attitude, some writers, administrators, and educators have attempted to reverse a traditional thrust in the American school system. It seems questionable that, in the opinion of another commentator, ". . . he who understands his own traditions is more likely to be sympathetic to someone else."[20] Regardless of how recent history books have compensated, by most standards *of our particular society,* the ancestors of American Indians, African Negroes, and, in some sense, even many Eastern Europeans are likely to compare unfavorably with those of Central and Western Europeans, the forebears of most of our population.

I think that, under these ethnic programs, the chances of divisiveness are increased, and, one is tempted to say as usual, for the sake of very vague ostensible objectives, of very questionable value. Fortunately, the more sensible influence of the white and non-white families and the children's innate common sense should largely negate such ill effects of these programs. The vast majority of children apparently have had higher morale than many alienated writers, administrators, and educators—in general they usually *have* been happy.[21] There may be some divisive effects of a "self-fulfilling nature" in the area of ethnic pluralism, but they should be minor compared to the possible effect on scholastic achievement. Such an ethnic-study program is bound to detract from the already reduced time available in the pupils' and teaching staff's day, which should be devoted to what concerns parents most—academic instruction in the basics. It will probably merely provide another group of easy electives likely to entice pupils away from more essential—and difficult—academic courses, the way "Art of Film"—watching movies—might very well be chosen instead of literature in an English department, or social studies instead of history.

The attitude some writers and educators seem to have about how children gather, interpret, and react to information, particularly regarding such realities as race and class, is perhaps most surprising in regard to textbooks. One author feels that primary-school reading textbooks portraying middle-class life could lead to frustration and raise questions. Underprivileged children would think: "Are no other families as poor as ours? Does everybody else live in a pretty white house? . . . On the other side, is it desirable for the well-to-do children to be unaware that there may be poor people living on the other side of the tracks?"[22]

Clearly one must challenge such premises. Children can and do identify with fanciful situations that have no relation to their lives. Fairy tales are full of princes and princesses, knights in shining armor. Adventure stories are filled with larger-than-life characters performing spectacular feats in strange places. If educators were to claim that children were bored with current reading material and that there were no incentives to read it, one could find common ground with them. To be concerned, however, that small children will feel frustrated because of the position of a child they *read about in a textbook,* or to imagine that unless the book enlightens them, they won't learn about the "other half," seems extremely farfetched. Small children, including most underprivileged children, have innumerable sources of information: television, comics, movies, what they see from car and bus windows, or stories by friends and family.

One also wonders why some educators can't recognize the validity of having people in books be models of what schools, and most parents, hope their children will grow up to be. It could bode ill for children in their care when educators and others fantasize to the extent that they truly feel that issues such as the danger of growing up unaware of their communities, are significant, and even dominant, in selecting *textbooks* for small children.

It is interesting to mention one reading textbook with Negro children as characters that uses the "look say" teaching method, in which whole words are to be recognized, rather than the "phonic" method in which letters are sounded out. There are quite convincing arguments against the "look say" methods; for one thing, it is a very ineffective method of teaching children with any degree of dyslexia. And, one writer states that, according to HEW figures, "one third of that class will not learn to read through the look say methods." Yet, because this particular book illustrates the life of Negro children and slum conditions, Negro parents in Harlem chose it for their children's school,[23] and despite its probable shortcomings for both Negro and white pupils, a progressive approach may put it in other schools.

One author cited earlier further states, ". . . the earliest impressions frequently develop attitudes that persist; it follows that it is never too early to tell children the truth."[24] We must question this "revisionist" attitude as a general premise. As mentioned before, we are at odds with these educators about giving young children their view of the "truth" about our noted but mortal men and great, but imperfect, system. One finds oneself in agreement with educators, however, about withholding from little children the fact that the wealthiest ethnic group in the country are the Jews, or that alcoholism is more prevalent among Gentiles, or that the majority of violent crimes in the United States is committed by Negroes, and so on.

It is important to consider the attitudes reflected in the positions we have been discussing not only because they were so widespread—though probably still not held by a majority in the late 1960s and early 1970s—but because they largely reflect the attitude of the "activists." In some instances, only by understanding the way such activists viewed things can reasons for changes in the school system that otherwise would be well-nigh incomprehensible at least be surmised. Their statements strongly indicate that many of these educators were probably as much "social engineers" as educators.

These points of view were also held down at the local level. For example, I sat in an open school board meeting in 1968 at which a mother, whose child was involved in a new cross-busing scheme, noted that her child had come home with a third grade reader in the fourth grade. The school superintendent said that this was to allow the new children in the class to catch up. The mother then asked how long this would continue. The superintendent replied, "I don't know, it may take a hundred years," presumably referring to integration, which, of course, had nothing to do with the mother's question. Later on, on a different occasion, I talked to a teacher in an affluent outlying suburb of New York City. I asked her what she thought students required, since there had been some question about the emphasis on reading, math, and history skills. She replied: "To learn how to survive in this world of pollution, wars. . . ."

Such attitudes at all levels tend both to downgrade the emphasis on scholastic achievement and to increase the feeling of self-righteousness of those who hold them. This, in turn, too often leads to a vigorous prosecution of untried academic and social reform programs, and the glossing over of difficult scholastic problems—which the untried programs often exacerbate —since it is all in the interest of a good cause.

10

SUMMARY

EXPENDITURES AND PRODUCT

The cost of primary and secondary school innovations in the past two decades has been truly prodigious, and over the last decade nothing less than spectacular. Figured in constant 1973–74 dollars—that is, eliminating inflationary effects—the estimated average amount spent per pupil nationally in public primary and secondary schools in 1973–74 ($1,364) approximates the average tuition per *private university* student in 1965.[1] New York State suburban high schools today often charge the taxpayer a price per pupil approximating the current tuition at Ivy League colleges; endowments of the colleges notwithstanding, this is an impressive figure for high school tuition. Those who felt the keys to academic excellence were low student/teacher ratios, new buildings, large amounts of audiovisual equipment, new media centers, specialized teachers, and high salaries certainly have been given a hearing during the last decade. A greater proliferation of inputs to our school systems would be hard to imagine. We are spending about $75 billion on primary and secondary schools this year.[2]

In fact, the quality of school systems has usually been measured by inputs such as those mentioned above. The graph on page 177 shows the annual cost of these inputs per public school pupil in constant dollars from the school year 1929–30 to 1973–74.

In contrast, superintendents, school board members, and educators have shown little inclination to discuss publicly or disclose the *outputs*. Yet there *are* measurable outputs, and they show a trend. The graph on page 178 is comprised of two sets of national test data: the renorming information for the Iowa Tests of Basic Skills (see Chapter 3) and Scholastic Achievement —College Board—Test (SAT) data (see p. 57).

With a few exceptions, state achievement data seem to show a similar decrease in achievement levels through the early 1970s. (See pp. 44–46 and the Appendix.)

Generally, we seem to have been experiencing a nationwide academic achievement decline, and not for the first time in this century. There appar-

TOTAL EXPENDITURES PER PUPIL IN AVERAGE DAILY ATTENDANCE
IN PUBLIC SCHOOLS, 1929-30 to 1973-74, IN CONSTANT DOLLARS

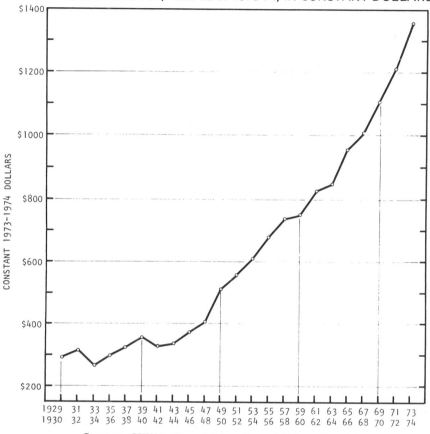

SOURCE: HEW, *Dig. of Educ. Stat.: 1975,* p. 71, table 72.

ently are some signs that things may be getting better in some sectors of the
student body, but it is too early to trace any trends, and SAT scores fell
again in the 1975–76 school year. Through the early 1970s, at least, data
seem to indicate that there is likely to have been a cyclical achievement
trend (see Chapter 3) over the past four decades that looks approximately
like the curve shown on the next page.

While the usual concern about possible financial neglect of the schools
over these periods of achievement slump is laudable, amount of expenditures does not necessarily account for the trends. Evidently in the 1940s,
as expenditures rose, achievement declined. On the other hand, as expendi-

NATIONAL TRENDS IN ACADEMIC ACHIEVEMENT

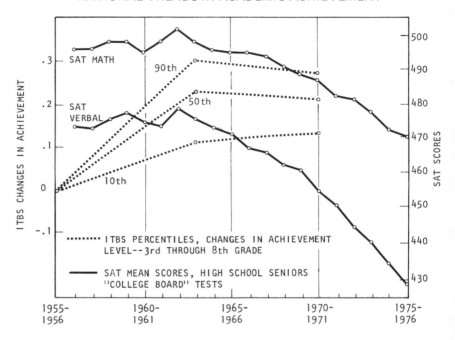

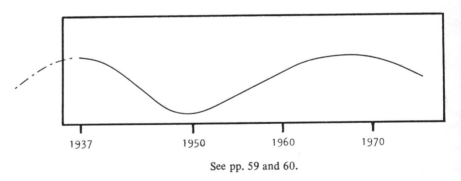

APPARENT CYCLICAL ACHIEVEMENT CURVE

See pp. 59 and 60.

tures continued to increase in the 1950s, achievement rose. Another divergence seems to have occurred in the mid-sixties. A composite graph of approximate achievement and expenditure trends shows that when the spurt in spending rate per pupil (in constant dollars) began its steepest climb, achievement began to fall:

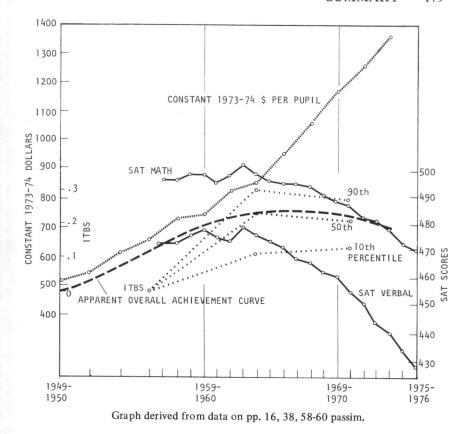

Graph derived from data on pp. 16, 38, 58-60 passim.

As the graph on the next page demonstrates, statistical data on such costly inputs as the student/teacher ratio show no correlation to this cyclical achievement curve over time.[3]

High academic achievement was apparent in the mid-1930s, when the average number of pupils per teacher was about thirty.[4] As the number decreased in the 1940s, academic achievement also fell. When the number of pupils per teacher rose slightly in the early 1950s, achievement apparently also began to rise, but in the mid-1950s these trends diverged when the number of students per teacher began to fall again and academic achievement continued to rise. As the plunge in student/teacher ratio continued, becoming somewhat precipitous in the mid-1960s, achievement began to decline and continued to do so through 1973.[5] Although data do not support the argument that a lower student/teacher ratio improves the quality of education, the student/teacher issue continues to be approached as though it does.[6]

Perhaps one should point out in passing that the premise that lower

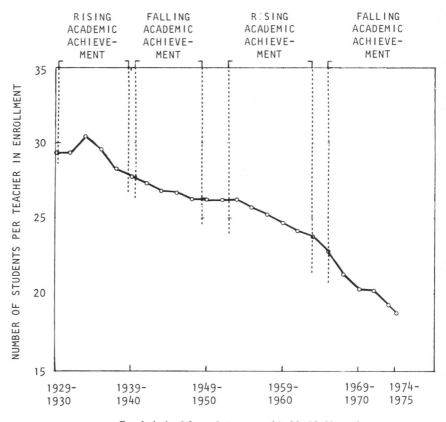

| RISING ACADEMIC ACHIEVE-MENT | FALLING ACADEMIC ACHIEVE-MENT | RISING ACADEMIC ACHIEVE-MENT | FALLING ACADEMIC ACHIEVE-MENT |

Graph derived from data on pp. 21, 38, 59-60 passim.

student/teacher ratio will improve the quality of education assumes that all teachers will be of equal quality, regardless of the increase in the instructional personnel pool. At some point along the expansion curve, this assumption could become increasingly risky; in other areas of expertise, as numbers go up, the probability of each additional recruit being equally qualified normally diminishes. If a similar drop in skill and dedication also occurs for teachers at some point along the expansion curve, one can logically see a possible explanation for achievement scores dropping as the number of teachers for a given number of pupils increases. Clearly, if a very good teacher is instructing a class of thirty pupils, there is no reason to be sure that the *average* achievement score will increase if the class is split in two and half the students are transferred to a much less competent teacher. In any event, within the limits of class sizes as we know them, one is forced to retreat to the position that student/teacher ratio per se and academic achievement have no clearly demonstrable relationship. Some other variables evidently dominate. But data also show no proven relationship between such factors as teachers' salary levels or age of buildings and achievement.[7] Furthermore, as indicated earlier, the decrease in student/teacher ratio does not necessarily indicate a similar drop in class size. Too often it merely means, even in the lowest grades, a relay of teachers who shift the same-size class to one another or relieve the classroom teacher one period a day.[8] "Specialist" teachers, such as remedial reading teachers, also relieve the classroom teacher of a former chore—helping slow learners after regular school hours.

The author once sat in a meeting with about two dozen educators who were complaining about lack of classroom space to which remedial reading teachers could take youngsters who needed help. They wanted new schools built. In that district, a child is taken out of some other class during the day for remedial work. He thus misses what is being taught in that class, but the complaint was that he is placed in a physically undesirable location for the extra help in reading the remedial reading teacher gives him when she gets around to him. The author suggested that it might be better for the classroom teacher to help him after three o'clock, when there is plenty of classroom space. Thus the child would not only be caught up to the class when it meets the next day, but this perhaps would eliminate the need and expense of the extra teacher.

This idea was unanimously rejected by the educators. One teacher said she had "tried that once," and it was a failure because some of the pupils looked on being kept after school as a form of punishment. When the author suggested that with some pupils one sometimes might have to use both the carrot and the stick to get them to apply themselves to the more difficult schoolwork, all these educators replied in unison, "*Never* the stick!" This situation also meant that classroom and specialist teachers could leave promptly at three o'clock, which is almost invariably the case in most schools today.

The division of responsibility for teaching a child to read, once considered the classroom teacher's job, is questionable. Teachers' aides and parents, as well as remedial reading teachers, now are also expected to be responsible for this task. One is reminded of the truth of the saying that something regarded as everybody's responsibility is nobody's responsibility.

The inflationary and, in other ways also, undesirable effect of this continuously increasing yearly per-pupil constant-dollar expense and the continuing drop in the measure of school productivity—that is, academic achievement—has reached very worrisome levels. Our educational system seems at least inefficient, if not downright wasteful. The yearly expenditure on education, including higher education, is approaching the figure of one out of every twelve dollars of the entire GNP, or close to $130 billion. Almost all of the $75 billion spent on primary and secondary education is extracted from the citizenry as taxes. Much of the balance is spent on private schools by parents who feel they can no longer entrust their children to the public school system. At the very time when the average citizen is beginning to feel hardships from spiraling taxes and other costs of education, it cannot be shown that additional expenditures over the recent past have been helping children to learn.

FACTORS EXTERIOR TO THE SCHOOL

Although direct causes for academic achievement fluctuations may exist outside the school system itself, they are hard to find. The "national IQ," based primarily on IQ scores of military-age men, as best as we can ascertain, seems to have held relatively constant at least until 1970.

MENTAL COMPETENCE OF MEN OF MILITARY AGE*

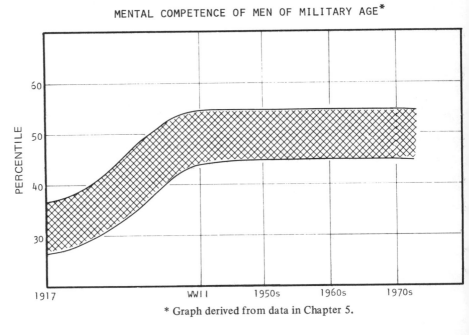

* Graph derived from data in Chapter 5.

The trend in Armed Forces Qualification Test score readings for men of military age should show the approximate trend in mean mental ability for high school students about five years before. The "then and now" study by

Thorndike's team (see p. 73) found 1972 10- and 15-to-18-year-old children superior in IQ to children of the early 1930s. There is some evidence, moreover, that they may have been testing the 1972 children on the downward side of the crest.

California pupil IQ scores show a decline after 1970, with the seventy-fifth percentile—the most intelligent pupils—in both sixth and twelfth grades falling faster than the twenty-fifth percentile (see Chap. 5). If California IQ and/or academic achievement dropped prior to the 1969–70 school year, we have no data to so indicate; our information begins with that year. We also have no way of knowing which came first—the drop in IQ or in academic achievement. As seen in Chapter 5, there seems reason to believe that California is not unique among the states in this IQ drop.

Tests in Iowa and New York State show that a drop in achievement began there in 1967, whereas the decline apparently started in 1969 in Hawaii. Only West Virginia data show both aptitude and achievement levels remaining stable according to the same test vehicles for several grades over a period of several school years, from 1970–71 to 1973–74.

Data cited in Chapter 4, though, tend to undermine one theory. Since all upper-grade achievement levels generally dropped simultaneously while lower grades held firm, the theory of an inherently less-talented peer-group ("cohort") moving through the school system becomes less convincing. Furthermore, the fact that statewide cohorts taking the identical test in one grade in different years show identical competence, and then show greatly changed competence later when taking identical tests in a higher grade in different years, also calls into question the idea that the decline in inherent IQ has triggered the decline in achievement. But the *grade* achievement trace had declined between the time the first cohort took the test in the higher grade and the second cohort took the same test (see pp. 53–56).

Minnesota data in Chapter 5 show a drop in aptitude scores for a couple of years after 1949, but achievement apparently fell steadily from 1939 through 1948, when we have no evidence that mental ability decreased; as seen in Chapter 3, our data for two states seem to indicate that it remained constant. Although it is conceivable that a drop in school systems' academic excellence could eventually trigger a decline in IQ, there is no evidence that a significant drop in IQ triggered the 1939–49 achievement slump.

Nor do we find that any particular socioeconomic factors outside the school system worsened significantly in the 1963–70 period compared to the 1955–63 period, times of significantly different achievement, according to the Iowa Tests of Basic Skills data cited in Chapter 3. Spendable weekly income was rising and unemployment was generally down in both periods. Furthermore, increased spending on Great Society programs as well as on established older programs such as federal housing improved conditions for the lowest income families in the late 1960s.

As we have seen, academic achievement apparently peaked during the Great Depression and declined in the relatively affluent 1940s. Also, as just indicated, peer groups of children can move down and sometimes even up in average achievement compared to other previously labeled equally competent cohorts, as measured in percentile level for their grade, in so short a time—a year or two, for example—that the socioeconomic and IQ status factors extrinsic to the school could not possibly have changed accordingly for whole state cohorts (see pp. 53–56).

Other trends (described in Chap. 3) also cast doubt on the socioeconomic-deprivation theories about academic achievement declines. Renorming of a national achievement test for third through eighth graders shows that the 1964–71 decline was sharpest among pupils in the ninetieth percentile (upper tenth percentile) achievement bracket, in California (1969–73) among the seventy-fifth percentile (upper twenty-fifth percentile) of twelfth grade students, and, according to New York City and State data, apparently among pupils outside great cities (see Appendix), though as yet core cities are normally still below other areas in the state. These ninetieth and seventy-fifth percentile pupils are most likely to be the offspring of parents with higher education, higher IQs, and higher income homes, where shelves of books and often encyclopedias are readily available. They are also most likely to travel and be exposed to people who use better grammar and a broad vocabulary.

Some achievement scores in big cities may show less decline than in the suburbs simply because core-city scores are so low to begin with that they cannot decline much further, particularly on multiple choice tests. Nationally, however, this "bottoming-out" explanation may not suffice. The renorming scores for the Iowa Tests of Basic Skills showed improvement in 1964–71 scores for the lower-tenth-percentile group, whose members currently show up among the poor in greater percentages than elsewhere. The rise was only 0.2 months compared to 1.1 months in the 1956–64 period, but it was still a rise, whereas the ninetieth and fiftieth percentiles were *declining* (see Chap. 3).

Furthermore, as we saw in Chapter 7, the longitudinal evidence from our almost century-old, universal, compulsory public school system suggests we question the excessive emphasis on socioeconomic factors per se when looking for factors influencing learning of the "three R's." The system has demonstrated its ability to educate children from all socioeconomic and ethnic backgrounds in the fundamental verbal, mathematical, and physical and social science skills. Severe depressions and vast influxes of non-English-speaking immigrants did not halt or disastrously disrupt its primary educational function. Moreover, it showed itself capable of teaching under conditions of crowding and deprivation no one would dream of asking educators to accept today (see pp. 77–93, 96).

Whether "sociopolitical" factors have affected schools is much harder to judge. The recent very permissive environment, particularly in larger cities, was not visible during the 1940s academic decline, although the 1940s environment may have been more permissive than in the 1930s.

Changes in societal attitudes of some groups may have had some effect on school-system operations. This seems particularly likely in view of such current fashionable attitudes as the "new morality" and the rejection of traditional values that have been accepted by the entertainment and news media. As we have seen, much of the public milieu in which children are now raised tends to undermine the fundamental principles once considered the foundation for all types of endeavors. The public legitimization of bad grammar, vulgarisms, and even lascivious behavior is clearly more prevalent today than previously. Magazines, records, movies, and even television shows depicting, and often championing, highly dubious mores are widespread, readily available to youngsters, and apparently often sanctioned by many adults normally considered authority figures. Some of these highly questionable diversions are specifically directed at the teen-age market. Looking around, we see this trend toward vulgarization legitimized everywhere: in clothes, fashions, the language and grammar in movies and television—including commercials—and popular music.

It should be recalled, however, that similar, though less intense, periods of loosening constraints in parts of the milieu children inhabited occurred in the 1890s and 1920s. Yet, during these periods, educators, probably supported by parents, seem to have been more successful in keeping undesirable effects of the changing milieu out of the schools. In any case, we have no evidence to suggest that primary and secondary schools were plagued with problems as severe as those they face today. Regardless of extra-school milieu, traditionally, schools staunchly maintained their positions as islands of scholastic and civilized environment. The products of the schools in the first decade of this century, though exposed to extreme deprivation at home, proved sufficiently educated to move, or to help their children move, far up the socioeconomic ladder. Moreover, available data indicate that the current attitudes of the majority of parents with regard to how they want their children to learn, to behave, and to study have probably not changed greatly, at least not in the past twenty years.[9] In addition, the much publicized "generation gap" of the sixties seems to have been basically little different from that of the 1950s.[10] Changed family attitudes and home environment thus seem inadequate explanations for the achievement decline, particularly considering the rapid drop in achievement of whole state peer groups, upper percentile brackets, and in northern, smaller city, suburban, and rural school districts.

EDUCATORS' ATTITUDES

The evidence leads us to the hypothesis that the problems of education are more likely to originate from forces within the schools than from outside factors. Perhaps at least a contributing factor was a loss of perspective by educators. The same educators who, in our opinion, tended to lose perspective in the area of achievement, also may have lost it in regard to adequate discipline. Language, dress, and behavior that would formerly have been deemed unacceptable are allowed in our schools today; sometimes they actually seemed to have been encouraged under the guise of a new "cultural" expression. In any event, many schools, particularly those in core cities, have become so chaotic—and some dangerous—that the educational process can hardly be conducted. Which teaching technique or curriculum is used is virtually irrelevant; very little teaching or learning can be accomplished under these conditions.

This current lack of orderliness and less than well-structured approach to education is not confined to core-city schools. Many schools in more affluent suburbs and small cities, including private schools, to some extent suffer from the same malaise. Furthermore, skilled, thoughtful approaches seem often to be sacrificed for spontaneity and pupil "involvement." Perhaps most disquieting about the new politics of current schooling is many educators' contention that schoolchildren should be treated as adults; children's judgment on the gamut of issues from curriculum to behavior is the ostensible rationale for change. It is difficult to dismiss the suspicion that this approach is self-serving for teachers as well as pupils. A child's objection to homework or learning the multiplication tables is likely to stem from dislike of demanding work, while the teacher's rationalizations are all too often apt to stem from aversion to teaching difficult subjects, remaining after school to help pupils, and correcting homework, weekly tests, and compositions. As William V. Shannon put it, after encouraging parents to "assert their natural authority" over children, "Teachers have to halt their headlong flight from intellectual and moral standards and make schools once again places of challenge and decorum."[11]

Our current educational difficulties may, therefore, stem from some fundamental problems that should be confronted. First, our primary and secondary universal, compulsory educational system has evolved over a period of almost a century into a highly sophisticated and effective mechanism suited to our unique society. This system nonetheless can be operated by our educators, *if they adhere to the standard operating procedures.* Recent experience suggests that productivity quickly declines when the system's operators tamper with the fundamental processes of this highly complex machine. It is doubtful whether many men today completely understand the ramifications of the various factors in the educational process; even fewer would be brilliant enough to make radical changes in the fundamental processes that would prove beneficial. Gradual, often minor improvements and increased pupil time in school within the normal structure and process seem to have fostered the system's growth. Radical, ill-conceived change seems to cause the machine to labor and lose momentum.

We must consider another possibility. Many primary and secondary school educators, once regarded, after clergymen and perhaps doctors, as the most responsible members of the educated class, may, at least from the traditional viewpoint, no longer fit that description. Though educators are still second only to doctors in inspiring public confidence,[12] many may no longer appreciate the gravity of their obligation to teach children fundamental scholastic disciplines and techniques for conducting intellectual activity, skills essential in seizing opportunities in employment and higher education. Unfortunately, some evidence suggests that this may be the case. It matters little in the short term whether this attitude stems from some educators' genuine belief that the academic disciplines no longer deserve the priority they once enjoyed, or from teachers' feelings that the old curriculum is too demanding. The reasons are less important than the fact that our implicit trust in many educators may not be well founded and that the problem we now have may be more difficult to solve than the one in the 1940s. But solve it we must. Perhaps the most important first step is to convince some of those with the final responsibility that a problem truly exists.

POLICY MAKERS AND THE NEED FOR INFORMATION

Even many of the federal government's education specialists may not have been aware of the extent of the problem, primarily because, at least until rather recently, they apparently did not systematically collect state academic achievement data (see p. 189). Billions of federal dollars, many of them for primary and secondary education, were dispensed without requiring evidence of the resulting output. Although state education departments are aware of this problem, local school districts traditionally have been independent and control the major part of the money spent on their schools. These local school boards seldom asked state officials or local superintendents for, and seldom knew anything about, trends in their own district's achievement level. (Superintendents compare their own district with another, pointing up the lower achievement, higher teacher salaries, or other features in that other district. These days they seldom bring the board's— or the public's—attention to a comparison of their district's current achievement scores and those of ten or even five years ago.)

When board members do hear of achievement problems in the state, they often perceive them as being in districts other than their own, particularly in any existing core-city areas, which are often thought to be lowering the state's educational standards. Sometimes changing school population is blamed. State education departments usually seem to have tended toward the fashionable progressive attitudes of the sixties. Their considerable power of the purse seems not to have been used as leverage on local school districts to raise academic achievement levels as it was used to enforce such standards as racial balance.

Perhaps understandably, local boards did not ask about academic achievement during the late 1960s. They were acting on the traditional assumption that highly responsible educators were in charge. School boards have always worried about raising money and allocating budgets rather than about whether children were being taught the fundamentals. But the assumption that concerns about achievement were the educators' domain was becoming questionable by 1970, as it had been in the 1940s. School boards today must learn something about education and how to measure schools' *outputs*. They can no longer limit themselves to following professional educators' advice as to what constitutes "quality education." Furthermore, these boards must not confine their attention to their own districts; they must be aware of national and state trends to avoid being misled by references to "changing pupil population."

The federal government should have maintained at least state-by-state—and possibly district-by-district—achievement data on schools that have received so much federal money over the last ten or fifteen years. A branch of HEW's Office of Education should have kept comprehensive, up-to-date longitudinal data on academic achievement in school districts receiving federal money. The collection and mere examination of such data would have been most valuable. For example, when the low-achievement problem was discovered in the 1960s in core-city slum schools, it was apparently thought by many to be a city problem, a problem of the underprivileged. Indeed, large amounts of Title I and other federal, state, and local money were spent to treat this "ghetto" problem. But a glance at state and national data since the second half of the 1960s clearly shows that *our entire primary and secondary school system was in jeopardy.* Tax money, and much private school effort, were poured in to patch up what were considered by many to be a few localized leaks in the "core-city areas," when, in actuality, the seams of the entire hull were giving way. The whole ship of education continued to founder despite vast amounts of money and effort expended to cure the local symptoms of a much broader problem.

Achievement data collected on the federal level would probably also have been useful in making stipulations when financial grants were allocated to school districts. Thus the Office of Education would have had to determine, by checking its programs and others against achievement data, which practices had not improved the teaching and learning processes. In addition to saving money, this approach could have diverted educators' attention from less demanding and often counterproductive programs and forced them again to consider time-tested, effective curriculums and methods. Since the data collection for the original Hudson Institute study (published in July 1975), HEW has been gathering state achievement test data and has also funded a study of a limited amount of state and national data, published in 1976, that verifies the achievement drop. It remains to be seen, however, whether federal education policy will be influenced by such documentation.

THE EXTENT OF THE PROBLEMS

Should the few pieces of possibly encouraging evidence cited earlier not signal a general upturn, and if this current slump in our primary and secondary educational system should continue, or even if the upturn comes but the return to the level of the mid-1960s is too slow, we may find that "going back to the fundamentals" will be more difficult than before. Students today in public and private school systems, in affluent suburbs as well as core cities, often are unaware of their lack of skills. In verbal skills, for example, they are poor in organizing and articulating concepts and ideas, particularly in written form; they often suffer considerable frustration when trying to express subtle, intricate ideas. These students often do not realize that the necessary skills for oral and written expression can be acquired without excessive difficulty; indeed, they were once normally acquired in primary and secondary schools.

This problem of improving academic achievement could become acute if many future teachers have not acquired such skills. Unfortunately, too many teachers today apparently share some of the same shortcomings as their pupils; one fears that teachers' colleges have been producing significant numbers of such teachers in recent years. Nor is there much basis for hope that the situation will soon improve. As indicated earlier, college textbooks are now to be written at a lower level of verbal skills, with "fewer abstractions and more repetition of concepts," since many of our current college entrants cannot read at the high school graduate level of their predecessors (see p. 61). One fears that state teachers' colleges, which were seldom considered "good schools," will be among those receiving these texts. We may also have similar problems with inadequately grounded mathematics and science teachers, and perhaps with social studies teachers, should we attempt to have this group teach history and geography. In the Sarasota, Florida, area, for example, of a group of fifteen applicants for teaching positions in the winter of 1975–76, "four could not read as well as the county's brightest eighth graders." On the math test seven scored below the lower 25 percent of the current Pinellas County teachers.[13]

The lack of computational ability and the confusion existing among many pupils who have been exposed to the "new math" in the lower grades are startling. Student inability to compute, however, is not as surprising as the apparent lack of understanding among some educators that children not only *can* be taught to compute; they *must* be taught. As noted earlier (see p. 233) in the New Jersey summary of state achievement tests results of 1972–73, a committee discussing multiplication and division in the fourth grade and noting the low achievement there actually considered the possibility that the children were not ready for this work, even though they had always been ready enough in the past. Pupils' inability to compute has already had some effect on decisions about teaching math. As we have seen, set theory and other new math approaches are being abandoned, and old methods of teaching computational skills restored in some large school systems (see p. 104).

The original deviation from the standard method of teaching math might have been not only confusing to many children, but beyond many teachers' competence. In any event, since computational ability plummeted along with other skills during the period when the new math flourished, we have no evidence that, at least in the current school milieu, this technique produced significant positive outputs. Nor have we any evidence suggesting that the new approach to social studies was generally successful. On the contrary, skills in social studies also declined during the application of these teaching approaches. Combining such subjects as geography, history, and current events into one subject in the lower grades is a questionable method. Expanding single courses in high school, which drastically increases the scope in time and geographic area covered, while simultaneously trying to make everything relevant is probably beyond many teachers' competence. These innovations have apparently also failed to increase academic achievement. Some of the effects of attempting this superficial spanning of vast areas of time and space in social studies seem obvious from achievement scores. But one wonders whether new teachers trained for these courses possess the depth of knowledge required, for example, to teach a solid course in Ancient History again.

Furthermore, today many pupils have poor study habits without realizing it; this includes many good students in "good" public and private schools in affluent suburbia. Many have little appreciation of the real meaning or value of meticulous work, and little idea that drill and the repeated use of a concept in homework can lead to the kind of skills allowing one to be "creative" in a discipline. These failings apparently do not originate in the home. On the contrary, parents normally stress these values, but children often seem to have acquired this lack of appreciation of work in the schools. As suggested earlier, *teachers* are often in league with pupils against parents in the ongoing battle over the need for homework; parents tend to think the lack of homework contributes to their children's low achievement.

A peripheral but very important problem existing today was relatively unknown prior to the mid-1960s. Textbooks used to be of such high quality and syllabuses so logical that the demands on teachers—and parents—to help youngsters learn were much less than today. It is difficult to understand how many current texts, written and organized as they are, can aid the normal, logical learning/teaching processes of both student and teacher. Of course, such texts greatly add to the burden of the parents, who often must teach their children what the schools fail to impart.

Generally speaking, the evidence on academic achievement seems to indicate that children in the first through third or fourth grades bring with them, apparently from the home, attitudes, background, and adult support conducive to the learning process. They seem to treat school as a new and different world; they tend to listen, behave, and learn in this atmosphere. Seen in this light, such rather recent innovations as the attempt to make learning "relevant" to neighborhood experiences and interests of children may be counterproductive. In my view, schools, as of old, should be striving for a higher ideal, one that sets them apart from the neighborhoods producing many of our underprivileged pupils. The result of the present strategy seems to be that, after the fourth grade, many schools tended to come down to the level of untrained children.

Perhaps due to the erosion of traditional values and the lack of disciplined training, some children leave school prepared for a world that does not exist. Certain things in life simply cannot be avoided or blamed on someone else; actions have personal consequences; outside the school environment, one has to produce to be promoted; work must satisfy the demands of the economy to be profitable for the worker; many trades and professions require work that gives no credit for good intentions or being nearly accurate—work must often be explicit, meticulous, and correct *every time;* it is important to be well informed and logical, not just spontaneous and talkative; and not everything is relative: young people's ideas, too, often can be simply incorrect and even worthless.

An unrealistic approach in schools may be reflected in educators' frequent preoccupation with quite subjective issues such as "interpersonal relations," (and reflected even in music and art education and the superlatives generously applied to their often barely mediocre products), as well as their ambiguity as to whether "arithmetical and punctuation skills . . . may or may not reflect the needs of given communities" (see p. 167). Today, though skills in art and music can be personally rewarding, few

Americans regard them as essential to their daily well-being as reading, writing, and arithmetic, which also happen to be subjects in which performance can be objectively evaluated and which are difficult to teach. It is not obvious that high school seniors who have had the ordinary attention of full-time art and music teachers from kindergarten through sixth grade are clearly superior in these specialized fields to pupils who had not had such training until junior or senior high school.

EFFECTS ON CHILDREN OF THE LESS AFFLUENT AND OTHERS

Despite many "assistance programs" in recent years for disadvantaged children, they, in common with all children, continue to pay a high price because of our relatively unproductive school systems. It might be said that, as mentioned earlier, even though the ninetieth and fiftieth percentile pupils declined in academic achievement, the fact that the lower tenth percentile pupils improved somewhat according to ITBS scores between 1964 and 1971, and that there was a possible reduction of the decline in "functional illiteracy," according to the National Assessment of Educational Progress between 1971 and 1975, shows the success of our recent school program among the poor. This phenomenon may be related to Title I and other efforts, but by no means are *all* underprivileged children inherently tenth percentile types. Indeed, it is probably the ones not in that category who traditionally have best used our public school system to equip themselves for socioeconomic upward mobility. In my view, if billions of federal, state, and local taxpayers' dollars have produced a program that only slightly improves achievement of the least gifted at the expense of more talented youngsters, the entire operation must be labeled a failure for the poor as well as all other students. Gap closing in education should be accomplished by bringing all students up—then the lowest students, too, make their greatest absolute gains—never by bringing the upper or middle groups down; if the whole system declines, those at the bottom suffer as much as, or more than, the rest.

11
WHAT CAN BE DONE?

Despite all the problems we have described, the attempt to upgrade our schools must be made once again. Some efforts to do so are already under way, and some indications could signal the beginning of a "bottoming out" or a "turnaround" of the performance of at least some sectors of the national student body. But there apparently continues to be resistance to such traditional efforts among many educators, a resistance even to admitting that the system has not been performing as well as it should and could.

In fact, a large part of the education establishment continues to avoid, if not obscure, the real issues in discussions of education at the local, state, and even federal levels. These educators too often still begin with the premise that educators have been doing a good job, and, as mentioned before, many seldom bring up comparisons of the academic achievement, or even the behavior, of current pupils of a school or district with that of their predecessors in the same school or district (or state). Nor are they likely to mention the falling relative achievement record of the same peer group of children as it proceeds up through the grades. If confronted with the evidence that the current products of the system somehow have seemed less adequately prepared to perform basic academic functions, many educators are still likely to respond that this is an unfair measure of school efficiency because new curriculums cover things the old academic achievement test vehicles don't probe for,[1] or because the youngsters have gained so many other "unmeasurable" but much more valuable benefits from school. Or they explain that causes of the problems, which educators cannot possibly compensate for, lie outside the school: the home, the parents, the environment, television, anything but the educators. Such attitudes, if they prevail, are likely to do much to prevent an upswing in academic achievement, or to retard one if it is already under way. It will take vigilance and effort by the community to start or continue an upturn in academic achievement to levels of the mid-1960s, and at reasonable cost to the taxpayer.

MONITORING MEASURED ACADEMIC
ACHIEVEMENT TRENDS

Probably the most important step in dealing with a school is to *acquire a historical record of the student body scores on standardized academic achievement tests.* These tests are regularly administered to most elementary and secondary school students throughout the country. Residents of school districts where "norm referenced" standardized achievement tests are not given should insist that the district do so. No school board should be without a continually updated historical record of the average achievement test scores of each grade in its district. School board trustees, parents, and all taxpayers should be alert for a downward trend in the average raw test score for each grade over the years. They should also check how each class performs in the grade over the years on the basis of how far above or below the "normal" average its average score falls.

It is truly unfortunate that, with all the other constantly increasing demands on parents—and school board trustees—laymen must acquaint themselves with such details. But we have reached a stage where we can no longer expect many of our professional school administrators and educators voluntarily to be really candid with us about such issues as the children's academic achievement or the justification for increasing costs of education. Fortunately, checking on these details is not beyond the comprehension of most school board trustees, or most parents, though it takes some concentration.

There are several types of tests that measure achievement for several basic subjects as well as overall competence. There are also IQ-type tests that are administered to pupils. For each of these tests there is also a national average score for each grade. The normal average ("norm") is determined by the test publisher by administering the test to a very large sample of a typical, national cross-section of pupils for the grade to be tested.

By comparing past average raw scores of students of the same grades who took the same tests over the years in a district, state, or school, a rising, falling, or stable trend in academic achievement can be discerned. Trends can also be determined by comparing the average score of classes over the years in relation to the national "norm." Classes will often score somewhat above or below the publisher's norm. For example, in one school district the sixth grades may, over the years, traditionally have an average raw score on the mathematics test that puts them in the 60 percent bracket—just in the upper 40 percent of the national sample of students who took the test —rather than the 50 percent bracket, where, by definition, the average score for the national sample lies. If, in subsequent years, the average scores for sixth grade classes taking the same test begin to compare to those in the 55 and then the 50 percent bracket of the test publisher's original national sample, the trend in that grade in mathematics is obviously down, and the teaching of math in sixth grade should be examined. In the jargon, such a grade would be said to have moved from the sixtieth "percentile" position to a fifty-fifth, then fiftieth "percentile" position. A point to remember is that, as we have seen, over the recent past, experience has shown that through the *third grade*—and sometimes the fourth grade—achievement scores almost always tend to *remain stable over the years,* regardless of what is happening in the other grades. Parents and other laymen should not be satisfied with the scores in these lower grades when they probe into pupil achievement. Always ask for scores in the *upper grades,* too—grades 4 through 9 or 12.

When a test is changed, or "renormed" (given again to a more recent typical group of students), the trend continuity is broken, and straight comparisons with past scores and positions compared to the old "norm," or "percentile" positions, are no longer valid for determining trends. Today, since the overall trend in academic achievement in the country as a whole is *down,* a new average score of a national sample of pupils ("norm") would be *lower* than the old one, so obviously comparing the achievement scores to a new *lower* norm will show an improvement in position of the average score with the new norm. This, of course, does not at all necessarily mean an improvement in academic achievement for your school. When seeking information on this trend in *"percentile"* position compared to the national sample, therefore, school board members, parents, and taxpayers should always ask for the *date* when the test was last renormed. If the test itself was not changed, the *raw* score comparisons should still be valid to indicate trends in academic performance for each grade.

Tests are changed too, however, so it is also important to check the *date* of the version of the test being administered to the pupils (this appears on the test), for the *names* of the tests often remain the same. Later versions of tests may tend to be "easier" these days. Of course, there are many test publishers, so an entirely different series of tests may be given; when that is done, the continuity is also broken.

In all cases, however, continuity is only broken for one year and the trend can be picked up again when, and if, the same test is given the next year. Of course, the longer the period the same test has been used, the better the academic achievement trend data. Note that in this process we are comparing a state school system, a school district, or individual grade *with itself* over time to determine the competence of the system. Of course, for purposes of choosing a new home, for example, one can use such data to compare one school with another, one district with another, one state with another, or a district with the "national average."

One can also keep a record of each peer group (cohort) of children as it moves through the grades. In most cases it is possible to track the general progress of such a group of children by comparing their position with norms established by the test producer ("percentile" rating) and the averages for preceding classes that took the same test. If, for example, the average of the fifth grade score for a mathematics test is identical with the average score of the fifth graders in the district who took the identical test in preceding years, then this group of pupils is average for the school district and should produce a traditional average score in the sixth grade too. If it scored somewhat below, or above, the average in the fifth grade, it should do about the same in the sixth grade, and so on; typically, throughout the 1950s and first half of the 1960s, pupils did perform at least this well as they advanced through the grades. Since the mid-1960s, however, as we have seen, we often find students with an average score equal to the past local norm for the fifth grade, for example, but scoring in a bracket several percentage points below the past local norm for the sixth grade when they attain that grade, then further below the traditional norm in the seventh grade, further below still in the eighth, and even further below in the ninth. In effect, what we are doing is comparing each *group* of children with *itself.* And each year we find that often such peer groups of children are falling further and further behind where they should be in their current grade (see pp. 53–56).

School systems through which such falling groups are passing should be carefully and meticulously scrutinized. Unless the makeup and basic competence of the groups are drastically changing—and changes in their average IQs, which are also periodically determined, should show this—a fundamental educational problem may well exist in the schools, districts, or states that are involved. In general, however, the speed of decline in these groups' academic competence, plus the much slower, or lack of, changes evident in the demographic and IQ data, and other evidence, suggest that we should be slow to accept the "changing student body" argument alone as explanation for most changes in academic achievement in the last decade (see pp. 124–127). Of course, the same caveat about the changing and renorming of tests mentioned before applies here, but the temporary nature of discontinuity in the trend statement also holds.

Carrying comparisons with past achievement beyond the ninth or tenth grade, when many students exceed the legal age for compulsory school attendance, requires a scrutiny for any changes in the dropout rate. If many pupils—usually the less competent children—who normally would have dropped out are suddenly kept on in the upper grades, they will draw *down* the *average* achievement rate in the *upper* grades. This does not hold for the lower grades, however, and even the upper grade "holding rate" has been rather constant, or going down, in most high schools in recent years, so most scores will not be affected in this way.

COST EFFECTIVENESS TRENDS AND BUDGETS

Armed with the achievement score data, school board members and the public can compare trends in changes in curriculums, teaching methods, expenditures per pupil, pupil/teacher ratios, and teachers' salaries, or any other changes with trends in academic achievement. We have seen that most current innovations—many of them extremely expensive—have generally not coincided with any salutary effect on overall academic achievement of pupils. Quite the contrary. All data on expenditures are in the public domain and should be closely compared with school *outputs*. If academic achievement, as measured by standardized tests, has been declining and expenditures per pupil have been increasing, as has generally been the case, school budgets should come under particular fire.

There is no great mystery, either, about how to separate the effects of increased or decreased student population to determine the causes of differences in budgets between one year and the next. One simply divides the total budget by the number of pupils to get a *cost per pupil.* If a school budget covers both elementary and high schools, the trend in cost per pupil in each category can and should be determined. It usually costs more to educate a high school pupil, so when the ratio of high school pupils to elementary pupils goes up or down, the average cost for all pupils moves somewhat in the same direction. But this should not be accepted as the sole cause for increased cost per pupil; the shift usually should not be more than one or two percent per year for a district. Furthermore, the individual sections of the budget covering high schools and grade schools can be identified. When the sections of the budget are broken down for the two categories of pupils, divide the high school section by the number of high school students, and the elementary section of the budget by the number of elementary students. Normally, one finds costs for both categories soaring, so regardless of a changing mix, the cost per pupil usually is up.

In addition, one should "deflate" the dollar value to compensate for the degree of inflation in the area. If one can't get this so-called "constant dollar" figure, a rough idea of the increased cost per pupil in constant dollars can be obtained by using the current (inflated) dollar difference between budgets of succeeding years and deducting the inflation rate for the area in percent. Getting a national constant dollar value for a budget is not so simple, but also not necessarily so difficult. Ask your local banker, CPA, or industrial economist to compute the constant dollar value of your school budgets for the past few years from the published cost figures. With some luck you may get a rough local constant dollar value, which is even better. Divide the number of pupils into *these* dollar costs and you have the cost per pupil in constant dollars—that is, a figure that eliminates arguments blaming inflation and rising student populations for increased school costs.

Most people will find that, above and beyond the results of inflation, the soaring *cost per pupil* has outstripped most other costs. Nationwide, in 1976, the costs for all types of éducation—elementary, secondary and college—were up 9 percent over 1975. The student body is unchanged at 60.1 million; the budget for 1976 is $130.2 billion. Inflation is currently 6.2 percent. The difference is only partly attributable to the one percent drop in elementary students, one percent increase in high school students, and four percent increase to 10.1 million in college students.[2]

Votes on school budgets are normally held each year; they are not only indicators of how hard pressed for money the taxpayers are but, particularly where school boards are appointed, are also, in effect, a sort of plebiscite on community satisfaction with the schools. Even where boards are elected, the budget vote is an important indicator of public opinion about the schools. Voting against a budget is not necessarily voting against education or better opportunities for the children, as many educators would have us believe. On the contrary, it often is the only opportunity the public has to vote against an inefficient, and even counter-productive, school system that may not be educating the children while wasting millions of the taxpayers' hard-earned dollars.

To really change the makeup of a budget, however, it is often necessary for the public to make its feelings known before the vote. This is a very bothersome process and, when carried to extremes, in some districts almost seems to fly in the face of representative democracy, on which at least our elected school board system is based. Let us take an example of voters of a school district who have voted down, or even barely passed, a budget the previous year and now are presented with a much higher budget for the coming school year. Clearly, the superintendent and the board should know that the budget would be in deep trouble by voting time. However, in some districts almost before the budget is voted on, usually in the spring, the number, salaries, and fringe benefits of the educators, which account for two-thirds or more of the budget, can just about be locked in by agreements with teachers' unions on income and advance notice of termination. It is reasonable that these actions come just about the time of the spring budget vote, since teachers who would be terminated in September because of a budget cut must have time to find new jobs. Unless the board has an alternate, detailed budget plan at hand, however, it is difficult to quickly determine which teachers are expendable—and some usually are—arrange for their termination, and reschedule a good September class schedule between a negative budget vote and the termination notice deadline. School boards normally don't like to, or can't, quickly do time-consuming, difficult jobs like this, so the electorate, on voting down a budget, in some states can, nonetheless, almost be faced with a *fait accompli.* If a new budget is submitted or, as in at least one state, an "austerity" budget automatically goes into effect, the vast salary monies, including any raises agreed on in previous union negotiations, are said to be "mandated" and cuts in pupil service monies are likely to be made. Hot lunches are cut out; in suburban and rural areas, minimum busing distances are increased, causing occasional pressure on some parents to drive their children to school, particularly in winter; athletic funds are reduced—and all at the saving of only a tiny fraction of the budget. In other states, when a budget is voted down, the boards must come up with a budget that will pass, even if teachers must be dropped, or they get no money.

In fact, this "mandated" argument can and does come up long before termination deadlines. Teachers' and service people's union contracts, and administrators' contracts, can run for two or more years, with written-in step increases in salary for such things as each additional year of service or additional graduate education. The public is thus often told that, since the school district is under contractual obligation, the huge salary block of money—about 70 percent of the budget in many cases—cannot be touched; it is "mandated" by binding contracts. Of course, this is not so. These contracts do stipulate salaries and fringe benefits, for the individual teachers, but they do *not* normally stipulate the *number* of teachers a school district must employ. Some union contracts have limits on class size written into them, which we think a mistake on the part of the boards who agree to them. But *pupil/teacher ratios* are almost invariably so low that, even in these cases, heavy cuts in staff can usually be made before this factor comes into play.

Thus, if the cost per teacher in the budget goes up, the way to keep that huge block of salary and fringe benefit money in the budget from increasing, without violating contractual obligations, is to cut the *number* of teachers and administrators. In other words, as in the traditional union-management agreements, more money per worker should normally be based on more productivity. This approach often is no hardship on the system, since student/teacher ratios are normally lower than need be and, with possible extreme exceptions, the ratio per se apparently has no discernible effect on academic achievement (see pp. 118, 179, 180, 181). Administrators also are often too numerous and too highly paid.

Contrary to some opinion, we submit that the general productivity of a teacher can be determined, or at least his or her *non*productivity determined, by comparing children's achievement test scores on entering her class with their scores upon leaving her class. Sometimes these scores may actually be lower at the end of the school year when children leave a class than when they entered. Clearly the teachers in these classes should always go in a staff reduction, and if staff has to be cut more, those of next lowest productivity should go, and so on. This kind of measurement is determined by the *previous* academic-achievement score trend of the group of children in the class of the teacher in question *this* year. If a group of children who were achieving rather well suddenly begin to do rather badly under the care of a teacher, that teacher should be on shaky ground. Conversely, if another teacher consistently has her pupils track with or better than previous trends —if their trend is up to par—she should feel secure. The problem with carrying out such a plan is the difficulty in removing teachers with tenure, even if they don't teach well. But it is a battle well worth fighting. Obviously, school districts should not grant tenure until they have data for enough years to insure a teacher's productivity.

The same criteria should be applied to administrators. If achievement scores decline, an administrator should be in trouble. This will tend to assure a school board that he will be careful about which teachers he recommends for tenure, which ones he keeps on, and which ones he gets rid of. He can also be held responsible for rising costs in constant dollars per pupil. Together, these two indicators should also discourage his loading the staff with nonacademic "baby-sitting" teachers, lightweight-electives teachers, and too many "administrators."

The noninflated dollar cost per pupil and the historic trend in academic achievement scores are valuable tools for other purposes too. In a district where pupils' academic achievement scores are falling, or not rising, and cost per pupil in constant dollars has been rising, it is legitimate for taxpayers to demand that school administrators hold down the budget, or even reduce it, to the constant dollar level it was years ago, particularly if the pupils were achieving better then. The money apparently was being spent for the wrong things, and these expenditures should be cut out. Furthermore, it is legitimate for parents to demand that, under this lower budget, if average IQ level of the student body has not dropped significantly, achievement levels be brought up to, or maintained at, the levels they were when that lower constant dollar per pupil budget was in effect. In school districts where scores are rising, a more careful look at what expenditures are for is necessary before recommendations for cuts can be made. Even in these instances, though, if much money is being spent on items that cannot be connected with academic achievement, no increases—or, if taxes are high, even cuts—may also be in order.

Theoretically, the way to assure that changes in the budget occur before it is "too late" is for the public to attend the open budget meetings and make its thoughts known. Showing up at these meetings, or even knowing when they will occur, is not always that simple for the average parent or taxpayer. Many fathers, particularly the heads of underprivileged families, are moonlighting on the evenings the school boards meet, to earn the money to pay the skyrocketing school taxes these boards cause to be imposed.

For the teachers, however, who get off work at about 3:00 P.M. and who have paid organization officers with a strong vested interest in keeping track of budget meetings, it is often a simple matter to pack these relatively small gatherings with themselves and their friends. Such groups, of course, do not necessarily indicate the opposition to school programs likely to be felt by the public as a whole. Nevertheless boards—even elected boards—often fall back on the supposed "public demand" demonstrated by this "participatory democracy" at these meetings to justify their inadequate opposition to teachers' and administrators' proposals that are likely to be at odds with the will of most of the parents and taxpayers. Boards of this type often underwrite academically weak, expensive educational programs and, where possible, sometimes bring up new substitute "supplemental budgets" for votes as quickly as previous ones are voted down. Unpopular school bonds sometimes have to be voted down again and again. Of course, if a bond or a budget passes, the electorate is never given another chance to reconsider *that* vote.

CURRICULUMS, TEACHING METHODS, AND THE "LAYMAN"

Despite, or perhaps because of, all these problems, it is essential that unsatisfactory local boards and state departments of education be taken in hand by the electorate, for it is not just our money that is being wasted. As we have seen, recent curriculum changes have affected the lives of millions of children, and track systems and "work-study" programs could, in effect, change the very nature of our American universal educational system.

It is in some important sense a shame and even a disgrace that "laymen" on school boards and amid the general public should have to take over the activities of our highly paid state and local school administrators. With regard to curriculum, teaching methods, and pupil behavior, again, however, there often seems to be no alternative. Clearly something has been awry in these areas in most school districts and states, and not just for our "manual arts" students. Standards have been lowered, and to think, as some would imply, that we can lower them only for the average and hard-to-teach pupils—many of them underprivileged children—without affecting the "better" students who take the "college oriented" programs is not only anathema to upholders of American principles, but apparently hard to support from available evidence. For example, as discussed previously, data indicating declining academic achievement scores outside "core-city" areas, similar achievement drops among upper ninetieth and seventy-fifth percentile students, the decline of reading and writing test scores administered with the SAT along with the decline of the average SAT scores themselves —all of this evidence—does not speak well for this approach. As we have seen, this may also hold for programs that concentrate on only the lowest achievers. A small increase over 1975 scores seen in the 1976 SAT scores of college-bound seniors in the 600 and above level, if it is the start of a continuing trend, might, however, indicate success for a *very small elite* group.[3]

School board members, parents, and taxpayers must force state and local administrators to discuss the *real* problems in our schools. Discussion is not enough, however; as just indicated, in states and districts where achievement test scores are declining, or where they fail to rise from unacceptably low levels toward past levels, school board members, parents, and taxpayers must now actually become involved in pressuring educators at all levels to rectify the situation. The available data seem to indicate that the "instincts" of the majority of parents and taxpayers on such "technical educational" items as classroom behavior, homework, and curriculum may in most cases have been more reliable than the "expertise" of the opposition educators. These parents will normally find a sizable number of dedicated, hardworking teachers on their side, though it may be more difficult for these teachers to be vocal about it. As mentioned before, the author has talked with many such teachers and has received letters from others, though some are reluctant to make their views public. The "layman," therefore, should not be reluctant to question the "experts" on these issues, and school board trustees and elected state officials should be careful not to be taken in by the minority of activists and self-appointed "spokesmen for the community." The majority attitudes of parents and taxpayers are not only available from opinion poll data but are obvious in most communities, if a little common sense is used in seeking them out. In fact, these days, it is almost only by restricting oneself to certain circles of "ideologues" that these common-sense opinions can be avoided.

In the area of curriculum, laymen may have to take a firm stand, for considerable changes will probably be necessary, particularly if it develops that we must reinstitute teaching methods that have been successful in the past. In order to spend the time required to really teach children the essentials in the limited hours of a school day, the number of courses may have to be reduced to what they once were. Many "specialized" courses in elementary schools are of light academic content, of little proven value, and take up a significant part of the school hours. Furthermore, they are very expensive. Even the more-or-less traditional nonacademic subjects in grade school have become very expensive, for reasons not clearly linked to improved pupil skills. As discussed earlier, it is not obvious, for example, that high school graduates who came from lower schools with full-time librarians, music, art, and gym teachers in kindergarten through fourth grade show superior skills in these areas, compared to students who did not have such teachers in the lower elementary grades. During the past decade, in which gym teachers and gym classes have proliferated, the physical fitness of our schoolchildren, as indicated by their ability to perform standard gymnastic tasks, has actually declined. Specialized teachers "baby-sitting" the classroom teacher's class one period each day in these lower grades, do shorten her work day still further, but it is an expensive luxury.

A course like "ecology," particularly at the elementary level, is of very doubtful scholastic value. Even the apparent current emphasis and increased money and time spent on such supposedly academically rich courses as science in elementary schools can be questioned as to their addition to the pupil's knowledge of the subject. There is little evidence as to achievement levels related to specialized courses in grade schools; tests are normally not administered, or at least results are not recorded. But what there is, is not encouraging. In Delaware, science achievement dropped in both the fourth and eighth grades between the 1971–72 and 1972–73 school years. In Hawaii, science achievement in both the fifth and seventh grades plummeted between 1965 and 1973 (see pp. 223–225 in the Appendix). A one-million-dollar survey in the 1972–73 school year compared 90,000 nine-, thirteen-, and seventeen-year-old pupils' knowledge of science with that of a similar group of children in the 1969–70 school year. The survey showed that between 1969–70 and 1972–73 all three age groups dropped an average of "about two percentage points. This appears to correspond to the loss of half a year of learning experience."[4]

All such new courses cut down on the time available for math and grammar—to say nothing of geography, a largely abandoned basic subject, the ignorance of which is often a bit shocking among current primary and secondary school pupils. Subjects like general science, biology, and chemistry are fine in high school, if the necessary time has been spent to prepare a pupil well in mathematics, the underpinning of sciences, in elementary school. If he is truly skilled in basic math—ratios, percentages, and so on —when he enters high school, the student can progress and be "creative" in science later. The value of even these "new" classes taking up the limited time in an elementary school day is, therefore, far from clear.

In high school the curriculum must be adjusted. One feels compelled to say that pupils simply must know the history of our civilization and great literature in our language. One also feels they should be exposed to some higher mathematics, some real science, and to at least one of the major foreign languages. They simply *must* be able to transform ideas into a moderate amount of written material in a comprehensible and generally grammatically correct way, to say nothing of transforming somewhat complex ideas and nuances into articulate, grammatically correct, accurate, and comprehensible speech.

This holds for manual arts students as well. It is wrong and against the principles of American education to brand a child at the age of thirteen with a lifetime occupation, foreclosing the option that he might someday become a professional person, regardless of what the child himself or even his parents think. That is the system widely used in Europe, but traditionally in this country, even though a person may enter the manual labor force upon graduating from high school, he has had the minimum requirements for survival under the normal college curriculum, if ever the opportunity arises. And, at least in this country, it often does arise, and not just through

GI bill opportunities. Furthermore, as mentioned earlier, apprenticeship program directors for skilled trades are also very interested in the academic side of schooling. Making manual arts programs a low-academic-content catchall for hard-to-teach students may make things easier for teachers, but it doesn't necessarily help the student or the work force.

Syllabuses and courses used in some states today simply may be inadequate tools for imparting the knowledge many children currently lack and which they used to acquire under the old system. Just as the "new math" courses and syllabuses were found wanting, and are beginning to be dropped in primary schools in favor of traditional ways of teaching mathematics (see page 104), the same course of action may be required in the social studies area in high school. What used to be history departments offer courses like "Asian and African Culture Studies," which are huge in scope from the viewpoint of centuries spanned, and geographic, historic, and cultural diversity suggested, but which have little depth and are simply no substitute for such courses as Ancient History. In English, modern writings like *Soul on Ice* simply do not impart the same important elements that substantial amounts of classical American and English literature do, to say nothing of the civilizing process accompanying the latter, which we wish to see advanced in our high schools. Nor are "rap sessions" about a current movie shown in class, or a TV show recently viewed for English credit, any substitute for teacher-scrutinized and corrected themes ("compositions") and written book reports on the great works of our culture.

The reemphasis on scholastically rewarding courses and reduction of academically weak electives, "enrichment" and "mini-courses" should, of course, not only tend to improve academic achievement, but, as indicated earlier, also save the taxpayers great amounts of money by permitting trimming of the huge teaching and administrative staffs. Many expensive facilities and much equipment may also prove to be unnecessary, though their costs are far less than salary costs.

School board trustees and parents should demand explicit explanations of the composition of each course. In districts and states where there are declining achievement records, and with the welfare of a generation of children at stake, this must be attended to *right now* while they are in school. Given no proven alternative, trustees and parents probably should insist *that elementary school students be given the same amount of class time on the fundamentals that they had in the past.* This would mean, for example, close to a full hour each day of reading, writing, and arithmetic in the first four grades plus some time on such subjects as spelling and penmanship each week. There are children from "good" schools who enter junior high school today who still print—they cannot write in script. In the upper elementary grades, the time on the three R's should continue, but grammar, geography, and history—substantive history—should receive more emphasis. (It is important to know, for example, that the Spanish settled Cuba before the Pilgrims settled Plymouth and that the Civil War came before the Spanish American War. Even if one has to memorize these things, that is no crime. It also helps to know where Spain, Plymouth, and Cuba are.) One of the great problems in our schools today is that there is simply too little class time spent on the more difficult-to-teach fundamental courses. This clearly seems wrong.

Some children have always had more trouble learning than others. Some are slow starters, but if the material is not too difficult, most children apparently suddenly find themselves reading, as though a light had gone on. Promoting a child so that he must deal with more difficult material when that light has just begun to flicker may be counter-productive. If he has not mastered the basics first, he can become frustrated and discouraged by the continually increasing difficulty of assignments as he is passed through the grades. These are the hardest students to "motivate," and it is among them that we usually find the most dropouts.

On the other hand, once a pupil really can read well, he is more likely to "take off" in later grades to the limit of his competence. There are slow learners who continue to need extra help, but, with the exception of some of the handicapped, *virtually all children can learn to read, write, do basic mathematics, and know some basic grammar, history, and geography.* As noted earlier, forty years ago a child who went through six or seven grades of school and could not read and write enough to get along on his own was virtually unknown. *Classroom* teachers were responsible for teaching them to read and write *and they did,* spending time after school with some of them to help them keep up. Today, the responsibility is often shared with still another full-time, fully paid "remedial reading" teacher, and vast numbers of the children *can't* read. Ninth grade students who couldn't do long division problems were virtually unknown forty years ago—today they are almost commonplace. Many can't make change for a dollar.

If nonhandicapped children who experienced reading and math difficulties in the lower and mid-primary grades were once again helped by the classroom teacher after school, sent to summer school, or, as a last resort, kept back a year or two, many reading and math problems in the upper primary grades and high school would probably be drastically reduced. Incidentally, it is no crime to keep a child back until "the light goes on" and he can cope with the more difficult material; it is no favor to the child to push him through and out of school without the basic skills. We know how to teach almost all nonhandicapped children to read, write, and do math problems. We have been doing it for almost one hundred years, for children of all types, large numbers of whom had not a glimmering of English when they entered school. We have had great success in this area in the recent past, right up to the mid-1960s. Even our core-city and lower-tenth percentile pupils appear to have done better nationally then than today. The method used to teach children in those days is no secret.

Parents must bring pressure on the school board trustees to induce administrators and classroom teachers to shoulder the responsibilities rightfully theirs, the job for which they are paid—to teach elementary schoolchildren the fundamentals, the foundation without which they cannot do the advanced work in high school and college or hold many productive jobs in our continually more technologically and service-oriented society.

High school curriculum standards simply must be raised. Again, in the face of declining academic achievement and no viable alternative, school board trustees and parents should insist on the mandatory minimum of two years of a foreign language, a year of a real science course, a year of algebra, a year of geometry (except, possibly, for business course pupils), three years of real history, and four years of traditional English courses. If students can't pass such courses, they should not receive a high school diploma. Also, the grades these pupils receive in class should be compared to their scores on standardized achievement tests, and any significant inflation of classroom grades should bring an immediate investigation of the teachers who gave them, and the principals who allowed, or encouraged, it to happen.

It is not enough for school board trustees and parents to examine the curriculums of the schools. It is also necessary these days to discover in detail such things as where the emphasis is being placed in the schools and what are the teaching methods being used. If a school district or state is experiencing a general continuing decline in achievement test scores, but is fortunate enough to have individual schools or districts that have maintained their usually relatively high academic standing of the mid-1960s, and if these well-performing districts or schools have not had a significant rise in average IQ of their pupils, parents and school board trustees should find out exactly how these schools do it. As mentioned before, for these trend purposes, the question is *not* how one state compares with another, or how one district or school compares with another, *so parents and school boards should not be diverted by such discussions;* the question is how each state, district, or school compares with *itself* over the last decade or so. Applying the methods used by the successful schools to less successful districts and schools with approximately the same student-body makeup may solve the problems. (But attempting to apply methods used in a school with pupils of exceptionally high average IQ to schools with pupils of normal average or even below normal average IQ could be a mistake.)

For districts without this particular advantage, however—and this means most of them—the task is going to be more meticulous and laborious, but much of it can be done rather quickly. For example, it is no lengthy procedure to summarize the available data on effectiveness or ineffectiveness of many of the inputs to school systems, as measured by student achievement. These might include audiovisual aids, facility expansion, new learning resource centers, new buildings, lower pupil/teacher ratio, more elective courses, specialized teachers, open classrooms, modular scheduling, team teaching, classrooms without walls, and so on.

Initially, this information is apt to demonstrate somewhat negative results because most recent, obvious innovations generally have not been proven to influence academic achievement. But this in itself is important information for school board trustees and parents. Where possible, school trustees should also try to find correlations between academic achievement and some other types of inputs to the school system: for example, statistical data on achievement comparing similar student bodies, some of which had significant amounts of teacher-graded, daily homework and others that had very little; some with much class-time blackboard work, others with little; some with frequent teacher-graded quizzes and others with few; some with more emphasis on rote learning, others with less; some with a structured, traditional curriculum, others with a more freewheeling, innovative curriculum; some with teachers who stay after school in the afternoon to help pupils—and there still are some who do—others with teachers who don't.

In most cases, school trustees and parents will find, as noted throughout this study, that schools in their districts practicing the traditional teaching methods, which are more demanding on the teacher, usually are few and far between. They may have to initiate such instruction programs to get samples for comparison. Taxpayers should press their elected representatives to see that state commissions of education and the federal Department of Health, Education, and Welfare include studies of the effects of *these* factors on education in their multimillion-dollar research programs.

Blackboard work by students, for example, which results in independent instruction by the teacher for each student, even in very large classes, apparently has become less emphasized. One temporary teacher who went in part time to help out a district in a "border state" told the author, "Hell, they didn't even have any chalk to use the blackboards." One junior high school math teacher with a small class in one of the most expensive private schools in the East only "asked for volunteers" to go to the blackboard. A high school math teacher in another school had the same approach, at least for the beginning of the term. But regardless of such things as class size or student/teacher ratio, if a teacher doesn't know what the pupils don't know, on a day-to-day basis, it is hard for him to bring up those who are behind. Kids seldom volunteer to show what they don't know. Insisting that *all* children go to the blackboard, take frequent teacher-corrected quizzes, be given substantial, daily teacher-corrected homework and weekly English compositions, and that parents get numerical or letter-graded report cards every four weeks for elementary school and six weeks for high school— these are ways to help assure that teachers, and parents, will be alerted to, and help with, problems a child may be having *as soon as they occur* rather than later, when a child is already far behind. But this means more work for the *teachers.* School board trustees and parents, therefore, should expect opposition to such plans from some, though seldom all, teachers and administrators, as well as rationalizations as to why, despite obvious drops in achievement, such efforts are unnecessary (see p. 105).

It seems obvious that much *time* must be spent by the teacher and that much drill is needed. Much *reading* must be done during and after normal class hours, in and out of school. This applies particularly to children beyond the third or fourth grade. They probably should not go past the fourth grade until they can read reading textbooks for that grade. Beyond this grade—or even beginning with it—we should be improving, honing, and expanding a skill, not teaching its most simple fundamentals.

Many math and other primary school problems might be reduced by a reemphasis of rote learning. For example, we know how to teach children the multiplication tables, and we know that this knowledge makes long division much easier. Children can and do learn the "times tables" by rote, chanting in unison if necessary.

We also know how to teach children the fundamentals of grammar and how to improve their verbal skills. Diagramming sentences, essay writing and correction by teachers, and the strictly enforced use of proper grammar, grade-equivalent vocabulary, and good diction at all times in school are essential.

With these activities too, blackboard work, in combination with diligent teacher assistance after school when needed, has traditionally facilitated pupils' progress, even in rather large classes. We also know how to teach history and geography, but the method is dependent upon learning a significant number of facts, a practice too many educators frown on today. In junior and senior high school, a good number of quizzes, including many "essay" type, are required. This too, of course, means more work for the teachers who must correct these essay tests, but it allows pupils to be creative and demonstrate a knowledge of the subject beyond that possible in multiple-choice test responses.

It is important that parents remain firm on these issues, for there is more than their logical, natural concern as loving adults to support their position; *the overwhelming evidence from all over the country casts the gravest doubt on the position of those who oppose them.*

VIOLENCE IN THE SCHOOLS

It should take very little to convince school districts to solve the more dangerous disciplinary problems. It is sad that the welfare and safety of our children, and even the teachers, should be an issue inside our schools; but to the extent that they are, all levels of government must use pressure to remedy this situation. We know how to do that, too: hoodlums should be expelled and educated in reform schools, not allowed to dominate our public schools. This minority of chronic troublemakers must be separated from the normal pupil population. If they refuse to abide by school decisions on the matter and resort to violence, it becomes a clear-cut police and court problem, and school trustees and administrators must work with the local police on its resolution. On this issue, though they may disagree on technique, all educators and the public are in accord—violence must be eliminated from our schools. In its extreme form, this problem applies only to a small minority of schools, however.

There may be less agreement on the degree of "permissiveness" that should be allowed in the classroom, an issue affecting perhaps the majority of our schools today. But most parents realize that the primary goals of the school relate to scholastic activities. Since an orderly classroom is required to accomplish these goals, more emphasis may have to be placed on discipline. Administrators and school board trustees, of course, must support the teachers—and parents—in achieving this. Finally, undesirable language and habits should be curtailed, to improve both discipline and verbal skills. None of this need lead to a "lock step," "repressive" environment. On the contrary, not only is an orderly, well-structured environment not harsh, nor should it be, but it is normally thought to be an environment in which children can be secure, creative, and happy.

SHOULD WE LOOK BACK?

The teaching methods that we have outlined are often thought to be "old-fashioned," as perhaps is the idea that the classroom essentially must have an orderly, well-structured, though by no means unhappy, environment. Many "innovative" educators may object to these methods, but until other proven techniques are developed, they are the only tried and true ones we have, and, at least in the lower grades, most current teaching staffs generally have the knowledge necessary to implement them. It is *the children who pay the price for continuing experimentation* in so many of our schools where achievement continues to drop, or not improve from unacceptably low levels. Without increased knowledge on the part of many teachers, however, they may not be able to teach the old curriculum in the upper grades and these children may still not attain their maximum achievement level.

It is true that, in many ways, this means returning to a system we had about twenty years and three quarters of a trillion tax dollars ago. This is certainly a bitter pill for us to swallow, but with the welfare of a generation of youngsters at stake, if our current teaching staffs can indeed meet the demands, we may have no other choice. Furthermore, no evidence suggests that most of the old late 1950s and early 1960s system was especially bad, nor that a normal, calmer environment in the schools precludes some real improvements. Such improvements can probably be wrought within the schools' traditional charter, as they have been in the past. Under such circumstances, the morale of the many dedicated, truly good teachers still in the schools should improve, their value be recognized, and their influence increase—in themselves important consequences that should greatly improve the schools' scholastic stature. As we have seen, we apparently have previously experienced dips in academic achievement levels and the system has usually recovered, largely through, it seems, a reemphasis of the fundamentals.

This teaching system need not carry "old-fashioned" titles and terminology. For example, a real "two track" system may be in order—one track emphasizing retentive abilities, the other one deductive. This process is likely to repel some educators who view rote learning as part of a "repressive" "lock step" system. Yet, we have no proof that considerable amounts of rote learning *per se* inhibit creativity or otherwise retard children. Pupils need not be wedded to either track, but should be shifted from the retentive to the deductive, or even vice versa. In fact, if absolutely necessary, pupils could be shifted back and forth between the two tracks more than once in the first few years of school, as they require help. Shifting between tracks, of course, would be significant only inasmuch as a greater concentration by pupils on one type of study than another would occur in certain subjects. All pupils would have to meet standard competence levels in either track for each subject in order to advance.

This two-track system may do much to allow more pupils to excel in some subject(s), and thus acquire an autocatalytic incentive to learn; normally lower-achieving children actually, and obviously, succeed in *learning* something. Such a "program," however, unlike several of the other processes that have been mentioned, requires greater concentration and diligence on the teacher's part, though little if any additional factual knowledge.

WHO OUTSIDE THE SCHOOL DISTRICT HAS INFLUENCE?

Of course, state commissions of education have great leverage with which to persuade local districts to improve academic achievement. Over the recent past, however, they have often done just the opposite; they lowered standards and brought in new curriculums and additional courses that reduced the scholastic richness of what was taught in the schools. The federal government also has considerable leverage when it comes to local school districts, through the money (again, our tax dollars) that it injects into the school systems. It, too, however, has done little over the past decade to insist on better outputs from our schools. Much federal money has gone to the schools of lowest achievement, and, at least until recently, there apparently was little checking to see whether these schools had improved when they came up again for grants. (I was surprised, some time ago, to hear a federal education specialist say that he approved of parents attempting to sue school districts in court as a way to force the schools to teach their children to read.) The constantly proposed solution of just "throwing money at the problem," however, probably must be rejected; in fact, an analytical approach to educational recommendations would probably result in the conclusion that it should have been rejected years ago. This is not to say that money should not be spent, but that after dispassionate, logical analysis, it is more likely to be spent carefully, on efforts with known goals within the standard charter of educational systems, and on proven methods to reach the goals. Almost by definition, this means less money spent and/or better academic achievement.

Finally, something will have to be done about personnel. We will need some teachers well-grounded in academic subjects. Many of the teachers who can meet the requirements of teaching children as they used to be taught are among the older teachers and will retire first. As indicated earlier, finding teachers with the qualifications necessary to replace them may be difficult without some improvement in teachers' colleges. It is interesting to note that some school districts, in order to maintain, or perhaps even further reduce, their present pupil/teacher ratio in a period of tight money, encourage the early retirement of the older, more highly paid teachers in order to replace them with younger, less highly paid instructors. Today, in spite of a drop in enrollment in primary schools and a glut of would-be and laid-off teachers on the job market, jobs are still not that easily filled with teachers competent in truly academic subjects. Teachers who really can teach math, even to junior high school children, are still not that easy to find. Classroom teachers who can and also want to take on the large amount of demanding work necessary to really teach children to read, learn grammar, and write an English composition, are also not that easy to find.

Something may also have to be done about the training of supervisory personnel. Although we still have a considerable number of good administrators, colleges teaching graduate courses in school administration apparently often make little impression on school superintendents as far as their implementing the teaching of academic subjects is concerned. Many also show little skill in working within reasonable budgets. Some superintendents seem to be less involved in these functions than they should be, and others, though deeply concerned, are for many reasons evidently relatively ineffective when they do become involved. The author knows of one superintendent who, aware of the present poor record in verbal skills among pupils, determined some time ago that high school students should write a theme a week. His English teachers insisted that they teach one less class a day under the theme-a-week plan.

Strong superintendents, dedicated to academic achievement and well trained in ways to supervise and assure the development of this achievement in a district's children—something the overwhelming majority of parents and taxpayers want—could help much in the reversal of the current downward trend in education. Finding enough such men may be more difficult than might be imagined; district superintendents (often, by law, former teachers), and heads of state departments of education too often have become attached to the easier, "gimmicky" way of "solving" academic achievement problems mentioned earlier, rather than employing the more difficult, head-on, proven methods of teaching children.

THE POWER OF THE BALLOT

Such people must be found, however, and the downward trend in academic achievement reversed. Under our system this can be done and has been done before (see Chapters 4 and 7). It is the local school districts that are responsible for seeing that the job is done. School board members must study the information and cut through the educators' jargon; they must become minor experts, able to look out for the welfare of the children and taxpayers in the milieu of all kinds of activist pressure and bargaining sessions with administrators and teachers' unions. Voters should check that potential school board members have the ability to perform these functions.

Other officials are deeply involved, too, and not just in seeing that competent people are placed on appointed school boards. Parents and taxpayers must have their elected state officials see to it that state commissions of education, which have often done so much to initiate highly questionable curriculums and teaching techniques, accept their part of the responsibility for our children's academic achievement. And where scores are falling, the commissions must be made to change their ways. The same can be said, though to a lesser degree, about our elected federal representatives and those Washington officials who have considerable influence on schools through their control of federal aid to education. School specifics must become issues in school board, and local, state, and even federal elections. It is primarily through this electoral process that those who control the destinies of our children can be directly or indirectly influenced to recover the proper perspective with regard to our educational system, which so many of them seem to have lost.

We must once again restore the notion that children's welfare, primarily as measured by their academic achievement, is the *paramount* concern for schools; the welfare of the taxpayers at local, state, and federal levels, or of parents who pay for private schools, comes second, and the welfare of other interested parties third. With these priorities reestablished, we should be able to reverse the trend of inferior education in so many of our schools before damage is done to too many more of our children.

Appendix
ANALYSIS OF ACHIEVEMENT AND OTHER TEST TRENDS, BY STATES
by Paul Bracken

Although millions of students are tested each year, not all states have programs allowing year-to-year comparisons. Many states, for example, leave decisions concerning standardized testing to the discretion of local school districts. Only where there is a statewide program has it been feasible to attempt comparisons of student populations over time. But even here we are limited by the relatively short time span during which a particular test is given. This appendix contains our collection of statewide data on academic achievement trends. It should be mentioned that in all cases the data were obtained as public information from the individual states. As of this writing there is no centralized federal data collection effort in this important area.

ARIZONA

Arizona has a limited testing program that examines reading and listening for grade 3 pupils.[1] The tests were administered to all students in October 1973. The instrument used was the 1973 Stanford Reading Achievement Test Form A, Primary Level II; about 35,000 pupils took this test. Results for reading show that Arizona grade 3 students scored slightly higher than the national average.

It will soon become apparent that this is not very surprising in that, as we shall see, many other lower grades in other states seemed to have been performing better over the past few years. Information on the effect of class size is available with reference to Arizona reading tests.

This merely confirms what almost all serious studies of this issue have found. Class size, per se, has little to do with learning.

Subtests	Items/Max. Possible	Mean Raw Score		Grade Equiv. of Mean Raw Score	
		Nat'l.	Ariz.	Nat'l.	Ariz.
Dictated Vocabulary	37	25.3	24.5	3.0	3.0
Word Reading	45	33.9	34.0	2.8	2.8
Paragraph Reading	48	32.0	31.5	2.8	2.8
Word Study Skills	65	46.1	47.0	2.8	2.8
Listening Comprehension (Total Tests)	50	34.6	34.7	3.0	3.0
Total Reading	158	112.1	112.7	2.8	2.8
Total Auditory	87	60.0	59.3	2.9	2.8

Pupils in Class	Number	Percent	Mean Raw Reading Score	G.E. Raw Reading Score
1- 4	56	0.16	111.57	2.8
5- 9	297	0.85	107.54	2.7
10-14	758	2.16	107.52	2.7
15-19	2014	5.74	107.19	2.6
20-24	10574	30.16	110.45	2.7
25-29	13224	37.71	113.82	2.9
30-34	6321	18.03	115.83	2.9
35-39	835	2.38	118.17	3.0
40-45	163	0.46	122.82	3.2
45 +	821	2.34	114.07	2.9

CALIFORNIA

California has been administering statewide achievement tests for the past several years to grades 1, 2, 3, 6, and 12. All public school students in the state participate in the program. Tests of fundamental skills such as reading and arithmetic are used.[2] Along with achievement scores, a wealth of other information on such things as pupil characteristics, average class sizes, and median teacher salaries is collected and analyzed. The trend in test scores is:

Grade 3 Reading Achievement

	50th California Percentile in Terms of Nation		Number of Pupils Tested
1966-67	34		313,380
1967-68	34	Stanford Reading Test	319,903
1968-69	36		329,447
1969-70	36		347,410
1970-71	38		336,845
1971-72	52	Cooperative Primary Reading Test	334,644
1972-73	52		329,187

Grade 6 Scholastic Aptitude and Achievement

The grade 6 testing program had consisted of the Lorge-Thorndike Intelligence Test for verbal ability and the Comprehensive Tests of Basic Skills (Form Q, Level 2) for other skill measurements.

Grade 6
Statewide 50th Percentile in Terms of
Publisher's Percentile Rank

	Verbal Ability	Reading	Language	Spelling	Arithmetic
1969-70	48	48	43	49	47
1970-71	46	46	43	49	43
1971-72	46	44	39	42	38
1972-73	43	44	39	42	38

There were more than 300,000 pupils taking each test for each year.

CALIFORNIA STATE TESTING PROGRAM RESULTS, 1969-73

GRADE 6

	Intelligence Test				Reading			
	1969-1970	1970-1971	1971-1972	1972-1973	1969-1970	1970-1971	1971-1972	1
75TH PERCENTILE State Raw Score	109.0	108.2	107.5	107.0	71.8	71.4	70.5	
Publisher's Percentile Rank	74	72	72	70	74	72	72	
25TH PERCENTILE State Raw Score	87.9	87.4	87.0	86.9	45.7	45.3	43.7	
Publisher's Percentile Rank	25	23	23	23	24	23	21	

GRADE 12

	Intelligence Test				Reading			
	1969-1970	1970-1971	1971-1972	1972-1973	1969-1970	1970-1971	1971-1972	
75TH PERCENTILE State Raw Score	113.2	112.8	110.5	110.1	29.8	29.4	28.8	
Publisher's Percentile Rank	74	74	70	67	74	71	71	
25TH PERCENTILE State Raw Score	90.5	90.2	88.7	88.3	15.4	15.1	14.9	
Publisher's Percentile Rank	22	20	18	16	24	24	24	

SOURCE: *California State Testing Program 1971–72 and 1972–73.*

Grade 12

	Verbal Ability	Reading	Expression	Spelling	Quantitative
1969-70	47 (101.5)	52 (21.5)	42 (40.8)	47 (8.2)	48 (13.2)
1970-71	45 (101.0)	49 (21.2)	40 (39.9)	47 (8.1)	48 (12.9)
1971-72	39 (99.1)	49 (20.8)	38 (38.6)	47 (7.8)	48 (12.8)
1972-73	39 (98.8)	47 (20.2)	36 (37.5)	47 (7.7)	48 (12.6)

Language				Spelling				Arithmetic			
69-70	1970-1971	1971-1972	1972-1973	1969-1970	1970-1971	1971-1972	1972-1973	1969-1970	1970-1971	1971-1972	1972-1973
8.4	67.9	66.5	66.7	25.7	25.7	25.5	25.4	84.8	83.2	81.5	81.6
8	68	65	65	73	73	73	64	74	68	65	65
4.3	43.2	41.0	41.2	17.6	17.3	16.4	16.3	58.9	56.1	52.9	53.6
1	19	17	17	22	19	16	16	24	21	18	19

Expression				Spelling				Quantitative			
69-70	1970-1971	1971-1972	1972-1973	1969-1970	1970-1971	1971-1972	1972-1973	1969-1970	1970-1971	1971-1972	1972-1973
0.8	49.8	48.4	47.3	11.1	11.0	10.7	10.5	19.0	18.7	18.4	18.3
8	65	60	57	72	72	72	72	77	77	74	74
0.3	29.6	28.6	27.7	5.4	5.3	5.2	5.0	8.8	8.6	8.5	8.4
2	22	21	19	26	26	26	26	25	25	25	20

Grade 12 Scholastic Aptitude and Achievement

Grade 12 has been taking the Lorge-Thorndike IQ Test and the Iowa Tests of Educational Development (Form X-4). Statewide raw scores are presented in parentheses beside the publisher's percentile rank of the California median score. For each test there were more than 200,000 pupils participating.

We see again the pattern of rising achievement in the lower grades 1, 2, and 3 and falling achievement in grades 6 and 12. A particularly interesting feature of these data is the drop in IQ score for grades 6 and 12 statewide. The drop is more pronounced for grade 12 than for grade 6. Unfortunately no data on IQ trends are presented for the lower grades.

In the upper grades *all* test scores have consistently fallen over time. The most precipitous drop is in grade 6 Arithmetic and in grade 12 Verbal Ability. Grade 12 Expression has also fallen quite a bit, as has grade 6 Spelling.

While the decline in verbal IQ scores may be speculated to be causing other drops in achievement, it is hard to reconcile this with the rising achievements in grades 1, 2, and 3. The rising achievement of pupils in the lower grades contrasts sharply with the drops in IQ and achievement since the same people are taking the test a few years apart. Furthermore, since this achievement drop in the upper grades is, as we shall see, apparently a national phenomenon, it is hard to use the argument that California is uniquely plagued with an influx of lower-achieving upper graders.

For this data set, as with those of so many other state school systems, one is struck by the consistent declines for all scores year after year. Although grade 12 Quantitative declines only slightly, one would expect there to be at least one random point that is higher than the preceding year's point. That is not the case. The trend shows up in many other achievement time series, including SAT scores. It is difficult not to conclude that declines in reading, expression, and spelling among *all* California grade 12 students have some influence on national SAT trends in verbal ability. Furthermore, as the above breakdowns show, in grade 12 the seventy-fifth percentile raw achievement scores, which are most likely to include the highest number of college-bound students, decline faster than those of the twenty-fifth percentile. Grade 6 does not show the same trend.

A final striking feature of the California data is the fact that grades 6 and 12 are both below the publisher's national average in all areas and have been so since the data begin in 1969–70.

DELAWARE

The Delaware Educational Assessment Program contains a testing program administered to pupils in grades 1, 4, and 8. Testing is in the spring and data are available only for the 1971–72 and 1972–73 school years.

The Cooperative Primary Test is given to grade 1 and the Sequential Tests of Educational Progress are given to grade 4. Grade 8 takes School and College Ability Tests. The results,[3] which follow, are expressed by a standardized T score and also in terms of the mean number of correct responses for Delaware and the national norm.

DIFFERENCE BETWEEN DELAWARE AND THE NATION
IN MEAN PERCENT CORRECT RESPONSES

	1971-72			1972-73		
	Total No. Items	No. Items Used for Comparison	Difference	Total No. Items	No. Items Used for Comparison	Difference
			GRADE 1			
Reading	50	50	.2%	50	46	1.6%
Mathematics	55	55	- .9	55	42	2.7
			GRADE 4			
Total Ability	100	100	-4.8%	100	100	-5.2%
Reading	60	44	-3.9	60	28	-3.6
English	100	90	-5.4	100	86	-5.3
Mathematics	75	58	-5.8	75	54	-3.9
Science	50	50	-3.8	50	26	-4.2
			GRADE 8			
Total Ability	100	100	-3.5%	100	100	-3.4%
Reading	60	58	-7.0	60	49	-6.6
English	100	98	-7.7	100	98	-6.9
Mathematics	75	70	-7.6	75	63	-6.5
Science	50	50	-4.6	50	41	-7.2

These data can be interpreted as the differences between the mean percent correct responses of Delaware pupils compared to national norms. For example, in grade 1 Reading, Delaware pupils in 1972–73 scored 1.6 percent more correct answers than students nationally. The number of items corresponds to the total number of questions for the particular test under consideration. Some questions were eliminated from statistical consideration because there were no corresponding national figures for comparison, as reflected in the number of items used. Note the substantial decrease in sample questions for 1972–73 over 1971–72. Although not mentioned in the Delaware assessment report, this would seem to make 1972–73 achievement level estimates less reliable than 1971–72 estimates.

For the most part, grade 1 scores are above national norms. As with other states, Delaware exhibits the usual pattern for the higher grades—that is, achievement is significantly below national achievement levels. Also note that achievement falls more for grade 8 than for grade 4. This is another familiar feature of recent achievement test data.

There does appear to be an increase in achievement for grades 4 and 8 in 1972–73 over 1971–72. In fact, the official state assessment report asserts that for grade 8, "A closer inspection of the [data] indicates, however, that the comparisons improved slightly, in Delaware's favor, from 1971–72 to 1972–73 on the English and Mathematics tests."[4]

It is not entirely clear, however, that for the mathematics test in grade 8 ample statistical consideration was given to the fact that more questions were screened from the comparison in 1972–73 than in 1971–72 (63 used out of 75 compared to 70 out of 75 respectively).

In conclusion, data from Delaware show that grade 1 is above the national norm and grades 4 and 8 are significantly below it. Also the upper grades are about two to three times more below the national norm than grade 1 is above it. Grade 4 English and grade 8 Science are the poorest subjects. Grade 8 Science is particularly interesting in that much of the new curriculum in mathematics was designed to further enhance scientific learning.

The ability level in Delaware is also below the national norm. This can certainly explain some of the achievement levels but an interesting issue would be the variability of IQ over time.

DISTRICT OF COLUMBIA

The District of Columbia has a citywide testing program for public school pupils in grades 1 through 9. The Metropolitan Achievement Tests (1970 edition) are administered to grades 1 and 2 and the Comprehensive Tests of Basic Skills (1968 edition) are given to grades 3 through 9. Tests were taken by all pupils in regular instructional programs, except that in May 1973, a 10 percent stratified sample was tested in grades 4 through 9.

An interesting feature of the D.C. data is that tests are given early and late in the year for the same grade. This permits an estimate of achievement gains for a grade in a given school year.

Scores are for reading and mathematics for grades 1 through 9:[5]

PERCENTILE STANDING OF MEDIAN SCORES
IN TERMS OF NATIONAL NORMS

	Reading				
	Fall 1970	Spring 1971	Fall 1971	Fall 1972	Spring 1973
National	50th	50th	50th	50th	50th
California Achievement Tests, Level 1					
Grade 1	*	45	*	*	43
Grade 2	15	39	24	28	38
Comprehensive Tests of Basic Skills, Levels 1-4					
Grade 3	15	28	20	23	27
Grade 4	17	29	21	*	22
Grade 5	19	28	21	*	22
Grade 6	23	30	23	*	22
Grade 7	19	19	12	*	17
Grade 8	17	24	14	*	20
Grade 9	19	24	18	*	17

	Mathematics				
	1970	Spring 1971	Fall 1971	Fall 1972	Spring 1973
National	50th	50th	50th	50th	50th
California Achievement Tests, Level 1					
Grade 1	*	41	*	*	36
Grade 2	10	39	20	20	38
Comprehensive Tests of Basic Skills, Levels 1-4					
Grade 3	9	29	16	25	30
Grade 4	14	26	9	*	23**
Grade 5	15	29	16	*	25**
Grade 6	20	29	23	*	21**
Grade 7	11	17	10	*	16**
Grade 8	14	21	11	*	19
Grade 9	14	18	15	*	14**

*Test not administered.

**Sample population for grade.

Here again we see the general tendency for the lower grades not only to be achieving more but to be steadily improving over time. Grade 3 Reading advanced from the twentieth (fall 1971) to the twenty-third percentile (fall 1972). This trend does not hold out for the upper grades, where achievement is lower and also downhill. According to data for grade 9 Reading, there is even the chance that achievement declined during the school year; students at the fifteenth percentile in the fall of 1971 were tested at the fourteenth percentile in spring 1973. Unfortunately, no tests were administered in fall 1972 that would provide evidence to substantiate this interesting possibility.

Achievement in mathematics is generally lower than reading for the upper grades. A phenomenon here is the tendency for scores to hit a certain rock bottom and then increase slightly. Although there are some scores at the tenth and eleventh percentiles, there is a general barrier at the fourteenth. This also seems to be true for scores in other large cities. Perhaps at this achievement level, certain random tendencies dominate year-to-year fluctuations. The literature has some citations on this phenomenon. The issue seems to be whether "below chance" scores are useful as measures of achievement. It is possible that very low scores may be due in part to lucky or unlucky guessing or to massive omission.[6] To some extent this may be happening in testing programs of America's large inner cities. Although a detailed study of this possibility is beyond the scope of this report, test results for Washington and Philadelphia lead one to consider the hypothesis, since it does explain some of the trends.

GEORGIA

Georgia has a statewide assessment program that also administers standardized tests. Grades 4, 8, and 11 were tested in 1972. In 1971 grade 12 was tested instead of grade 11.

The reporting of test scores in Georgia is a very complicated procedure.[7] Only test score comparisons within a defined category are possible. A category consists of schools that have similar characteristics: Average Daily Attendance (ADA), Cognitive Ability Test Scores, percentage of students in ADA in a school above a minimal income level. A Georgia Department of Education report states:

> While comparisons cannot be made across categories, it should be possible to compare schools or systems within a given category. For example, since the systems in Category 1 are all large systems with students who are high

in academic abilities and family income, it is reasonable to expect their achievement test scores to also be similar. . . .[8]

However, it was possible to obtain some meaningful statewide data over time and these are presented.

Of eight possible comparisons with these data, eight have declined. Given this statewide achievement decline, it would be difficult to argue that education in Georgia is improving over time.

GRADE 8
(RAW SCORES)

	1971	1972	1973
Vocabulary		92.5	91.1
Reading		94.1	92.5
Language		91.8	90.7
Work-Study		94.2	93.0
Mathematics		95.2	92.7
Verbal Ability	92.4	91.9	
Nonverbal Ability	91.9	92.9	

GRADE 11
(STANDARDIZED T.A.P. SCORES)

		1972	1973
Composition	--	46.9	45.3
Reading	--	47.0	45.9
Mathematics	--	46.8	45.2

HAWAII

Hawaii has a statewide compulsory testing program for students in grades 4 through 11. The Sequential Tests of Educational Progress (STEP) and the School and College Ability Tests (SCAT) are administered.[9] The trend speaks for itself.

STEP, TABULATIONS OF HAWAII AVERAGES, FALL 1965-1973
(IN MID-PERCENTILES)

Grade	Publisher's Average	1965	1966	1967	1968	1969	1970	1971	1972	1973	
					Reading						
4	(50)	50	46	50	50	50	46	46	46	46	
6	(51)	58	54	58	58	58	54	51	46	46	
8	(50)	54	54	54	54	54	50	45	45	42	
10	(49)	43	43	49	43	43	43	39	39	35	
					Mathematics						
4	(51)	62	51	62	51	62	51	51	51	51	
6	(48)	48	48	48	42	42	42	36	36	36	
8	(50)	56	50	56	50	50	43	43	43	38	
10	(43)	43	43	43	43	43	39	39	39	35	
					Writing						
4	(52)	52	45	52	45	45	45	45	39	39	
6	(48)	48	44	44	44	44	40	36	36	33	
8	(51)	56	56	56	51	51	47	47	44	44	
10	(49)	53	53	58	53	53	49	49	43	43	
					Science					Spring/Fall	
5	(48)	48	54	48	48	48	48	43	43	38	32
7	(50)	50	57	57	50	50	50	41	42	36	31
9	(52)	N/A	N/A	60	60	52	60	52	43	43	36
11	(46)	N/A	39	39	33	33	33	33	33	33	28
				Social Studies							
5	(53)	53	53	46	46	46	39	39	34	34	34
7	(50)	56	56	56	56	50	50	50	43	43	38
9	(52)	N/A	N/A	52	52	37	45	45	37	37	31
11	(49)	N/A	49	49	43	49	49	43	43	39	39

In 1965 Hawaii was at or above the publisher's national average in most areas. From this level the state's achievement has fallen to very low levels. The drop in achievement is present in *all* skills and for *all* grades. Seventh grade Science has dropped an amazing 26 percentile points in six years and grade 10 Quantitative has fallen 18 points. On a statewide basis this is truly a massive decline.

An interesting feature of the Hawaii data is the decline in all areas, including science and social studies. If the new curriculum is accompanied by drops in reading, mathematics, writing, science, and social studies achievement, then what can one infer about the new curriculum?

SCAT, TABULATIONS OF HAWAII AVERAGES, FALL 1965 TO 1973
(IN MID-PERCENTILES)

Grade	Publisher's Average	1965	1966	1967	1968	1969	1970	1971	1972	1973
				Quantitative						
4	(51)	62	62	62	62	62	62	62	62	62
6	(47)	55	55	55	55	55	47	47	39	N/A
7	(51)	-	-	-	-	-	-	-	-	51
8	(52)	52	52	52	46	46	41	41	41	N/A
10	(49)	58	58	54	54	49	44	44	40	40
				Verbal						
4	(55)	55	55	55	55	55	55	46	46	46
6	(56)	56	56	61	56	56	56	51	51	N/A
7	(48)	-	-	-	-	-	-	-	-	48
8	(50)	56	56	56	56	56	50	50	50	N/A
10	(46)	42	38	46	46	42	42	42	38	38

IDAHO

Idaho has a voluntary statewide testing program for pupils in grades 9 and 11. Grade 9 students take the Differential Aptitude Tests (DAT) and grade 11 students take the Iowa Tests of Educational Development (ITED). Although school participation is not required, 98 percent of those eligible participated. Approximately 11,000 students were tested in 1972. Data were available for only two years for each grade.[10]

Although only two years of data were available for each grade, it is striking that out of 17 possible comparisons (10 for grade 9 and 7 for grade 11), 12 are down and none is up. The largest drops appear to be in grade 9 Grammar and grade 11 Expression. Also note that all but reading in grade 11 are below the national average.

GRADE 9, DAT MEAN STANDARD SCORES

	Fall 1972		Fall 1973	
	Male	Female	Male	Female
Verbal Reasoning	22.9	23.4	22.2	22.8
Numerical Ability	18.7	19.1	18.4	18.9
Abstract Reasoning	31.0	31.5	29.6	30.6
Spelling	59.7	66.4	59.2	66.0
Grammar	22.5	25.8	20.8	23.8

GRADE 11, ITED AVERAGE NATIONAL
PERCENTILE RANKINGS

	1971-72	1972-73
Social Studies	40	40
Natural Science	47	43
Corr. of Expression	37	32
Quantitative Think.	49	49
Reading Literature	47	47
Reading Average	51	51
Vocabularly	47	47

IOWA

Iowa has a statewide testing program for grades 1 through 12. Not surprisingly, the instrument for grades 1 through 8 is the Iowa Tests of Basic Skills. Although participation is not mandatory, about 95 percent of eligible schools were included in a recent administration. During 1972–73, over 293,000 pupils were tested in grades 1 through 9. Data for grades 3 through 8 are shown.[11]

IOWA, ITBS COMPARISONS, 1965-72
IN TERMS OF 1965 "BASE-YEAR" PERCENTILE RANKS
GRADE 3

YEAR	VOCAB-ULARY	READ-ING	LANGUAGE SKILLS				WORK-STUDY SKILLS			MATH SKILLS	
			SPELL-ING	CAPITAL-IZATION	PUNC-TUATION	USAGE	MAPS	GRAPHS	REFER-ENCES	CON-CEPTS	PROB-LEMS
1965	50.0	50.0	50.0	50.0	50.0	50.0	50.0	50.0	50.0	50.0	50.0
1966	51.7	50.9	50.8	50.8	50.9	50.5	52.5	51.4	51.2	51.1	52.2
1967	52.4	52.0	50.6	49.7	50.9	51.2	52.5	51.7	52.6	51.8	54.0
1968	52.4	52.0	51.3	50.5	50.9	51.7	54.1	52.5	53.0	51.8	55.0
1969	50.3	50.4	48.0	46.8	47.0	49.1	52.2	51.4	50.4	49.6	50.4
1970	51.0	50.6	48.2	46.8	47.2	48.6	52.9	51.7	51.2	50.4	53.1
1971	51.0	50.9	46.5	46.0	46.0	47.9	52.5	51.0	50.0	49.0	51.8
1972	51.3	51.3	46.5	48.4	50.3	49.1	54.1	52.1	52.1	50.0	54.5

GRADE 4

YEAR	VOCAB-ULARY	READ-ING	LANGUAGE SKILLS				WORK-STUDY SKILLS			MATH SKILLS	
			SPELL-ING	CAPITAL-IZATION	PUNC-TUATION	USAGE	MAPS	GRAPHS	REFER-ENCES	CON-CEPTS	PROB-LEMS
1965	50.0	50.0	50.0	50.0	50.0	50.0	50.0	50.0	50.0	50.0	50.0
1966	49.8	51.2	51.3	50.8	47.8	51.0	52.1	51.9	51.2	51.4	50.6
1967	50.2	51.2	50.7	49.7	49.3	50.7	52.1	51.9	51.2	49.6	48.9
1968	49.1	51.4	49.5	50.3	49.8	50.7	53.4	53.6	51.8	51.4	49.2
1969	48.5	51.4	49.5	49.8	49.6	50.7	53.4	56.0	53.0	50.9	47.8
1970	47.8	49.5	48.1	47.7	47.4	48.6	52.8	55.5	51.8	49.6	46.7
1971	46.8	49.2	48.4	44.9	47.4	49.3	52.5	55.2	51.5	49.0	46.2
1972	48.1	49.6	48.8	45.7	47.4	48.4	54.5	55.2	53.0	50.4	47.0

GRADE 5

YEAR	VOCAB-ULARY	READ-ING	LANGUAGE SKILLS				WORK-STUDY SKILLS			MATH SKILLS	
			SPELL-ING	CAPITAL-IZATION	PUNC-TUATION	USAGE	MAPS	GRAPHS	REFER-ENCES	CON-CEPTS	PROB-LEMS
1965	50.0	50.0	50.0	50.0	50.0	50.0	50.0	50.0	50.0	50.0	50.0
1966	50.8	50.4	51.1	51.3	52.3	50.6	52.2	51.9	51.1	50.9	49.2
1967	50.3	50.7	51.1	50.0	50.6	50.9	52.2	51.9	51.1	49.8	47.8
1968	49.3	50.2	49.2	48.5	49.8	49.8	52.2	52.1	50.9	48.8	46.6
1969	49.8	49.6	47.5	46.6	48.1	48.9	50.9	52.4	51.1	46.8	43.8
1970	49.6	49.6	47.8	46.4	47.9	47.3	51.5	53.2	51.3	46.4	43.2
1971	49.8	48.4	47.7	45.8	48.1	47.3	50.3	52.7	51.3	44.3	42.9
1972	49.3	48.2	47.7	45.8	47.2	47.0	52.2	54.1	51.3	46.0	43.8

GRADE 6

YEAR	VOCAB-ULARY	READ-ING	LANGUAGE SKILLS				WORK-STUDY SKILLS			MATH SKILLS	
			SPELL-ING	CAPITAL-IZATION	PUNC-TUATION	USAGE	MAPS	GRAPHS	REFER-ENCES	CON-CEPTS	PROB-LEMS
1965	50.0	50.0	50.0	50.0	50.0	50.0	50.0	50.0	50.0	50.0	50.0
1966	50.9	50.0	51.4	51.6	51.0	49.9	50.4	51.0	51.0	50.8	49.
1967	50.5	49.6	51.0	51.4	50.6	49.3	51.0	50.8	50.8	48.8	47.2
1968	50.2	50.3	51.2	52.3	51.4	49.9	53.2	52.6	52.3	49.2	46.
1969	50.2	49.3	50.3	49.8	50.2	48.0	52.0	52.3	51.4	46.0	43.0
1970	49.2	48.0	49.0	48.9	49.1	47.0	51.5	51.9	51.4	44.6	41.7
1971	49.7	49.0	50.1	49.6	49.6	47.3	51.2	51.0	52.1	43.5	43.5
1972	49.1	48.2	49.7	48.3	47.9	46.1	51.8	51.7	51.4	43.5	42.9

GRADE 7

YEAR	VOCAB-ULARY	READ-ING	LANGUAGE SKILLS				WORK-STUDY SKILLS			MATH SKILLS	
			SPELL-ING	CAPITAL-IZATION	PUNC-TUATION	USAGE	MAPS	GRAPHS	REFER-ENCES	CON-CEPTS	PROB-LEMS
1965	50.0	50.0	50.0	50.0	50.0	50.0	50.0	50.0	50.0	50.0	50.0
1966	51.0	49.6	50.5	50.8	50.5	50.2	51.8	49.8	50.3	49.1	48.4
1967	51.0	49.0	50.3	50.8	51.1	49.3	51.8	50.3	50.6	48.8	47.7
1968	49.0	47.3	49.2	48.6	47.8	47.0	49.8	49.0	49.8	46.7	44.2
1969	48.8	46.9	48.9	47.2	46.3	46.0	49.5	49.0	49.3	44.5	42.2
1970	47.3	44.8	48.0	45.3	45.0	44.5	49.2	48.2	49.8	43.5	41.1
1971	47.1	44.8	48.0	45.9	45.7	45.0	49.3	48.2	49.1	44.0	40.5
1972	46.9	45.6	48.3	44.6	44.4	44.4	50.5	49.0	49.5	42.0	40.5

GRADE 8

YEAR	VOCAB-ULARY	READ-ING	LANGUAGE SKILLS				WORK-STUDY SKILLS			MATH SKILLS	
			SPELL-ING	CAPITAL-IZATION	PUNC-TUATION	USAGE	MAPS	GRAPHS	REFER-ENCES	CON-CEPTS	PROB-LEMS
1965	50.0	50.0	50.0	50.0	50.0	50.0	50.0	50.0	50.0	50.0	50.0
1966	50.8	50.2	50.8	51.5	51.8	49.2	51.1	49.8	51.0	48.0	48.1
1967	49.8	49.1	51.0	50.4	50.9	48.2	50.3	48.8	50.3	46.5	46.1
1968	49.0	48.5	50.8	50.7	51.5	47.2	51.1	47.8	50.5	46.1	44.4
1969	48.7	47.4	49.7	49.1	49.7	45.8	49.8	47.6	50.0	44.0	42.8
1970	46.9	46.2	49.7	47.9	49.0	44.7	50.3	46.9	50.7	43.8	41.5
1971	47.3	45.7	50.4	49.1	49.5	45.1	50.5	48.1	51.0	44.0	41.5
1972	46.9	46.0	49.0	47.4	47.8	44.6	50.5	48.1	51.0	44.0	41.5

While again some basic skills in the early grades have improved over time, the results for the upper grades (above 4) are uniformly declining. The rise in work-study skills in most grades has very little to do with basic achievement in reading, language, and mathematics. Mathematics skills seem to have suffered the most decline since 1965.

It is particularly troubling to observe achievement losses in Iowa, where isolation from much of the turmoil surrounding education in the past few years would have seemed more likely than in other places. It is remarkable that the drop in Iowa achievement parallels the decline in so many other areas one is led to believe have such "different" problems. The trend in basic skills shows little evidence of any difference. Achievement is apparently falling throughout the country; only the parameters of the decline need to be determined.

MICHIGAN

The Michigan Educational Assessment Program has had a controversial history that will not be examined here. This program does administer a statewide testing program for pupils in grades 4 and 7 in public schools. Parochial school students do not participate. A specially developed instrument, the Standardized Michigan Educational Assessment Test, was developed to measure mathematics, word relationships, reading, and the mechanics of written English. A special equating procedure is employed by the state education department that allows year-to-year comparisons of test scores so that it is possible to measure progress.[12] Scores are expressed in terms of the 1970 results, which have a mean of 50 and a standard deviation of 10 (T scores).[13]

Comparing 1973 with 1970 results, it is seen that achievement has fallen in varying degrees in both grades in all subjects except mathematics. The rise in grade 7 scores in mathematics is particularly interesting since no other state for which we have data seems to have accomplished this over this time frame. In fact, achievement in mathematics in the Detroit public schools for grade 7 has also increased over this time. A closer investigation of this desirable trend in Michigan appears to be warranted since it may be unique in the United States.

The most obvious drops in achievement for both grades are in word relationships. The losses overall in grade 7 have been rather consistent— that is, except for mathematics, each year is lower than the last. Grade 4 exhibits some increases over the time in question. This is perhaps again an

MEANS IN EQUATED STATE STANDARD SCORE UNITS, MICHIGAN

GRADE 4

	1970	1971	1972	1973
Reading	50.0	50.5	50.4	49.9
Mathematics	50.0	50.5	50.6	50.9
Mechanics of Written English	50.0	50.0	49.4	49.5
Word Relationships	50.0	50.6	49.0	48.6

GRADE 7

	1970	1971	1972	1973
Reading	50.0	49.4	50.1	49.6
Mathematics	50.0	50.0	50.0	50.3
Mechanics of Written English	50.0	49.6	49.4	49.2
Word Relationships	50.0	49.8	49.5	48.8

example of the pattern that achievement in the United States has been declining faster in the higher grades. Broadly speaking, it is in grades 4 and 5 that achievement drops begin to appear.

MISSISSIPPI

The Mississippi State Department of Education has been administering the California Achievement Tests (1970 edition) to grades 5 and 8 since 1970–71. Although participation is optional, about 87 percent of school districts participate. About 38,000 pupils are tested in each grade.

It is important to note in the following statewide summary that there was a change in the method of computing the statewide mean after the 1971–72 school year. Thus the increase in 1972–73 scores is the result of statistical factors and not necessarily the result of achievement gains.[14]

We can see slight drops in grades 5 and 8 from the 1970–71 to 1971–72 school years in all areas with the exception of language. Disregarding the 1972–73 change because of scoring differences, we see that 1973–74 scores increased over the 1972–73 results. These changes may be said by some to be random changes that might be expected over time, but it should be noted that a truly random variation would be characterized by gains and losses for each particular test. When all tests go down and up together in a particular year, it is less likely to be random. The safest assumption would probably be that though Mississippi may not have started at the highest of academic achievement levels, it

MEAN STATEWIDE RAW SCORES, MISSISSIPPI

GRADE 5

	Reading	Mathematics	Language	Spelling
1970-71	39.03	53.88	52.41	16.71
1971-72	38.69	53.14	52.44	16.54
(Note change in computing mean)				
1972-73	40.7	56.2	55.1	17.3
1973-74	41.4	57.0	55.5	17.3

GRADE 8

	Reading	Mathematics	Language	Spelling
1970-71	41.56	44.44	59.80	16.48
1971-72	41.31	43.98	59.95	16.19
(Note change in computing mean)				
1972-73	42.2	45.9	61.5	16.5
1973-74	42.2	46.3	62.2	16.5

may be one of the few states that has been holding steady in achievement over the past four years.

NEBRASKA

Although we have been able to obtain scores for only a single year for Nebraska, the data are nonetheless significant. The Nebraska scores reflect one of the very few instances that a testing population has scored above the national norm.

NEBRASKA GRADE 11 SCORES, 1972

	Median Percentile Score in Terms of National Percentiles	Sample Size
Reading	51	11,242
Language Arts	52	11,217
Mathematics	62	11,204
Social Studies	50	11,179
Science	54	11,166

The testing instrument for these data was the Iowa Tests of Educational Development.[15] Note that reading, language arts, and social studies are fairly close to the national average; only mathematics is far above this norm. It is also important to note the number of pupils taking the test—only 11,000 compared to the 200,000 who typically take the eleventh grade tests in California.

NEBRASKA GRADE 7 SCORES, 1971

	Median Percentile Score in Terms of National Percentiles	Sample Size
Reading	61	11,225
Language Arts	59	11,201
Mathematics	60	11,221
Social Studies	58	11,200
Science	64	11,200

NEW JERSEY

New Jersey administers tailor-made, criterion-referenced achievement tests to pupils in public schools. Grades 4 and 12 are tested and participation is mandatory. In 1972–73, approximately 250,000 students were included in the program. Only results from the November 1970 administration are presently available.[16]

It is fairly difficult to summarize the results of criterion-referenced tests. The only comparisons usually made consist of looking at the percentage of students who answer a particular question correctly versus the number expected to do so. The expectation is frequently determined by a group of educators and usually consists of simple comments such as "excellent," and "good achievement," or "poor" on statewide percentage of students scoring correctly. This means that a different group of educators might rate a certain performance differently; the same educators may even rate achievement differently from one year to the next, depending on a host of other factors. It thus becomes impossible to compare the educational effectiveness of one state with another; it is difficult to compare a state with itself over time. In fact, the New Jersey presentation of results precludes comparison of one district with another. The only comparisons are among urban, suburban, rural, and vocational regions. This makes evaluation of educational effectiveness difficult. For example, the official state report concludes that ". . . beginning fourth grades in the State of New Jersey generally perform well when results are related to the minimal primary reading skills stated as objectives noted in varied types of primary reading programs." The report does not define "well" nor specify with whom students are compared. Since objectives are not quantitatively stated and evaluators may change, there is little hope of meaningful comparison. Studying examples of test problems and the number of correct responses to those problems is virtually the only way to understand such a program.

With respect to grade 4 Multiplication and Division, the summary results state:

> Particularly low achievement was noted throughout this cluster. There was some question by committee members as to whether the students are "ready" for these items at this grade level. It was assumed that achievement for this cluster would increase with advancing grade levels, but the present scores were uniformly low. There were very few differences noted across the geographic regions but the urban community type was consistently lower as compared to other community types.[17]

One cannot help assuming that achievement levels are not improving when the state questions whether today's fourth graders are ready for something that has normally been taught in the fourth grade for many decades. It is interesting to speculate on what would replace multiplication and division, were they to be removed from the grade 4 curriculum. The same trend appears to hold for pupils in grade 12: "Students showed a weakness in the area of multiplication and division of fractions and to a lesser extent in using least common denominators."[18]

NEW MEXICO

New Mexico has a statewide testing program for pupils in grades 1, 5, and 8.[19] In addition, records are kept of the score achieved by high school students on the American College Testing Program (ACT). Participation in the program is required of both public and nonpublic schools.

The trend in grade 1 IQ scores has gradually been increasing, as shown in the table on page 234. This table should be kept in mind when considering the trend in academic ability for grade 5 pupils. It is important also to note that in the following tables a change in testing instruments in 1971–72 makes comparison impossible across the entire time frame.

GRADE 1

COMPARISON OF MEAN TEST SCORES ON OTIS-LENNON
MENTAL ABILITY TEST, 1971-72 TO 1973-74

Group	1971-72	1972-73	1973-74	N-Count 73-74
Anglo	103.9	105.2	105.4	8,972
Spanish	90.0	92.7	94.0	8,349
Indian	83.6	85.1	86.1	1,802
Black	89.8	90.3	91.2	467
Asian American	-	-	102.9	61
Other	98.9	100.8	101.5	109
Non-Public	100.0	101.2	102.5	1,140
Public	95.7	97.3	98.3	19,434
Total State	96.0	97.6	98.5	20,574
National	100.0	100.0	100.0	-
Spanish Language Administration	-	84.0	87.7	229

GRADE 5

ACADEMIC APTITUDE SCORES, 1969-70 TO 1973-74

Group	1969-70	1970-71	1971-72[*]	1972-73[**]	1973-74
Anglo	111	109	103	-	102
Spanish	96	95	91	-	90
Indian	92	91	85	-	85
Black	92	93	89	-	88
Asian American	-	-	-	-	96
Other	103	104	98	-	98
Non-Public	NA	108	101	99	101
Public	102	102	96	96	95
National	100	100	100	100	100

[*]Note change in testing instruments.

[**]Academic aptitude scores for ethnic groups were not provided for school year 1972-73.

GRADE 5

TOTAL BATTERY ACHIEVEMENT SCORE
AND NATIONAL REFERENCE GROUP, 1969-70 TO 1972-73
(IN MEAN GRADE EQUIVALENT)

Group	1969-70	1970-71	1971-72[*]	1972-73
Anglo	5.5	5.5	5.3	5.3
Spanish	4.3	4.3	4.3	4.3
Indian	3.7	3.9	3.8	3.8
Black	3.9	4.2	4.1	4.1
National	5.1	5.1	5.1	5.1

[*]Note change in testing instruments.

GRADE 8

ACADEMIC APTITUDE SCORES[*]
1971-72 TO 1973-74

Group	1971-72	1972-73[**]	1973-74
Anglo	103	-	103
Spanish	91	-	92
Indian	85	-	86
Black	88	-	90
Asian American	-	-	99
Other	100	-	100
Non-Public	100	102	103
Public	97	97	96
State Total	-	-	97
National	100	100	100

[*]Based on a standard scale with a range of 1-150, a mean of 100, a standard deviation of 16.

[**]Academic aptitude scores for ethnic groups were not provided for school year 1972-73.

GRADE 8

TOTAL BATTERY ACHIEVEMENT MEAN GRADE EQUIVALENT
1971-72 TO 1973-74

Group	1971-72	1972-73	1973-74
Anglo	8.2	8.2	–
Spanish	6.2	6.4	–
Indian	5.4	5.5	–
Black	5.8	6.1	–
Other	7.7	7.6	–
Under 500	6.8	7.3	–
501-1000	6.4	6.5	6.5
1001-5000	6.6	6.7	6.6
Over 5000	7.4	7.4	7.1
Non Public	7.6	7.7	7.6
Public	7.2	7.2	7.1
Total			7.1
National	8.1	8.1	8.1

There has been an increase over time of grade 5 performance for blacks and a decline for Anglo students.

The ability and achievement results for grade 8 students are shown here and on page 235. It is seen that academic aptitude for grade 8 (see first of the two preceding tables) has apparently held steady for Anglo pupils and is increasing for various minority groups. It is also interesting to note the drop in ability for public school pupils and the corresponding gain for those in nonpublic schools. There has been a drop in public school achievement (see the preceding table). There is also an achievement increase for minority group students but none for Anglo students.

Scores of New Mexico students on the ACT follow.

Here too there has been an overall decline since 1967–68. The largest drop appears to be in the social sciences. This drop in New Mexico is compared with the nationwide decline in SAT scores and the general decline in national ACT scores. The official report of the New Mexico Department of Education notes:

> This corresponds to the finding that scores on the Scholastic Aptitude Test, another widely used college entrance test, are dropping nationwide. This phenomenon was a topic of discussion at a conference of directors

NEW MEXICO, ACT MEANS

YEAR	Number of Pupils Tested	ENGLISH			MATHEMATICS			SOCIAL STUDIES			NATURAL SCIENCE			COMPOSITE		
		BOY	GIRL	TOTAL	BOY	GIRL	TOTAL	BOY	GIRL	TOTAL	BOY	GIRL	TOTAL	BOY	GIRL	TOTAL
1967-68	8,239 B - 4,348 G - 3,891	17.5	19.5	18.5	19.6	17.0	18.4	19.8	18.8	19.3	21.5	19.9	20.3	19.7	18.7	19.2
1968-69	7,843 B - 3,947 G - 3,896	17.9	19.5	18.7	20.2	18.0	19.1	20.2	18.9	19.6	21.7	19.2	20.5	20.0	19.1	19.5
1969-70	8,771 B - 4,403 G - 4,368	17.2	18.8	18.0	20.4	18.0	19.2	19.7	18.1	18.9	21.5	19.7	20.6	19.8	18.8	19.3
1970-71	9,091 B - 4,478 G - 4,613	16.4	18.2	17.4	19.3	17.0	18.1	18.2	17.4	17.8	21.2	19.3	20.3	18.9	18.1	18.5
1971-72	9,107 B - 4,501 G - 4,606	16.3	17.9	17.1	19.3	16.7	18.0	18.2	17.2	17.7	21.3	19.1	20.2	18.9	17.9	18.4
1972-73	8,701 B - 4,151 G - 4,550	16.8	17.7	17.2	19.5	16.5	18.0	18.1	16.2	17.1	21.6	19.1	20.3	19.1	17.5	18.3
							NATIONAL NORMS									
1970-73	2,647,873 B-1,321,470 G-1,326,403	16.7	18.6	17.7	19.7	17.7	18.7	18.7	17.9	18.3	21.2	19.5	20.4	19.2	18.6	18.9

ACT
(NATIONAL)

	1967-70	1970-73	Difference
English	18.2	17.7	- .5
Mathematics	19.0	18.7	- .3
Social Studies	19.4	18.3	-1.1
Natural Science	20.1	20.4	.3
Composite	19.3	18.9	- .4

of state testing programs held in Princeton, New Jersey, on November 4 and 5, 1973. It was reported that the Minnesota College Testing Program mean scores had experienced an increase until approximately 1961–62 where they plateaued until about 1969–70 when the mean scores began dropping approximately ½ raw score point annually. In addition, it has been noted [also at the Conference of Directors of State Testing Programs] that national scores on the reading and math portions of the Iowa Tests of Basic Skills are showing "substantial drops," particularly in the higher grades.[20]

NEW YORK STATE

The State Education Department of New York has administered several testing programs that attempt to measure a wide range of skills and abilities. While most of these testing programs are not designed to give a continuing score scale for performance over the years, the Pupil Evaluation Program (PEP) does allow a time series analysis. PEP is a fall testing program required of *all* New York State pupils in grades 3, 6, and 9 and consists of reading and mathematics achievement tests.[21] The program was initiated in October 1965 and data on PEP scores are available since 1966. According to a New York State description the program has value as a "statewide product evaluation and continuous inventory system." Although the test forms have been revised since 1966, the newer norms were obtained by equating raw scores on the revised tests to those on the original tests, using the equi percentile method.[22] The original PEP norms are based on the 1966 statewide results. Thus it is possible to compare students of recent years with 1966 students as far as reading and mathematics achievement is concerned.

The Bureau of Pupil Testing and Advisory Services provides percentile ranks of median raw scores for PEP based on the definition that 1966 pupils would serve as the median comparison group. Students in 1966 therefore will fall at the 50th percentile in each grade and for each test. The results are shown for grades 3, 6, and 9.

Overall, there has been an upward trend in grade 3 Mathematics test scores and no significant changes in the reading scores.

GRADE 3
(PERCENTILE RANKS OF MEDIAN RAW SCORES)

	1966	1967	1968	1969	1970	1971	1972	1973
Reading								
Public	47	47	49	48	46	46	48	NA[*]
Nonpublic	57	58	57	58	56	57	58	NA
Total State	50	50	51	50	49	49	50	50
Mathematics								
Public	49	49	52	52	51	52	53	NA
Nonpublic	54	55	56	61	59	59	60	NA
Total State	50	51	53	54	53	53	54	54

[*]Not available.

GRADE 6
(PERCENTILE RANKS OF MEDIAN RAW SCORES)

	1966	1967	1968	1969	1970	1971	1972	1973
Reading								
Public	47	46	47	44	42	41	41	NA[*]
Nonpublic	57	56	56	55	53	53	53	NA
Total State	50	49	49	47	44	44	44	44
Mathematics								
Public	48	45	46	42	39	39	39	NA
Nonpublic	54	51	50	51	50	49	49	NA
Total State	50	47	47	44	42	41	41	39

[*]Not available.

GRADE 9[*]
(PERCENTILE RANKS OF MEDIAN RAW SCORES)

	1966	1972	1973
Reading			
Public	NA**	40	NA
Nonpublic	NA	59	NA
Total State	50	42	41
Mathematics			
Public	NA	38	NA
Non Public	NA	58	NA
Total State	50	41	39

[*]Data for intervening years not available from New York State Education Department.

**Not available.

The time series trend in the higher grades is obvious enough. Between 1966 and 1973 grade 6 lost 6 reading and 11 mathematics percentile points. The grade 9 results are more bleak in that reading fell by 9 points and mathematics by 11 points. An important statistical feature of the trend is its monotonic quality. While one might expect some random variations to cause increases in the year-to-year trend, none seems to be present. Grade 6 statewide scores have never increased in either reading or mathematics since 1966. It should be recalled that PEP scores cover virtually *all* New York pupils.

There are some special breakdowns of the data by community type and by percentages scoring below an established Statewide Reference Point. For different communities the trend in average percentile test scores for grade 6 is shown on the following table.

As far as the *trend* of grade 6 Reading and Mathematics achievement is concerned, New York City pupils have had the *least* achievement loss among all community types considered. Achievement in New York State for grade 6 has fallen faster in the suburban areas than it has in the New

GRADE 6

	1966	1967	1968	1969	1970	1971	1972	1973
Reading								
New York City	37	36	37	34	32	32	32	NA[*]
Large Cities	47	44	42	40	38	35	35	NA
Medium Cities	54	52	51	48	47	46	45	NA
Small Cities	53	52	52	50	48	47	47	NA
Vl & Lg Central	59	58	57	56	54	53	53	NA
Large Rural	55	53	54	51	51	49	48	NA
Small Rural	52	50	50	50	48	47	46	NA
Total State	50	49	49	47	44	44	44	44
Mathematics								
New York City	34	30	32	30	28	30	29	NA
Large Cities	49	48	46	39	37	33	33	NA
Medium Cities	51	50	48	46	43	43	42	NA
Small Cities	54	52	51	48	46	44	43	NA
Vl & Lg Central	58	56	54	54	51	50	49	NA
Large Rural	59	54	53	51	50	47	45	NA
Small Rural	59	56	54	52	50	47	45	NA
Total State	50	47	47	44	42	41	41	39

[*]Not available.

York City school system. Of course the New York City scores are the lowest and the fact that these tests are multiple choice may mean that New York City public schools, particularly in mathematics, may be approaching the lowest point possible on these tests.

The New York State Education Department also issues the yearly percentage of pupils in each grade who score *below* a certain statewide standard. This standard was defined to be the lower 23 percent scores according to the 1966 administration of the PEP test. The percentage of students annually falling into this is used for policy-making and resource-allocation purposes. The statewide reference points do not change from year to year so that a comparison over time is possible just as it was for the statewide median raw score percentiles. Therefore, they both provide baselines against which the state can measure educational effectiveness over time. In grade 3 Reading, for example, if fewer pupils score below the Statewide Reference Point in subsequent years than in 1966, this reduction indicates improvement in the reading skills of grade 3 pupils.

A glance at the percent of pupils in this "below average achievement range" from 1966 to 1972 reveals the same trend as in the statewide median percentile scores.

PERCENT OF PUPILS SCORING BELOW AVERAGE
IN STATEWIDE ACHIEVEMENT RANGES

	1966	1967	1968	1969	1970	1971	1972
Grade 3							
Reading	23	23	22	23	24	24	23
Mathematics	23	22	20	20	19	19	18
Grade 6							
Reading	23	24	24	25	27	27	27
Mathematics	23	25	25	27	29	29	30
Grade 9							
Reading	NA*	NA	NA	NA	NA	NA	30
Mathematics	NA	NA	NA	NA	NA	NA	32

*Not available.

Grade 3 is apparently improving over time and grade 6 is declining. While no time series data are available for grade 9, the nearly universal pattern of higher grades doing worse is present: 1966, 23 percent; 1972, 30 and 32 percent.

It is important to keep in perspective the reason for the growth or decline of percentages of pupils falling below the Statewide Reference Point. The fact that there have been increases in grade 6 target groups should not be viewed in isolation from the effectiveness of the rest of the state educational system. If one views it alone, one might conclude that the problem is one of special groups of students performing poorly for some reason. However, when it is looked at with the decline in the statewide median scores, one sees that the increase in percentage of the priority group is caused more by a gradual diminution in quality of the entire system. It is likely that there is a greater percentage of grade 6 underachievers because there is a greater percentage of students scoring lower *on the average*. The *entire distribution* of grade 6 test scores has been shifting downward, not just those from any particular achievement level. Discussions centering on resource allocation for pupils below the Statewide Reference Point must consider the tendency of the entire system to deteriorate in achievement, which can be seen if one looks at the percent of pupils scoring below the Statewide Reference Point over time broken down by community type.

The fact that achievement loss is centered on *all* types of communities makes it difficult to accept the notion that any local changes in population or racial makeup of communities is causing the drop.

PERCENT OF GRADE 6 PUPILS SCORING BELOW
STATEWIDE REFERENCE POINT, 1966-1972

	1966	1967	1968	1969	1970	1971	1972
Reading							
New York City	36	36	36	39	40	40	39
Large Cities	23	25	28	30	32	36	36
Medium Cities	19	19	20	22	24	24	25
Small Cities	17	18	18	20	22	22	22
Vl & Lg Central	13	14	14	16	17	17	17
Large Rural	16	17	17	19	19	20	21
Small Rural	18	18	19	19	20	22	23
Mathematics							
New York City	38	41	40	42	44	42	42
Large Cities	21	22	25	30	33	37	37
Medium Cities	20	20	22	23	26	27	28
Small Cities	16	18	18	20	22	24	25
Vl & Lg Central	13	15	16	16	19	20	20
Large Rural	13	16	17	18	20	21	23
Small Rural	13	15	16	17	19	21	22

In summary, following the general trend of the lower grades doing better than the upper grades, grade 3 achievement in New York State has been holding steady in reading and had been improving in mathematics since 1966. The higher grades have been steadily declining in achievement with grade 9 doing worse than grade 6. Achievement has fallen fastest *outside* New York City, and contrary to the grade 3 trend, mathematics achievement has fallen faster than reading in grades 6 and 9.

NORTH CAROLINA

The Division of Research in the North Carolina Department of Instruction administers a statewide testing program of pupils in grade 6. Although school participation in the program is not required, 100 percent of eligible schools participated. About 12,000 grade 6 students were tested as a representative probability sample of all sixth graders.

Test results are only available for a single year (1971–72) so there is no way to study North Carolina's educational system over time. The testing instruments used were the Iowa Tests of Basic Skills and the Lorge-Thorndike Intelligence Test.[23]

Test	Median		Averages in North Carolina	
	State	Nation	White	Nonwhite
IQ	94.4	100	98.6	85.1
Reading	57	67	63.0	49.4
Vocabulary	57	67	61.5	46.6
Language Skills	58	66	63.6	50.8
Mathematics	58	66	63.3	52.1

North Carolina is below the national median in all areas of achievement.
Some final statistics reveal the growth of innovative practices within North Carolina schools. While there has been a national trend in the late 1960s toward the use of such innovations, it is rare that reliable quantitative estimates of their growth are available.

PERCENTAGE OF SCHOOLS WITH PROGRAMS/INNOVATIONS

Program/Innovation	1968-69	1969-70	1970-71	1971-72
1. Using a competitive grading system (A-B-C)	78.0%	77.3%	70.1%	69.6%
2. Using a non-competitive grading system	15.2	21.3	35.6	40.6
3. Team teaching for Math	13.8	20.2	28.6	34.9
4. Non-graded classes	8.4	12.7	14.3	16.6
5. Open classroom concept	4.1	6.6	13.6	28.8
6. Teachers using behavioral objectives	27.7	29.5	45.1	54.9
7. Special resource centers (other than the library)	23.8	29.3	42.2	54.9
8. School has regular meeting advisory committee of students	11.6	13.8	21.3	27.0
9. Instructional media ("listening" centers, single concept film loop, cassette tapes, T.V., etc.)	56.9	66.7	81.2	88.2

OHIO

The Ohio Survey Test program is administered to pupils in grades 4, 6, 8, and 10. Participation by the schools is optional, but most schools take part in the program. Data for grades 8 and 10 are shown. Grades 4 and 6 are not included because of difficulties in obtaining interpretations. The interested reader may consult the official state reports for the raw data from all tests for all years.[24]

GRADE 8

	1968(Jan.)	1968(Nov.)	1969(Nov.)	1970(Nov.)	1972(Jan.)
Total Ability	59.9	59.4	59.0	59.2	58.6
Reading	38.5	37.9	37.5	37.1	NA*
English	51.5	50.6	50.1	49.5	48.8
Mathematics	27.0	26.5	26.2	25.8	25.2

GRADE 10

	1968(Jan.)	1968(Nov.)	1969(Nov.)	1970(Nov.)	1972(Jan.)
Total Ability	61.4	60.5	61.1	60.3	60.1
Reading	37.7	37.2	36.9	36.4	NA*
English	49.9	49.3	48.8	47.9	46.8
Mathematics	28.4	27.9	27.5	27.1	26.7

*Not available.

We see in both grades the loss over time of skills in the basic subject areas. Test changes were made in the 1972–73 administration so that continuation of the trend is impossible to interpret. Note that for both grades achievement consistently falls off—even when there is an increase in total ability.

RHODE ISLAND

The Rhode Island Department of Education administers the Iowa Tests of Basic Skills and the Lorge-Thorndike Intelligence Test to pupils in grades

4 and 8. Participation of all students is required by law. Only data for the October 1972 administration are available.

AVERAGE ACHIEVEMENT SCORES
(IN NATIONAL PERCENTILE)

GRADE FOUR

Vocabulary	45
Reading	46
Mathematics	46
Total IQ	100.9
Language	49

GRADE EIGHT

Vocabulary	50
Reading	53
Mathematics	53
Total IQ	102.1
Language	55

SOURCE: *A Report of Achievement Test Information,*
Fall 1972, Rhode Island Dept. of Education, Oct. 1973.

Although grade 4 scores are uniformly below the national norm, grade 8 scores are above it, a phenomenon that seems to be the reverse of the general trend of lower grades doing better than upper grades in recent years. Unfortunately, data for one year do not allow us to assess the effectiveness of Rhode Island's schools over time. However, it is notable that these scores are above the national average.

SOUTH CAROLINA

South Carolina has a statewide testing program for grades 4, 7, 9, and 12. In 1972–73, all fourth and seventh grade students in participating schools and a sample of ninth and twelfth grade students were tested. Approximately 85 percent of eligible students were tested—about 105,000 pupils.

The instruments used for grades 4 and 7 were the Comprehensive Tests

of Basic Skills and the Short Form Test of Academic Aptitudes. Grades 9
and 12 took the Iowa Tests of Educational Development.

SOUTH CAROLINA STATEWIDE TESTING PROGRAM RESULTS:
PUPILS BELOW THE NATIONAL MEDIAN*
(PERCENT)

	Grade 4	Grade 7	Grade 9	Grade 12
Reading	69.6	73.0	71.7	67.2
Language	71.3	71.9	67.1	63.5
Mathematics	72.9	82.9	67.7	64.9
Social Studies	NT**	NT	66.7	68.2
Science	NT	NT	69.4	67.5

*National Median = 50.0%.

**Not tested.

SOURCE: *Initial Report of the Fall 1972 South Carolina Statewide Testing Program,*
Vol. 1, No. 1, May 1973, State Dept. of Education.

Unfortunately, South Carolina changed tests in 1973 from CTBS Form
Q to CTBS Form S. However, it is more than evident that South Carolina
is substantially below the national average in *all* grades for *all* achievement
areas. Grade 7 Mathematics appears to be the area most in need of improvement. One feature that is evident is that, unlike most other states, South
Carolina has a fairly even distribution of underachievers across the grades.

SOUTH DAKOTA

South Dakota has had a yearly statewide testing program for many years.
Grades 9 and 11 take the Iowa Tests of Educational Development (ITED).[25]
Although participation is not required in the program, about 95 percent of
the eligible schools participate.

Beginning in the 1970 administration, ITED was revised and renormed.
Consequently, the scores for 1970, 1971, and 1972 are not really comparable
to the previous data. However, they are comparable to themselves.

The scores are presented as the mean percentile score in terms of a
national average.

The interesting feature of these data is their consistency—up to 1970.
Notice the last three years show general declines. These scores are comparable since they were made on the same test. Although grade 11 scores for

GRADE 9

	1960	61	62	63	64	65	66	67	68	69	70	71	72
Social Studies	61	68	68	67	67	67	67	59	59	59	59	57	47
Natural Sciences	69	75	75	56	56	56	62	56	62	62	62	54	54
Correctness of Expression	66	66	66	61	68	68	68	68	68	68	-	-	-
Quantitative	75	75	75	75	75	75	80	69	75	75	69	59	59
Reading Lit.	66	66	66	61	61	61	61	61	61	61	-	-	-
Vocabulary	59	66	66	57	57	57	63	63	57	57	57	53	49

GRADE 11

	1960	61	62	63	64	65	66	67	68	69	70	71	72
Social Studies	62	62	67	65	65	59	65	65	59	59	59	50	50
Natural Sciences	59	59	65	60	60	60	60	60	65	60	60	54	54
Correctness of Expression	57	57	57	55	55	63	63	63	63	63	-	-	-
Quantitative	68	68	68	68	68	68	68	68	72	68	64	58	58
Reading Lit.	57	63	63	55	55	55	55	60	55	55	-	-	-
Vocabulary	56	56	63	57	57	57	57	57	57	57	57	47	47

1972 are the same as in 1971, they are significantly below the 1970 scores. Over the final three years, the largest drops have been in grade 9 Quantitative (Mathematics) and grade 11 Vocabulary. Between 1960 and 1967 for grade 11 there appears to have been an increase in achievement in all areas except mathematics, which held its own. This shows the importance of a time-series look at achievement; the longer sequences demonstrate that in the early 1960s, *gains* in achievement were more usual. Note also that South Dakota is still above the national average in a majority of areas.

TEXAS

The Texas Education Agency Needs Assessment Program tests sixth grade pupils in reading and mathematics.[26] As in the case of New Jersey, the tests are criterion referenced, and data are available only for 1971. Thus, it is not possible to compare Texas with itself over time or even with other states or the nation. However, the test results do point to the internal strengths and weaknesses of educational achievement.

The findings for reading can briefly be summarized as follows:

> The performance of girls was superior to that of boys, particularly on those objectives concerned with study skills.
>
> On all objectives the white students outperformed both the Mexican-Americans and the Negroes.
>
> The Mexican-Americans outperformed the Negroes.
>
> Suburban communities had the highest percentage of achievers.
>
> Cities of over 500,000 had the lowest percentage of achievers.

The findings for mathematics were identical.
An example of the kind of math problems given on the test is:

$$\begin{array}{r} 20{,}408 \\ -\,19{,}535 \end{array}$$

Only 57 percent of the grade 6 pupils could solve this subtraction. Fractions seemed to be a particular weakness of the students; for example, only 1 percent of the sixth graders could solve the following problem:

$$\tfrac{7}{8} \div 3\tfrac{2}{3} = ?$$

The difficulty in summarizing criterion-referenced tests is the tendency to pick out the highlights. Examining those problems where students scored particularly high and low does not reveal the totality of what these tests were designed to measure. However, students seem to score higher on "conceptual areas" than they do on areas involving computational skill.

UTAH

Utah does not have a statewide testing program. However, the performance of Utah pupils is reflected in a publication that compared Utah with the rest of the nation.[27]

All grades are considered and are lumped into this assessment. The result is shown:[28]

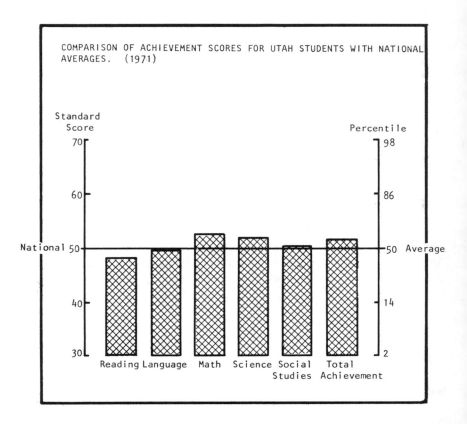

COMPARISON OF ACHIEVEMENT SCORES FOR UTAH STUDENTS WITH NATIONAL AVERAGES. (1971)

NOTE: Reprinted from "How Good Are Utah Schools?" Utah State Board of Education, 1971.

Since there is no breakdown by grade, it is impossible to detect differences by grade level. However, an earlier 1967 study in Utah found that Utah pupils compared better nationally in the early than the later grades. The 1971 data show Utah students above the national average in most areas. It is impossible to conclude very much about Utah for the past few years due to the lack of recent data.

WEST VIRGINIA

West Virginia has a State-County Testing Program for students in grades 3, 6, 9, and 11. Approximately 119,000 pupils were tested in 1972. Schools are required to participate in the program. The instrument used in all grades was the STS Educational Development Series. See the table on page 252.

In West Virginia there is no strong trend up or down in achievement test scores overall. Grade 9 appears to have been falling in the area of basic skills while increasing in academic ability. Grade 3 has had random changes in ability and a small decline in basic skills achievement in 1973–74. Grade 12 has been holding steady in achievement and improving in ability.

In the higher grades, ability seems to have been improving, with achievement either holding steady or slightly declining.

Grade 11 is only below the national norm by a slight amount. It is much closer to this "national average" than almost all other states. When one considers the popular notions about education in Appalachia, this is somewhat surprising. The fact that grade 11 achieves more than Grade 6 or grade 9 is also surprising since the reverse tendency seems to hold in most other areas.

PHILADELPHIA

The School District of Philadelphia administers a testing program for the city's public school students. Tests were given for grades K and 1 for the first time in 1972 and for grades 2 through 8 since 1968. Grades 3 through 8 have been taking the Iowa Tests of Basic Skills,[29] and year-to-year comparisons are possible. The results for the ITBS in grades 3 through 8 are shown on page 253 expressed in terms of the national percentile rank of the Philadelphia public school median score. Tests were not given in 1973 due to a teachers' strike in the early part of the year.

Again we see the steady pattern of the lower grades (3 and 4), with the higher grades exhibiting significant and steady declines in achievement. In fact the critical turning point seems to be well defined for these data.

WEST VIRGINIA

	1970-1971	1971-1972	1972-1973	1973-1974
		GRADE 3		
Total Ability	3.6	3.5	3.6	3.5
Basic Skills	3.6	3.6	3.6	3.5
National Norm	3.7	3.7	3.7	3.7
		GRADE 6		
Total Ability	6.5	6.5	6.5	6.5
Basic Skills	6.4	6.4	6.4	6.3
National Norm	6.7	6.7	6.7	6.7
		GRADE 9		
Total Ability	8.9	8.8	8.8	9.0
Basic Skills	8.9	8.8	8.7	8.7
National Norm	9.2	9.2	9.2	9.2
		GRADE 11		
Total Ability	10.9	10.9	11.1	11.0
Basic Skills	11.1	11.1	11.1	11.1
National Norm	11.2	11.2	11.2	11.2

SOURCE: West Virginia Dept. of Education, *Eleventh Report: State-County Testing Program.*

The striking feature about Philadelphia grade 7 achievement in reading and mathematics is its remarkably low level. In 1972, for example, the median public school Arithmetic score was at the 13th percentile. This means that *half* of these students fell below the national 13th percentile. For grade 8 there is a sharp decline in 1969 scores compared to those of 1968. However, recent data for 1974, 1975, and 1976 indicate a possible turnaround in Philadelphia scores. Grades 5, 6, 7, and 8 all had *higher* reading and mathematics scores in 1976 than in 1974.[30]

PHILADELPHIA CITY-WIDE TESTING PROGRAM
IOWA TESTS OF BASIC SKILLS
NATIONAL PERCENTILE RANK OF MEDIAN SCORE*

	Reading	Vocabulary	Total Language	Total Work Study	Arithmetic
Grade 3					
1968	29	30	35	–	32
1969	29	30	35	–	30
1970	29	30	35	–	32
1971	29	33	35	–	32
1972	29	35	35	–	32
Grade 4				–	
1968	21	22	22	–	22
1969	21	22	22	–	22
1970	21	22	27	–	22
1971	21	22	25	–	22
1972	21	24	25	–	22
Grade 5					
1968	22	23	22	21	23
1969	22	26	24	21	20
1970	16	21	22	14	18
1971	16	19	22	14	16
1972	18	23	22	17	18
Grade 6					
1968	22	27	23	22	21
1969	20	27	24	22	19
1970	17	23	23	18	15
1971	14	21	19	16	13
1972	17	24	21	18	15
Grade 7					
1968	22	26	26	21	16
1969	22	25	25	23	18
1970	21	25	25	21	15
1971	16	20	20	18	13
1972	16	23	23	20	13
Grade 8					
1968	23	28	28	25	18
1969	20	24	24	21	16
1970	20	22	22	21	16
1971	17	22	22	20	13
1972	17	22	22	21	14

*National norm for all grades in all areas is 50.

SOURCE: "1971–72 Philadelphia City-Wide Testing Program," Spring 1972 Achievement Testing Program, City Performance Distribution and Medians, Office of Research and Evaluation, Division of Testing, School District of Philadelphia, 72–146-G, June 1972.

NOTES

1. SCHOOL BUDGETS

1. U.S. Census Bureau, *U.S. Stat. Abst.: 1975* (Wash.: GPO, 1975), p. 111, table 176. HEW, *Dig. of Educ. Stat.: 1975,* Pub. No. NCES 76–211 (Wash.: GPO, 1976), pp. 6, 24. (See list of abbreviated forms, p. 14.)

2. HEW, *Dig. of Educ. Stat.: 1975,* pp. 6, 24.

3. Ibid., p. 71, table 71.

4. U.S. Census Bureau, *U.S. Stat. Abst. 1975,* p. 111, table 176. HEW, *Dig. of Educ. Stat.: 1975,* p. 6, table 1. and p. 71, table 71.

5. Tax Credits for Nonpublic Education. Hearings Before the Committee on Ways and Means, House of Representatives, 92nd Congress, Part 1 (Aug. 14–16, 1972), pp. 68, 94, 97.

6. HEW, *Dig. of Educ. Stat.: 1975,* p. 71, table 71.

7. HEW, National Center for Education Statistics, *The Condition of Education: 1976,* Pub. No. NCES 76–400 (Wash.: GPO 1976), p. 9, chart 1.6.

8. U.S. Census Bureau, *U.S. Stat. Abst.: 1973,* (Wash.: GPO, 1973), p. 257, table 404. HEW, *Dig. of Educ. Stat.: 1973,* Pub. No. (OE) 74–11103 (Wash.: GPO, 1974) p. 25, table 27.

9. *U.S. News & World Report,* Sept. 13, 1976, p. 32.

10. HEW, *Dig. of Educ. Stat.: 1975,* p. 24, table 21.

11. This figure was derived by upping the per-pupil expenditure for 1950 ($331.33) as it appears in Vol. 1, p. 17, of *The Fleischmann Report on the Quality, Cost, and Financing of Elementary and Secondary Education in New York State* (New York: The Viking Press, 1973) to $400 and multiplying that number by about 2 million pupils (ibid., p. 5) to equate to the figure of $8 billion in the next line. The original $331.33 figure did not contain capital and other costs; the 1973–74 figure contains such costs.

12. The New York *Times,* Oct. 1, 1976, p. B2.

13. HEW, *Dig. of Educ. Stat.: 1975,* p. 67, table 68.

14. *The Fleischmann Report on the Quality, Cost, and Financing of Elementary and Secondary Education in New York State* (New York: The Viking Press, 1973), Vol. 1, p. 5.

15. HEW, *Dig. of Educ. Stat.: 1973,* p. 30, table 29.

16. HEW, *Dig. of Educ. Stat.: 1975,* p. 32, table 26.

17. Ibid., p. 71, table 71.

18. Ibid.

19. Ibid.

20. See 1976–77 school budgets for school districts in Rockland and Westchester counties, e.g., Nyack School District, a medium-income area in Rockland County.

21. Mark R. Arnold, "Public Schools," in Sar A. Levitan, ed., *The Federal Social Dollar in Its Own Back Yard* (Washington, D.C.: U.S. Bureau of National Affairs, 1973), p. 41.

22. Ibid.

23. HEW, *Expenditures and Revenues for Public Elementary and Secondary Education: 1970–71,* Pub. No. (OE) 73–11407 (Wash.: GPO, 1973), pp. 8, 9.

24. HEW, *Dig. of Educ. Stat.: 1975,* p. 67, table 68. See also *Expenditures and Revenues for Public Elementary and Secondary Education: 1970–71* for a breakdown of costs of "local" vs. "state and intermediate administrators."

25. HEW, *Dig. of Educ. Stat.: 1975,* pp. 33, 67.

26. *The Fleischmann Report,* Vol. 1, pp. 18, 19, 22.

27. See pp. 117, 118; 179–181.

28. *The Fleischmann Report,* Vol. I, pp. 18, 19, 22.

29. HEW, *Dig. of Educ. Stat.: 1975,* pp. 33, 51.

30. HEW, *Statistics of Public Elementary and Secondary Day Schools: Fall 1973,* Pub. No. (OE) 73–11402 (Wash.: GPO, 1973), pp. 23, 24.

31. HEW, *Dig. of Educ. Stat.: 1975,* p. 54, table 52.

32. Ibid.

33. U.S. Census Bureau, *U.S. Stat. Abst.: 1975,* p. 370, table 603.

34. HEW, *Dig. of Educ. Stat.: 1975,* p. 33, table 27.

35. The New York *Times,* Jan. 16, 1974, p. 20.

36. HEW, *Dig. of Educ. Stat.: 1975,* p. 55.

37. Derived from U.S. Census Bureau, *Current Population Reports,* P-60, No. 85, Dec. 1972, "Money Income in 1971 of Families and Persons in the U.S." (Wash.: GPO, 1972), pp. 112–19, 155–57.

38. HEW, *Dig. of Educ. Stat.: 1975,* p. 55.

39. Derived from U.S. Census Bureau, *Current Population Reports,* P-60, No. 101, Jan. 1976, "Money Income in 1974 of Families and Persons in the U.S." (Wash.: GPO, 1976), pp. 113–14, 116–20.

40. U.S. Census Bureau, *U.S. Stat. Abst.: 1972* (Wash.: GPO, 1972), p. 112.

41. HEW, *Dig. of Educ. Stat.: 1973,* Pub. No. (OE) 74–11103 (Wash.: GPO, 1974), p. 11, table 10.

42. U.S. Census Bureau, *U.S. Stat. Abst.: 1975,* p. 131.

43. U.S. Census Bureau, *Current Population Reports,* P-60, No. 101, Jan. 1976, "Money Income in 1974 of Families and Persons in the U.S.," (Wash.: GPO, 1976), pp. 113–116, 120.

44. U.S. Census Bureau, *U.S. Stat. Abst.: 1975,* p. 131.

45. HEW, *Dig. of Educ. Stat.: 1975,* p. 50.

46. U.S. Census Bureau, *Current Population Reports,* P-60, No. 101, Jan. 1976, "Money Income in 1974 of Families and Persons in the U.S.," (Wash.: GPO, 1976), pp. 112–13, 116, 120.

47. James B. Conant, *The Education of American Teachers* (New York: McGraw-Hill, 1963), p. 237.

48. U.S. Census Bureau, *U.S. Stat. Abst.: 1973,* p. 130.

49. U.S. Census Bureau, *Current Population Reports,* P-60, No. 101, Jan. 1976, "Money Income in 1974 of Families and Persons in the U.S.," (Wash.: GPO, 1976), p. 116.

50. "Once a teacher or administrator is hired he can be reasonably assured of tenure regardless of his performance." Quoted from *The National Observer,* Mar. 9, 1974, p. 22.

51. *U.S. News & World Report,* Oct. 4, 1976, p. 31.

52. Ibid.

53. The New York *Times,* Sept. 22, 1974, p. 1.

54. Ibid., Aug. 4, 1974, Section E, p. 9.

55. See Chap. 8.

3. A LONGITUDINAL STUDY OF ACADEMIC ACHIEVEMENT

1. In summarizing this study, however, Archibald W. Anderson apparently did not realize this and stated:

> In spite of the fact that the unselected group of 1919 pupils were being compared with a highly selected group of "superior" 1845 pupils, and in spite of the fact that the 1919 pupils were taking some examinations on subjects no longer taught as such, they did much better on the examinations as a whole than the pupils of 1845. The median score for the 1919 group was 45.5 as compared with a median score of 37.5 for the 1845 group. In general, the 1919 pupils tended "to make lower scores on pure memory and abstract-skill questions, and higher scores on thought and meaningful questions."

> —As quoted in C. Winfield Scott and Clyde M. Hill, eds., *Public Education under Criticism* (Englewood Cliffs, NJ: Prentice-Hall, 1954), p. 277. Anderson's study originally appeared in "The Charges Against American Education: What Is the Evidence?" *Progressive Education* 31 (1952), 91–105.

2. Otis W. Caldwell and Stuart A. Courtis, *Then and Now in Education, 1845–1923: A Message of Encouragement from the Past to the Present* (Yonkers, NY: World Book, 1924).

3. D. A. Worcester and Anne Kline, *Reading Achievement in Lincoln, Nebraska, Schools 1921 and 1947* (Lincoln, Neb.: Univ. of Nebraska Teachers College, 1947).

4. Arthur I. Gates, *Reading Attainment in Elementary Schools: 1957 and 1937* (New York: Teachers College Press, 1961), p. 20.

5. Diane Ravitch, *The Great School Wars, New York City 1805–1973: A History of the Public Schools As Battlefield of Social Change* (New York: Basic Books, 1974), p. 237.

6. Although testing in this program is not mandatory, the participation rate is quite high.

7. Minutes of the Conference of Directors of State Testing Programs, Educational Testing Service, Princeton, NJ Nov. 4–5, 1973, p. 2. From a discussion of Dallis Perry, "A Loss in Test Scores, The Minnesota Experience," Univ. of Minn., 1972.

8. Benjamin S. Bloom, "The 1955 Normative Study of the Tests of General Educational Development," *School Review* 64 (1956) 110–24.

9. It is interesting to note that a study funded by the HEW on reading achievement in 1971 cited the Gates study and summarized it based on age rather than grade, *with no mention of the superiority of 1937 children by grade:*

> Gates (1961a) compared the reading achievement of children tested in 1957 with the attainment of children tested 20 years earlier in 1937. Some 31,000 children were tested in 1957 with the test on which the 1937 norms were based. Gates reported that 1957 children in the range from grades 4 to 6.5 reached a particular level of reading ability about 5 months earlier than did the 1937 pupils. Essentially, compared to 1937, 1957 pupils were about a half year advanced.

> —Reginald Corder, "The Information Base for Reading: A Critical Review of the Information Base for Current Assumptions Regarding the Status of Instruction and Achievement in Reading in the United States," Educational Testing Service, Berkeley, Calif., 1971, p. 49. Prepared for the U.S. Office of Education, Grant No. OEC–0–70–4792 (508).

This citation is included to exemplify the frequently low-quality studies that unfortunately plague educational research. Failure to mention the grade comparison criteria leads to some very misleading concepts about comparative education.

10. Joseph R. Sligo, "Comparison of Achievement in Selected High School Subjects in 1934 and 1954" (Ph.D. diss., State Univ. of Iowa, 1955).

11. William B. Schrader, "Test Data As Social Indicators," Educational Testing Service, Statistical Report Nos. 68–77, Princeton, NJ, Sept. 1968.

12. A. N. Hieronymus and E. F. Lindquist, *Manual for Administrators, Supervisors, and Counselors,* Levels Ed., *Forms 5 & 6, Iowa Tests of Basic Skills* (Boston: Houghton Mifflin, 1974).

13. Donald Ross Green, Senior Research Psychologist, CTB/McGraw-Hill, Monterey, Calif. to Richard A. Shaffer, *Wall Street Journal,* Apr. 1, 1974.

14. Stephen A. Roderick, "A Comparative Study of Mathematics Achievement by Sixth Graders and Eighth Graders, 1936 to 1973, 1951–55 to 1973, and 1965 to 1973" (Ph.D. diss., Univ. of Iowa, July 1973).

15. Ibid., pp. 255–56.

16. Iowa Tests of Educational Development Forms X-5 and Y-5, Science Research Associates, 1972.

17. John C. Flanagan and Steven M. Jung, *Progress in Education: A Sample Survey (1960–1970)*, 2nd ed. (Palo Alto, Calif.: American Institutes for Research, Sept. 1972), p. 12.

4. TRENDS IN RECENT ACHIEVEMENT TESTS

1. See the Appendix, pp. 231–232.

2. Ibid., pp. 245–246.

3. Ibid., pp. 247–248.

4. Ibid., pp. 250–251.

5. Ibid., pp. 251–252.

6. Ibid., pp. 230–231.

7. See Appendix.

8. An exception apparently occurs in mathematics achievement in Michigan. See the Appendix, pp. 229–230.

9. See the Appendix, pp. 232–233, 249.

10. See the Appendix, pp. 214–218 and 238–243, and Calif. State Dept. of Education, *Profiles of School District Performance, California State Testing Program, 1971–72 and 1972–73,* Sacramento, 1974.

11. See the Appendix.

12. This phenomenon was noted by the New York press in the 1972–73 time period.

13. See the Appendix, pp. 251–253.

14. 1975–76 Phila. City-Wide Testing Program, *February 1976 Achievement Testing Program, Citywide Summaries,* Report #7692, Office of Research and Evaluation, May 1976, pp. 33, 34.

15. See the Appendix, p. 241.

16. The New York *Times,* Mar. 18, 1973, p. 1.

17. Mark R. Arnold, "Public Schools," in Sar A. Levitan, ed., *The Federal Social Dollar in Its Own Back Yard* (Washington, D.C.: U.S. Bureau of National Affairs, 1973), p. 25.

18. Ibid., p. 43.

19. The New York *Times,* Feb. 15, 1974, p. 16.

20. Ibid., Apr. 30, 1973, p. 64.

21. Ibid., Nov. 2, 1974, p. 32.

22. Ibid., Feb. 15, 1974, p. 16.

23. Ibid., p. 16.

24. Ibid., Dec. 24, 1974, pp. 1, 17.

25. Ibid., Oct. 3, 1975, p. 45.

26. Ibid.

27. Los Angeles *Times,* Aug. 15, 1976, p. 23.

28. 1975–76 Phila. City-Wide Testing Program, *February 1976 Achievement Testing Program, Citywide Summaries,* Report #7692, Office of Research and Evaluation, May 1976, pp. 33, 34.

29. *Profiles of School District Performance,* and *California State Testing Pro-*

gram 1971–72 and 1972–73, Calif. State Dept. of Education, Sacramento, 1974, p. 34.

30. Ibid., p. 318.

31. Ibid., pp. 53–56.

32. Ibid., p. 364.

33. Ibid., p. 363.

34. Ibid., p. 426.

35. See further along in this study and the Appendix for some demographic data on shifting minorities and their inferior achievement records, as well as data on the trivial shift in California over this time period. See also the Appendix, pp. 233–238, for information on improvement in Negro achievement in New Mexico while Anglo achievement remained unchanged.

36. U.S. Census Bureau, *U.S. Stat. Abst.: 1974* (Wash.: GPO, 1974), p. 110, table 173. (See list of abbreviated forms, p. 14.)

37. U.S. Census Bureau, *U.S. Stat. Abst.: 1975* (Washington, D.C.: GPO, 1975), p. 111.

38. Data obtained from the College Entrance Examination Board, New York, NY.

39. William H. Angoff, ed., *The College Board Admissions Testing Program: A Technical Report on Research and Development Activities Relating to the Scholastic Aptitude Test and Achievement Tests* (New York: College Entrance Examination Board, 1971).

40. The New York *Times,* Dec. 16, 1973, p. 26 L.

41. *National Report, ATP, College-Bound Seniors, 1975–1976,* Admissions Testing Program of the College Entrance Examination Board, pp. 6–7.

42. *Time* magazine, Dec. 31, 1973, p. 45.

43. *National Report, ATP,* pp. 7–9, and data obtained from the College Entrance Examination Board.

44. *Time* magazine, Dec. 31, 1973, p. 45.

45. The New York *Times,* Dec. 16, 1973, p. 26 L.

46. *Time* magazine, Dec. 31, 1973, p. 45.

47. The New York *Times,* Dec. 16, 1973, pp. 1, 26L.

48. Karl Shapiro, "Is This Really the Brightest Student Generation?" speech before the California Library Association, San Francisco, as reported in *Human Events,* July 11, 1970.

49. Los Angeles *Times,* Aug. 15, 1976, p. 26.

50. J. Mitchell Morse, "Riting Inglish Real Good," The New York *Times,* Oct. 21, 1976, p. 39 (Op Ed).

51. Los Angeles *Times,* Aug. 15, 1976, p. 26.

52. The New York *Times,* Nov. 7, 1974, p. 47.

53. Morris Kline, *Why Johnny Can't Add: The Failure of the New Math* (New York: St. Martin's Press, 1973), pp. 111, 112.

54. Joseph J. Schwab, *College Curriculum and Student Protest* (Chicago: the Univ. of Chicago Press, 1969), p. 36.

55. The New York *Times,* June 29, 1973, p. 40, quoting the secretary of HEW, Casper W. Weinberger.

56. "The 1971 National Reading Difficulty Index: A Study of Functional Reading Ability in the U.S. for The National Reading Center," Aug. 1971, Louis Harris and Associates.

57. HEW, *National Health Survey,* Series 11, No. 131, Dec. 1973, "Literacy Among Youths 12–17 Years: U.S.," Pub. No. (HRA) 74–1613 (Wash.: GPO, 1973), App. 1, p. 1.

58. Wallace Roberts, "Right to Read: Lost in PR," *The Washington Monthly,* Sept. 1973, p. 35.

59. U.S. Census Bureau, *U.S. Stat. Abst.: 1973* (Wash.: GPO, 1973), p. 115, table 175.

60. The New York *Times,* Feb. 20, 1972, p. 55.

61. Dr. Jerome Kagan, Harvard Univ., "The Poor *Are* Educable," The New York *Times,* Jan. 16, 1974, p. 81.

62. *The Fleischmann Report on the Quality, Cost, and Financing of Elementary and Secondary Education in New York State* (New York: The Viking Press, 1973), Vol. 1, pp. 33–37.

63. Los Angeles *Times,* Aug. 17, 1976, p. 1.

64. *The Citizen Register* (Ossining, NY), Oct. 18, 1976, p. A2.

65. Education Commission of the States, *National Assessment of Educational Progress Newsletter,* Aug. 1976, p. 9.

66. National Assessment of Educational Progress, *Reading in America, A Perspective on Two Assessments,* Oct. 1976, pp. xi, 5–21.

67. The New York *Times,* Sept. 22, 1976, p. 1.

68. Los Angeles *Times,* Aug. 15, 1976, p. 26.

69. Education Commission of the States, *National Assessment of Educational Progress Newsletter,* Aug. 1976, p. 7.

70. Ibid., p. 9.

71. See p. 64 for the "bottoming out" of automatic promotions through sixth grade between 1970 and 1974, which may affect this.

72. See pp. 57–58 and *National Report, ATP.*

73. See pp. 36–39 for the greater rate of improvement of the lower tenth percentile on the ITBS tests while the whole group was rising.

74. See pp. 56–59; and *National Report, ATP.*

5. IQ LEVELS FROM WORLD WAR I TO THE PRESENT

1. Read D. Tuddenham, "Soldier Intelligence in World Wars I and II," *American Psychologist* 3 (1948), pp. 54–56.

2. Robert M. Yerkes, ed., *Psychological Examining in the United States Army,* Vol. 15, Memoirs of the National Academy of Sciences, 1921.

3. Christopher Jencks et al., *Inequality: A Reassessment of the Effect of Family and Schooling in America* (New York: Basic Books, 1972).

4. There are theoretical reasons for this phenomenon, but they are beyond the

scope of the present discussion. The interested reader can consult Robert Cancro, *Intelligence, Genetic and Environmental Influences* (New York: Grune and Stratton, 1971).

5. Lester R. Wheeler, "A Comparative Study of the Intelligence of East Tennessee Mountain Children," *Journal of Educational Psychology* 33 (1942), 321.

6. See the Appendix, pp. 214–218.

7. Ibid.

6. SOME INTERPRETATIONS OF IQ DATA

1. See the Appendix.

2. Los Angeles *Times,* Aug. 16, 1976, p. 3.

3. See the previous chapter for the drop in mean AFQT score and Categories I and II (the brightest men) in 1955. Some data that show no such trough in the mid-1950s AFQT scores can be found on p. 71.

4. See p. 1–2–5 of *The Report of the President's Commission on an All Volunteer Army* for a drop in the percentage of "Trainables" (total Categories I, II, and Upper III) in Navy recruits in 1955 and 1956.

5. Read D. Tuddenham, "Soldier Intelligence in World Wars I and II," *American Psychologist* 3 (1948), p. 55.

7. THE EDUCATIONAL PROCESS

1. V. T. Thayer and Martin Levit, *The Role of the School in American Society* (New York: Dodd, Mead 1966), p. 25. Used by permission of Dodd, Mead & Company, Inc.

2. See Chap. 8.

3. Thayer and Levit, *The Role of the School,* p. 167. Used by permission of Dodd, Mead & Company, Inc.

4. Ibid.

5. Ibid., p. 123.

6. Ibid., p. 167.

7. Ibid.

8. See p. 100.

9. See Chap. 8.

10. Charles B. Spahr, *America's Working People* (New York: Longmans, Green and Company, 1899), pp. 137, 138.

11. Ibid., p. 141.

12. The New York *Times,* Jan. 16, 1974, p. 59.

13. Peter Binzen, *Whitetown, U.S.A.* (New York: Random House, 1970), p. 45.

14. Ibid., p. 44.

15. HEW, *Statistics of Public Elementary and Secondary Day Schools: Fall 1972* (Washington, D.C.: GPO, 1972), p. 17, table 4.

16. Allon Schoener, ed., *Portal to America: The Lower East Side 1870–1925* (New York: Holt, Rinehart and Winston, 1967), pp. 127–28.

17. Ibid., pp. 129–30.

18. U.S. Immigration Commission, *Reports,* Vol. 29: *The Children of Immigrants in Schools,* S. Doc. No. 749, 61st Cong., 3rd sess. (Wash.: GPO, 1911).

19. Oscar Handlin, *The Uprooted: The Epic Story of the Great Migrations That Made the American People* (Boston: Little, Brown, 1951), pp. 220–21.

20. U.S. Immigration Commission, *Reports,* Vol. 29, p. 97.

21. Binzen, *Whitetown, U.S.A.,* p. 44.

22. U.S. Census Bureau, *Historical Statistics of the United States: Colonial Times to 1957* (Wash.: GPO, 1960), pp. 9, 214.

23. U.S. Census Bureau, *U.S. Stat. Abst.: 1972* (Wash.: GPO, 1972), p. 112, and p. 91 of this work.

24. See Chap. 8.

25. U.S. Department of Labor, Manpower Administration, *Career Thresholds,* Manpower Research Monograph, Vol. 1, No. 16, p. 37, as noted in Andrew Levison, *The Working Class Majority* (New York: Coward-McCann & Geoghegan, 1974), p. 121. The author considers that the large discrepancy between these figures and the much greater number of white collar workers' sons in both categories of college attendees reflects "the effects of . . . class bias in the educational system." He further points out that many workers' children attend "two-year community colleges which teach essentially skilled working-class jobs." He adds, "The number of workers who can afford to finish a four-year college course are far fewer, and, in a final irony, for many the degree no longer guarantees a good job as it once did."

26. Peter F. Drucker, *The Age of Discontinuity* (New York: Harper and Row, 1969), p. 324.

27. Norman Frederiksen and William B. Schrader, *Academic Achievement of Veteran and Non-veteran Students,* Psychological Monographs: General and Applied (Washington, D.C.: American Psychological Association, 1952).

28. Thayer and Levit, *The Role of the School,* pp. 125–26. Used by permission of Dodd, Mead & Company, Inc.

29. See Chap. 8 for the results of public opinion surveys of whites and Negroes on this issue and see also Manie Culbertson, *May I Speak?* (Gretna, La.: Pelican, 1972), pp. 119–20, for the attitude of Negro pupils in her class on this point.

30. Lawrence A. Cremin, *The Transformation of the School* (New York: Random House, Vintage Books, 1961), p. 324.

31. Ibid., p. 348.

32. This and preceding three quotes are from Diane Ravitch, *The Great School Wars, New York City 1805–1973: A History of the Public Schools As Battlefield of Social Change* (New York: Basic Books, 1974), pp. 236–38.

33. Fredrik S. Breed, "Education and the Realistic Outlook," *Philosophies of Education,* National Society for the Study of Education, Forty-first Yearbook, Part 1 (Chicago: the Univ. of Chicago Press, 1942), p. 128.

34. I. L. Kandel, *The Impact of the War upon American Education* (Chapel Hill, NC: the Univ. of North Carolina Press, 1948), p. 65.

35. Ibid., pp. 77–78.

36. Ibid., p. 78.

37. Ibid., p. 86.

38. Ibid., p. 106.

39. Ibid., p. 108.

40. Ibid., pp. 77–109 passim.

41. Ibid., p. 86.

42. Ravitch, *The Great School Wars,* pp. 236–38.

43. Cremin, *The Transformation of the School,* p. 335.

44. Ibid., pp. 338–45.

45. Ibid., pp. 344–45.

46. Ibid., p. 347.

47. Alan B. Wilson et al., "Education of Disadvantaged Children in California: A Report to the California State Committee on Public Education, 1966," mimeographed (Berkeley, Calif.: Survey Research Center, Univ. of California, 1966), p. 35.

48. See Chap. 8. p. 128. See also Herbert Ginsburg, *The Myth of the Deprived Child* (Englewood Cliffs, NJ: Prentice-Hall, 1972), p. 23, for data on variance in children's average IQ level in relation to the skill inherent in fathers' crafts.

49. Gray and Klaus, as cited in Harry A. Averch et al., *How Effective Is Schooling? A Critical Review and Synthesis of Research Findings,* R-956-PCSF/RC (Santa Monica, Calif.: The Rand Corp., 1972), p. 117.

50. HEW, *A Study of the Achievement of Our Nation's Students,* Pub. No. (OE) 72–131 (Wash.: GPO, 1973), p. 144.

51. George C. Kohn, " 'Grammar don't Matter'?" *Christian Science Monitor,* July 15, 1974, p. 9.

52. Wilson et al., "Education of Disadvantaged Children," p. 35.

53. Ibid.

54. The New York *Times,* Nov. 18, 1973, p. 59 L.

55. James S. Coleman, et. al., *Equality of Educational Opportunity* (Washington, D.C.: GPO, 1966), p. 325.

56. Thayer and Levit, *The Role of the School,* p. 124. Used by permission of Dodd, Mead & Company, Inc.

57. Andrew Mayes, "Remember, Remember," *New Society,* Nov. 1, 1973, p. 468. This extract is taken from an article which first appeared in *New Society,* London, the weekly review of the social sciences.

58. Ibid., p. 469.

59. Thayer and Levit, *The Role of the School,* p. 365. Used by permission of Dodd, Mead & Company, Inc.

60. Arthur R. Jensen, *Genetics and Education* (New York: Harper and Row, 1972), pp. 242–43.

61. Mayes, "Remember, Remember," p. 470. This extract is taken from an article which first appeared in *New Society,* London, the weekly review of the social sciences.

62. Morris Kline, *Why Johnny Can't Add: The Failure of the New Math* (New York: St. Martin's Press, 1973) pp. 1–3.

63. Ibid., p. 39.

64. Ibid., pp. 48–49.

65. *The Fleischmann Report on the Quality, Cost, and Financing of Elementary and Secondary Education in New York State* (New York: The Viking Press, 1973), Vol. 1, p. 29.

66. Kline, *Why Johnny Can't Add,* p. 49.

67. Ibid., p. 110.

68. Ibid., p. 55.

69. Ibid., p. 110.

70. The New York *Times,* Jan. 8, 1973, p. 84.

71. Kline, *Why Johnny Can't Add,* p. 103.

72. The New York *Times,* Jan. 8, 1975, p. 84.

73. Paul Lissandrello, Jr., "The Last Days of Homework," *Changing Education,* journal of the American Federation of Teachers, Winter/Spring 1974, p. 38.

74. Ibid.

75. Los Angeles *Times,* Aug. 16, 1976, p. 20.

76. Ibid.

77. See Chap. 5 and the Appendix by Paul Bracken.

78. National Assessment of Educational Progress, *Reading in America, A Perspective of Two Assessments,* Oct. 1976, p. 21.

79. Karl Shapiro, "Is This Really the Brightest Student Generation?" speech before the California Library Association, San Francisco, as reported in *Human Events,* July 11, 1970.

80. The New York *Times,* May 9, 1975, p. 16E.

81. HEW, *Patterns of Course Offerings and Enrollments in Public Secondary Schools: 1970–71,* Pub. No. (OE) 73–11400 (Wash.: GPO, 1972), p. 5.

82. Los Angeles *Times,* Aug. 16, 1976, p. 3.

83. Ibid.

84. HEW, *Patterns of Course Offerings,* p. 5.

85. Los Angeles *Times,* Aug. 16, 1976, p. 19.

86. Ibid., p. 3.

87. Ibid., p. 19.

88. Such courses were offered in an affluent upstate New York school in 1974, and may still be; nor does this school seem to be alone in offering courses like this.

89. Professor Ron Edmonds, Harvard Graduate School of Education, the New York *Times,* Nov. 18, 1973, Section 1, p. 59 L.

90. Kohn, " 'Grammar Don't Matter'?" p. 9.

91. Ibid.

92. F. Ray Marshall and Vernon M. Briggs, Jr., *The Negro and Apprenticeship* (Baltimore, Md.: Johns Hopkins Univ. Press, 1967), pp. 39, 55–57.

93. U.S. Census Bureau, *U.S. Stat. Abst.: 1974* (Wash.: GPO, 1974), p. 133, table 218.

94. Daniel Klepak, New York State's so-called education watchdog, declared that a study made by his office had demonstrated that "schools can teach inner-city

children to read," and that it was time to scrap "self-fulfilling prophecies that disadvantaged children simply can't learn." The New York *Times,* Apr. 4, 1974, p. 17.

95. The New York *Times,* Dec. 31, 1975, p. 19.

96. Fred M. Hechinger, "What Happened to the Best and the Brightest?" *Saturday Review/World,* Feb. 9, 1974, p. 65.

97. Ibid.

98. The New York *Times,* May 9, 1975, p. 16E.

99. Lester G. Crow et al., *Educating the Culturally Disadvantaged Child* (New York: David McKay, 1966), p. 85.

100. Clara M. Dobay, "The Sick Classroom," *The National Observer,* Mar. 9, 1974, p. 22, reprinted from the *Texas Outlook,* publication of the Texas State Teachers Association.

101. *The National Observer,* Oct. 13, 1973, p. 1.

102. *Daily News,* Jan. 29, 1974, p. 5.

103. The New York *Times,* Jan. 28, 1974, p. 31.

104. Ibid.

105. The New York *Times,* Feb. 26, 1974, p. 41.

106. *Student Activism in the High Schools of New York State: A Report to the New York State Commissioner of Education,* Mar. 1969, as quoted in the *Student Rights Handbook for New York City,* published by the Student Rights Project of the New York Civil Liberties Union, New York, 1969, p. 16.

107. Ibid., p. 13.

108. Ibid., p. 14.

109. Irving Kristol, "A Foolish American Ism—Utopianism," *The New York Times Magazine,* Nov. 14, 1971, p. 102.

110. Robert F. Biehler, *Psychology Applied to Teaching* (Boston: Houghton Mifflin, 1971), p. 262.

111. The New York *Times,* July 14, 1976, p. 27.

112. Ibid.

113. *The National Observer,* Oct. 13, 1973, p. 1.

114. These were truly tough kids, with the inherent capability of being very dangerous late adolescents. A very few years later, before some of them had reached voting age, these sons and grandsons of immigrants were jumping into Europe with the airborne divisions, landing on the islands in the Pacific as Marines, and filling the ranks of all our combat units, fighting German Waffen-SS panzer troops and Imperial Japanese Marines to a standstill—man for man when necessary.

115. Mark R. Arnold, "Public Schools," in Sar A. Levitan, ed., *The Federal Social Dollar in Its Own Back Yard* (Washington, D.C.: U.S. Bureau of National Affairs, 1973), p. 47.

116. Ibid., p. 48.

117. Shapiro, "Is This Really the Brightest Student Generation?"

118. For example, see the considerable statistical evidence of the failure of even voluntary busing programs in the North to achieve either goal in David J. Armor, "The Evidence on Busing," *Education Yearbook 1973–74* (New York: Macmillan Educational Corp., 1973), and the accusation by Thomas F. Pettigrew et al. in

"Pierced Armor," an article reprinted from *Integrated Education,* Nov.–Dec. 1972, in *Education Yearbook 1973–74,* p. 60, that Armor not only demanded unreasonably high results but ignored equally voluminous and valid evidence, which is listed, that proves just as conclusively that busing programs are successful on both counts. Averch et al., after a considerable survey of the evidence available at the time, stated their conclusions in the Rand Corporation report *How Effective Is Schooling?:* "There is no strong evidence that student-body effects exist. In particular, there is no evidence that the racial composition of a student body affects the performance of individual members of that student body." (p. 43)

A recent survey of the South by the National Opinion Research Center, the University of Chicago, carried out for the U.S. Office of Education, reported that Negro boys, who usually are the highest dropout risks, have gained half a grade level in southern schools receiving federal desegregation aid. The report said that black male students in high school had probably benefited more from an improved racial climate than from superior instruction. The study also checked on Negro high school girls and fifth-grade Negro boys and girls, but no such improvement was noted among these groups. (*Southern Schools: An Evaluation of the Effects of the Emergency School Assistance Program and of School Desegregation,* Vol. 2, Report No. NORC-R-124B, Oct. 1973.)

"UCLA psychologist Harold Gerard has completed an extensive study that he believes demonstrates that five years of school busing in Riverside, Calif., has failed to benefit minority children, and perhaps even harmed them." (*The Wall Street Journal,* Mar. 7, 1974, p. 14.) This argument continues.

119. Armor, "The Evidence on Busing," *Education Yearbook 1973–74,* p. 56.

120. For example, *The Fleischmann Report* (Vol. 1, pp. 307–427) goes into detail about the number of "White," "Black," "Spanish surnamed," "Indian and Oriental" pupils in every school district in the state; The New York *Times* (Oct. 23, 1973) carries similar data released by the Board of Education for every school in New York City and the District of Columbia.

121. As quoted in Arnold, "Public Schools," in Levitan, ed., *The Federal Social Dollar,* p. 25.

122. *Manpower Report of the President,* Apr. 1974 (Wash.: GPO), p. 97.

123. Even in the immigrant period of 1908–09, children who transferred into New York City schools from elsewhere in the United States were more likely to be behind scholastically than those who had been in the system from the beginning. U.S. Immigration Commission, *Reports,* Vol. 32: *The Children of Immigrants in Schools* S. Doc. No. 749, 61st Cong., 3rd sess. (Wash.: GPO, 1911).

124. George Gallup, "The Third Annual Survey of the Public's Attitudes Toward Public Schools," *United Teachers Magazine,* Nov. 21, 1971, p. M-1.

125. The New York *Times,* Dec. 3, 1973, pp. 1, 19.

126. Some say Mr. Anker's program of keeping students back until they can read near the grade level into which they are to be promoted has already broken down.

127. We have letters as well as verbal assurance from teachers who espouse this approach.

128. See the New York *Times,* Sept. 15, 1974, p. 15E, for a description of such a trend in Palo Alto, California.

129. The New York *Times,* May 25, 1975, p. 16E.

130. See pp. 189–190 for some less than reassuring indicators that bring up this question of adequacy and competence of teachers, particularly in the future.

8. PARENTS, THE HOME ENVIRONMENT, AND EDUCATION

1. HEW, *A Study of the Achievement of Our Nation's Students,* Pub. No. (OE) 72–131 (Washington, D.C.: GPO, 1973), p. 147.

2. This may be because better educated people tend to come from more influential families who help them progress, because of people they meet at school, or because of some other subtle reason. Christopher Jencks et al. in the book *Inequality: A Reassessment of the Effect of Family and Schooling in America* (New York: Basic Books, 1972), discuss this question. If such factors dominate, however, they are less easily understood, and less relevant to the average person than the above figures.

3. Andrew Levison, *The Working Class Majority* (New York: Coward-McCann & Geoghegan, 1974), pp. 121, 122. Levison feels that since two-thirds of workers "saw their children enter working-class jobs and many of the others saw only slight advances for their children, into clerical jobs or small, often marginal, businesses like franchise operations," and that since in 1962 "only 10 percent of the sons of manual workers . . . entered the professional and technical 'elite,' " there is "nothing even approaching a fair deal in education for the young blue-collar workers." Even with the increased opportunities since 1962, he still feels this is true and the "statistics on mobility bear out the failure of the schools."

4. HEW, *A Study of the Achievement of Our Nation's Students,* p. 145.

5. Kim Marshal, *Law and Order in Grade 6-E* (Boston: Little, Brown, 1970), p. 39. Mr. Marshal, a white Harvard graduate, was a teacher in a heavily black school in Roxbury, a Boston suburb.

6. See *The Gallup Poll: Public Opinion 1935–1971,* 1st ed., 3 vols. (New York: Random House, 1972), Vol. 2, *1949–1958,* pp., 1281, 1282, 1364, 1514, 1581, 1582; Vol. 3, *1959–1971,* pp. 1587, 1612, 1715, 1791–92.

7. The New York *Times,* Aug. 4, 1974, p. E 9.

8. *Gallup Opinion Index,* No. 119 (Princeton, NJ: American Institute of Public Opinion, May 1975), p. 18.

9. Ibid.

10. The New York *Times,* Sept. 21, 1976, p. 9.

11. The New York *Times,* Mar. 5, 1974, p. 29.

12. *The Journal-News,* Rockland County, NY, Mar. 18, 1974, p. 1 B.

13. David J. Armor, "The Evidence on Busing," *Education Yearbook 1973–74* (New York: Macmillan Educational Corp., 1973), p. 51.

14. The New York *Times,* July 14, 1974, p. 7.

15. Jean Heinig, "A Tale of Two Cities," *The Public Pulse,* Apr. 1970.

16. V. T. Thayer and Martin Levit, *The Role of the School in American Society*

(New York: Dodd, Mead, 1966), pp. 125–26. Used by permission of Dodd, Mead & Company, Inc.

17. HEW, *A Study of the Achievement of Our Nation's Students,* p. 146.

18. Ibid.

19. Ibid., p. 14.

20. Oscar Handlin, *The Uprooted: The Epic Story of the Great Migrations That Made the American People* (Boston: Little, Brown, 1951), p. 294.

21. Herbert Ginsburg, *The Myth of the Deprived Child* (Englewood Cliffs, NJ: Prentice-Hall, 1972), p. 23, table 2–1, "Mean Stanford-Binet I.Q.s of 2,757 Children Classified According to Parental Occupation" (McNemar, 1942, p. 38).

22. Arthur R. Jensen, *Genetics and Education* (New York: Harper & Row) pp. 110, 107.

23. Ginsburg, *The Myth of the Deprived Child,* p. 25, table 2–3, "Race and Class Difference in I.Q. Scores" (Deutsch and Brown, 1964, p. 26).

24. Alan Wilson et al., "Education of Disadvantaged Children in California: A Report to the California State Committee on Public Education," Mimeographed (Berkeley, Calif.: Survey Research Center, Univ. of California, 1966), p. 36.

25. Theodore Dobzhansky, *Genetic Diversity and Human Equality* (New York: Basic Books, 1973), p. 23, quoting Scarr-Salapatek (1971 a, b).

26. Ibid., p. 22.

27. HEW, *A Study of the Achievement of Our Nation's Students,* p. 14.

28. Jerald G. Bachman, *The Impact of Family Background and Intelligence on Tenth-Grade Boys,* Vol. 2, *Youth in Transition,* (Ann Arbor, Mich.: Institute for Social Research, Univ. of Michigan, 1970), p. 128.

29. These days the labor market includes 52.4 percent married women, with husbands present, and with children between six and seventeen years of age. Many of the women from the 14.6 percent of the female work force that is widowed or divorced also have school-age children. U.S. Census Bureau, *U.S. Stat. Abst.: 1975* (Wash.: GPO, 1975), p. 347, table 565, and p. 346, table 563.

30. For a discussion of the non-generation gap between parents and high school pupils and supporting data, see Frank E. Armbruster, *The Forgotten Americans: A Survey of the Values, Beliefs, and Concerns of the Majority* (New Rochelle, NY: Arlington House, 1972), pp. 174, 175, 190.

31. U.S. Immigration Commission, *Reports,* Vol. 3: *Statistical Review of Immigration, 1820–1910,* S. Doc. No. 756, 61st Cong., 3rd sess. (Wash.: GPO, 1911), pp. 6, 7, 10, 11.

32. U.S. Census Bureau, *U.S. Stat. Abst.: 1973* (Wash.: GPO, 1973), p. 34.

33. Handlin, *The Uprooted,* p. 145.

34. Ibid., p. 148.

35. Ibid., pp. 149–50.

36. Ibid., pp. 151, 153.

37. Allon Schoener, ed., *Portal to America: The Lower East Side 1870–1925* (New York: Holt, Rinehart and Winston, 1967), pp. 210–12.

38. Ibid., p. 210.

39. U.S. Immigration Commission, *Reports,* Vol 29: *The Children of Immigrants in Schools* S. Doc. No. 749, 61st Cong., 3rd sess. (Wash.: G.P.O., 1911), p. 97.

40. Peter Binzen, *Whitetown, U.S.A.* (New York: Random House, 1970), p. 44.

41. U.S. Immigration Commission, *Reports,* Vol. 29: p. 97.

42. U.S. Census Bureau, *Historical Statistics of the United States: Colonial Times to 1957* (Wash.: GPO, 1960), pp. 206–14.

43. U.S. Census Bureau, *U.S. Stat. Abst.: 1973,* p. 116. In 1952 it was found that 1.3 percent of those with five years of schooling (the limit used from 1947 to 1952 for those asked about literacy) were, nonetheless, illiterate. See U.S. Census Bureau's *Historical Statistics of the United States,* p. 206.

44. See p. 61.

45. Handlin, *The Uprooted,* pp. 145–46.

46. Roger Lane, "Urbanization and Criminal Violence in the 19th Century: Massachusetts As a Test Case," *Journal of Social History* 2 (1968), as reprinted in National Commission on the Causes and Prevention of Violence, Staff Reports, Vol. 2: *Violence in America: Historical and Comparative Perspectives,* eds., Hugh Davis Graham and Ted Robert Gurr (Washington, D.C.: GPO, 1969), p. 367.

47. Maldwyn Allen Jones, *American Immigration* (Chicago: the Univ. of Chicago Press, 1960), p. 133.

48. The New York *Times,* Mar. 23, 1975, p. 41 L.

49. U.S. Immigration Commission, *Reports,* Vol. 36: *Immigration and Crime,* S. Doc. No. 750, 61st Cong., 3rd sess. (Wash.: GPO, 1911), pp. 10, 36.

50. U.S. Immigration Commission, *Reports,* Vol. 1: *Abstracts of Reports of the Immigration Commission,* S. Doc. No. 747, 61st Cong., 3rd sess. (Wash.: GPO, 1911), p. 151.

51. This situation no longer seems to apply to the degree that it once did in our larger cities like New York.

52. Lane, "Urbanization and Criminal Violence," in *Violence in America,* p. 364.

53. Oliver Jensen et al., *American Album* (New York: American Heritage, Ballantine, 1970), p. 189.

54. U.S. Immigration Commission, *Reports,* Vol. 1: *Abstracts of Reports of the Immigration Commission,* p. 151.

55. Schoener, ed., *Portal to America,* p. 210.

56. *The New York Times,* Dec. 5, 1933, as reproduced in Cabel Phillips, ed., *The New York Times Chronicle of American Life: From the Crash to the Blitz, 1929–1939* (London: the Macmillan Co., Collier-Macmillan Ltd., 1969), p. 176.

57. U.S. Census Bureau, *U.S. Stat. Abst.: 1974* (Wash.: GPO, 1974), p. 25.

58. Schoener, pp., 62, 63.

59. *Gallup Opinion Index,* No. 89, Nov. 1972, p. 23.

60. Elmer H. Johnson, *Crime, Correction and Society,* rev. ed. (Homewood, Ill.: Dorsey, 1968), p. 35.

61. National Commission on the Causes and Prevention of Violence, *Staff Reports,* Vol. 12: *Crimes of Violence,* ed. Donald J. Mulvihill et al. (Wash.: GPO, 1969), p. 705.

62. Sheldon Hackney, "Southern Violence," *American Historical Review* 74 (1969), as reprinted in National Commission on the Causes and Prevention of Violence, *Staff Reports,* Vol. 2: *Violence in America,* pp. 389–92.

63. The New York *Times,* Sept. 8, 1970, p. 32.

64. Frank E. Armbruster et al., *Can We Win in Vietnam?* (New York: Praeger, 1968), pp. 255–58.

65. Schoener, ed., *Portal to America,* p. 62.

66. This section of William B. Saxbe's testimony is quoted verbatim in *The American Rifleman,* Mar. 1974, p. 45.

67. The New York *Times,* Mar. 23, 1975, pp. 1, 41 L.

68. The New York *Times,* Feb. 26, 1974, p. 41.

69. U.S. Census Bureau, *U.S. Stat. Abst.: 1975,* p. 158 Table 266.

70. Though one still hears those who more or less support this view. On March 4, 1974, in a television report on the spectacular deterioration of a modern high-rise, low-income public housing project in Newark, broadcast by WNBC, Channel 4, New York, some of those interviewed tended to express this theme.

71. U.S. Census Bureau, *U.S. Stat. Abst.: 1975* (Wash.: GPO, 1975), pp. 151, 388.

72. Ibid., p. 926.

73. Ibid., pp. 890, 908.

74. Ibid.

9. FASHIONABLE EDUCATION ATTITUDES

1. James E. McClellan, *Toward an Effective Critique of American Education* (New York: Lippincott, 1968), pp. 6, 7.

2. Ibid, p. 8.

3. Walter Loban, "A Sustained Program of Language Learning," in Marjorie B. Smiley and Harry L. Miller, eds., *Policy Issues in Urban Education* (New York: Free Press, 1968), pp. 233, 237.

4. See p. 99.

5. Nathan Caplan, "Street Skills of Many Hard-to-Employ Youths May Hinder Success in Job Training Programs," *Institute for Social Research Newsletter,* Univ. of Michigan, Vol. 1, No. 19 (Autumn 1973), pp. 5–7.

6. Smiley and Miller, eds., *Policy Issues,* p. 284.

7. Neil Postman and Charles Weingartner, *Teaching As a Subversive Activity* (New York: Delacorte, 1969), p. 1.

8. *A Report of Achievement Test Information, Fall 1972, in Grades 4 and 8,* Research, Planning, and Evaluation, Statewide Testing Program, State of Rhode Island, Dept. of Education, Oct. 1973.

9. "EAP State Report 1972–1973 Educational Assessment Program," New Jersey Dept. of Education, Division of Research, Planning, and Education/Field Services.

10. *Report of Achievement Test Information.*

11. "Summary Report of Statewide Testing Program 1972–73," Report No. 83, Office of Instructional Services, Evaluation Section, Hawaii Dept. of Education, Oct. 1973, p. 19.

12. For example, Dunbar High School, in Washington, D.C.

13. See the statement by New York City schools' Chancellor Irving Anker on WINS, Sept. 1, 1973.

14. Postman and Weingartner, *Teaching As a Subversive Activity,* p. 3.

15. See Irving Sloan, "Balance and Imbalance: 'New' History Texts and the Negro," in Smiley and Miller, eds., *Policy Issues,* pp. 184–200.

16. Ibid., p. 189.

17. Dr. Will Herberg, *U.S. News & World Report,* June 4, 1973, p. 57.

18. The New York *Times,* Jan. 28, 1974, p. 11.

19. Andrew M. Greeley, *Why Can't They Be Like Us?* (New York: Dutton, 1971), pp. 90, 92.

20. The New York *Times,* Jan. 28, 1974, p. 11.

21. A Louis Harris poll of 15- to 21-year-olds taken in 1970—the year of Kent State and the "student strike"—for *Life* (Jan. 8, 1971) showed that 90 percent said they were happy and 93 percent expected to be "as happy or even happier in the future."

22. Otto Klineberg, "Life Is Fun in a Smiling, Fair-Skinned World," in Smiley and Miller, eds., *Policy Issues,* pp. 173, 174.

23. Louise Clarke, *Can't Read, Can't Write, Can't Takl Too Good Either: How to Recognize and Overcome Dyslexia in Your Child* (New York: Walker, 1973), p. 207.

24. Klineberg, in Smiley and Miller, eds., *Policy Issues,* p. 174.

10. SUMMARY

1. U.S. Census Bureau, *U.S. Stat. Abst.: 1974* (Wash.: GPO, 1974), p. 136, table 225. HEW, *Dig. of Educ. Stat.: 1975,* Pub. No. NCES 76–211 (Wash.: GPO, 1976), p. 71, table 72.

2. HEW, *Dig. of Educ. Stat.: 1975,* p. 24, table 21.

3. See pp. 20 and 118 for a discussion of the difference between student-teacher ratio and average class size.

4. See Chap. 3 and Chap. 4 for academic achievement data.

5. Incidentally, Arizona achievement data (see p. 214 in the Appendix) contain mean reading scores for third grade pupils by class size. These, again, show no correlation between class size per se and achievement scores, except that coincidentally, I am sure, the mean raw reading scores list showed increasing scores as class sizes increased, with the highest scores by far occurring in classes of forty to forty-five children. Possibly these last were largely parochial school classes.

6. "New York has the lowest pupil/educator ratio. The state has made a massive investment in reducing class size in order to raise quality." From *The Fleischmann Report on the Quality, Cost, and Financing of Elementary and Secondary Education in New York State,* Vol. I (New York: The Viking Press, 1973) p. 12.

7. See pp. 117–119. See also Christopher Jencks et al., *Inequality: A Reassessment of the Effect of Family and Schooling in America* (New York: Basic Books, 1972),

pp. 94–96; Christopher Jencks, "The Effects of High Schools on Their Students," Harvard Center for Educational Policy Research, 1972; *New York City School Fact Book*, 2nd ed., Institute for Community Studies, Queens College, City Univ. of New York, 1972, pp. iii, iv; James S. Coleman et al., *Equality of Educational Opportunity* (Washington, D.C.: GPO, 1966), pp. 218–30 and supplementary Appendices 9, 10. Also note the achievement levels vs. class size for Arizona on pp. 213–214 of the Appendix.

8. Full-time art, music and gym teachers as well as librarians (who read stories to classes of children daily) are now found in kindergarten through fourth grade schools.

9. See *The Gallup Poll: Public Opinion 1935–1971*, 1st ed., 3 vols. (New York: Random House, 1972), Vol. 2, *1949–1958*, pp. 1281, 1282, 1364, 1514, 1581, 1582; Vol. 3, *1959–1971*, pp. 1587, 1612, 1715, 1791–92. See also *The Gallup Opinion Index*, No. 87, Sept. 1972, as reproduced on pp. 132 and 133.

10. See Frank Armbruster, *The Forgotten Americans: A Survey of the Values, Beliefs, and Concerns of the Majority* (New Rochelle, NY: Arlington House, 1972), pp. 190–94 and 238 for data derived from Purdue Opinion Panel polls of high school pupils over the years.

11. William V. Shannon, "Too Much Too Soon," The New York *Times*, Sept. 8, 1976, p. 37.

12. Though showing the public's fluctuating confidence in all types of people in places of responsibility, the Harris Surveys found those in charge of education second only to those in charge of medicine in having the public's confidence. National Opinion Research Corp. surveys of 1973 and 1974 support this ranking. See *The Harris Survey*, Nov. 13, 1972; *The Harris Survey* as reported in *Confidence and Concern: Citizens View American Government*, A Survey of Public Attitudes by the Subcommittee on Intergovernmental Relation of the Committee on Government Operations, U.S. Senate, Part 2, Dec. 3, 1973.

13. Sarasota *Herald Tribune*, Aug. 30, 1976 (Editorial page).

11. WHAT CAN BE DONE?

1. See *The Wall Street Journal*, Aug. 2, 1976, p. 9, "Letters to the Editor," from a school superintendent.

2. *U.S. News & World Report*, Sept. 13, 1976, p. 32.

3. *National Report, ATP, College-Bound Seniors, 1975–1976*, Admissions Testing Program of the College Entrance Examination Board, pp. 6, 7.

4. *The Journal-News*, Rockland County, NY, Mar. 27, 1975, Gannett News Service, dateline Washington.

APPENDIX: ANALYSIS OF ACHIEVEMENT AND OTHER TRENDS, BY STATES

1. Data in this section from "Analysis of Standardized Testing Results 1973–1974," State Dept. of Education, Phoenix, Ariz., Apr. 1974.

2. For the data source and more complete information on the program, see *California State Testing Program 1971–72 and 1972–73,* Calif. State Dept. of Education, Office of Program Evaluation and Research, 1974.

3. See Preliminary Report of the Spring 1973 Testing Program, Delaware Educational Assessment Program 1972–73, Delaware Dept. of Public Instruction, Sept. 1973.

4. Ibid., p. 14.

5. Data from A Summary of Reading and Mathematics Test Results as Measured by Norm-Referenced Tests, 1970–73, District of Columbia Public Schools, July 1973.

6. For further discussion, see William H. Angoff, ed., *The College Board Admissions Testing Program: A Technical Report on Research and Development Activities Relating to the Scholastic Aptitude Test and Achievement Tests* (New York: College Entrance Examination Board, 1971).

7. See "8th Grade Schools Category Report," Office of Instructional Services, Georgia Dept. of Education, Jan. 1974.

8. Ibid., p. 1.

9. Data from "Summary Report of Statewide Testing Program 1972–73," Report No. 83, Office of Instructional Services, Evaluation Section, Hawaii Dept. of Education, Oct. 1973, p. 19.

10. "Differential Aptitude Tests, Idaho Percentile Norms," 1972–73 and 1973–74. "Tables of Standard Scores with Corresponding Percentile Norms for Iowa Tests of Educational Development," 1971–72 and 1972–73. State of Idaho, Dept. of Education.

11. Data from Iowa Basic Skills Testing Program, Univ. of Iowa.

12. For the statistical details of this equating procedure, see "The Equating Report: Year-to-Year Analysis of the Cognitive Tests of the Michigan Educational Assessment Program," Michigan Dept. of Education, Mar. 1973.

13. Data from Report No. 3, "Detroit Schools' Standing on State Assessments 1970 through 1973," Dept. of Research and Development, Division of Curriculum and Educational Research, Detroit Public Schools.

14. Data from "Frequency Distribution Summary for California Achievement Tests, 1970 Edition," State of Mississippi, Dept. of Education.

15. See "11th Grade Statewide Norms for the 1972 Fall Testing Program using the SRA Iowa Tests of Educational Development," State of Nebraska, Dept. of Education, Mar. 1973.

16. For information and data on this program, see "EAP State Report 1972–1973 Educational Assessment Program," New Jersey Dept. of Education, Division of Research, Planning, and Evaluation/Field Services.

17. "EAP State Report 1972–1973 Educational Assessment Program."

18. Ibid., p. 27.

19. All data in this section from "Analysis of Standardized Testing Results 1973–1974," State Dept. of Education, New Mexico, Apr. 1974.

20. "Analysis of Standardized Testing Results 1973–1974," p. 32.

21. For more detailed information on the Pupil Evaluation Program, see "New York State Pupil Evaluation Program, School Administrator's Manual," The State Education Dept., Bureau of Pupil Testing and Advisory Services, Oct. 1973.

22. For a mathematical description of the equi percentile method, and other score-equating considerations, see the Michigan Education Department booklet "The Equating Report," Mar. 1973.

23. See State Assessment of Educational Progress in North Carolina 1971–72, Division of Research, State Dept. of Public Instruction, Dec. 1972.

24. See Statewide Reports—Ohio Survey Tests, 1968–73, Ohio Testing Services, State Dept. of Education.

25. Information available from Guidance and Counseling Service, Division of Elementary and Secondary Education, Pierre, S. Dak.

26. See "Sixth Grade Reading—A Needs Assessment Report" and "Sixth Grade Mathematics—A Needs Assessment Report," Texas Education Agency, 1972.

27. See "How Good Are Utah Schools?" Utah State Board of Education, 1971.

28. Ibid., p. 27.

29. For a detailed description of the Iowa Tests of Basic Skills see A. N. Hieronymus and E. F. Lindquist, *Manual for Administrators, Supervisors, and Counselors, Levels Ed., Forms 5 & 6, Iowa Tests of Basic Skills* (Boston: Houghton Mifflin, 1974).

30. See *1975–76 Philadelphia City-Wide Summaries,* Office of Research and Evaluation, Division of Testing Services, School District of Phila., T 76–111–G, Report #7692, May 1976, p. 2.

BIBLIOGRAPHY

GENERAL

ANDERSON, Archibald W. "The Charges Against American Education: What Is The Evidence?" *Progressive Education* 31 (1952). Quoted in *Public Education under Criticism*. Eds. C. Winfield Scott and Clyde M. Hill. Englewood Cliffs, NJ: Prentice-Hall, 1954.

ANGOFF, William H., ed. *The College Board Admissions Testing Program: A Technical Report on Research and Development Activities Relating to the Scholastic Aptitude Test and Achievement Tests.* New York: College Entrance Examination Board, 1971.

ARMBRUSTER, Frank E., et al. *Can We Win in Vietnam?* New York: Praeger, 1968.

ARMBRUSTER, Frank E. *The Forgotten Americans: A Survey of the Values, Beliefs, and Concerns of the Majority.* New Rochelle, NY: Arlington House, 1972.

ARMOR, David J. "The Evidence on Busing." *Education Yearbook 1973–74.* New York: Macmillan Educational Corp., 1973.

AVERCH, Harry A., et al. *How Effective Is Schooling? A Critical Review and Synthesis of Research Findings.* R-956-PCSF/RC, Mar. 1972. Santa Monica, Calif.: The Rand Corp., 1972.

BACHMAN, Jerald G. *The Impact of Family Background and Intelligence on Tenth-Grade Boys,* Vol. 2, *Youth in Transition.* Ann Arbor, Mich.: Institute for Social Research, Univ. of Michigan, 1970.

BERDIE, Ralph F., et al. *Who Goes to College? Comparison of Minnesota College Freshmen 1930–1960.* Minnesota Studies in Student Personnel Work, No. 12. Minneapolis: Univ. of Minnesota Press, 1962.

BIEHLER, Robert F. *Psychology Applied to Teaching.* Boston: Houghton Mifflin, 1971.

BINZEN, Peter. *Whitetown, U.S.A.* New York: Random House, 1970.

BLOOM, Benjamin S. "The 1955 Normative Study of the Tests of General Educational Development." *School Review* 64 (1956).

BOSS, Mabel E. "Reading, Then and Now." *School and Society* 51 (1940).

BREED, Fredrick S. "Education and the Realistic Outlook." *Philosophies of Education.* National Society for the Study of Education, Forty-first Yearbook, Part 1. Chicago: the Univ. of Chicago Press, 1942.

CALDWELL, Otis W., and Courtis, Stuart A. *Then and Now in Education, 1842–1923: A Message of Encouragement from the Past to the Present.* Yonkers, NY: World Book, 1924.

CANCRO, Robert. *Intelligence, Genetic and Environmental Influences.* New York: Grune and Stratton, 1971.

CAPLAN, Nathan. "Street Skills of Many Hard-to-Employ Youths May Hinder Success in Job Training Programs." *Institute for Social Research Newsletter. Univ. of Michigan,* Vol. 1, No. 19 (Autumn 1973).

CLARKE, Louise. *Can't Read, Can't Write, Can't Takl Too Good Either: How to Recognize and Overcome Dyslexia in Your Child.* New York: Walker, 1973.

College Entrance Examination Board, New York, New York. Unpublished data.

CONANT, James B. *The Education of American Teachers.* New York: McGraw-Hill, 1963.

CORDER, Reginald. "The Information Base for Reading: A Critical Review of the Information Base for Current Assumptions Regarding the Status of Instruction and Achievement in Reading in the United States." Berkeley, Calif.: Educational Testing Service, 1971.

CREMIN, Lawrence A. *The Transformation of the School.* New York: Random House, Vintage Books, 1961.

CROW, Lester G., et al. *Educating the Culturally Disadvantaged Child.* New York: David McKay, 1966.

CULBERTSON, Manie, *May I Speak?* Gretna, Louisiana.: Pelican, 1972.

DAVIS, Percy R., and Morgan, M. Evan. *A Balanced Educational Program for Santa Monica.* Santa Monica, Calif.: Board of Education, 1940.

DOBAY, Clara M. "The Sick Classroom." *The National Observer,* Mar. 9, 1974. Reprinted from the *Texas Outlook,* publication of the Texas State Teachers Association.

DOBZHANSKY, Theodore. *Genetic Diversity and Human Equality.* New York: Basic Books, 1973.

DRUCKER, Peter F. *The Age of Discontinuity.* New York: Harper and Row, 1969.

FLANAGAN, John C., and Jung, Steven M. *Progress in Education: A Sample Survey (1960–1970)* 2nd ed. Palo Alto, Calif.: American Institute for Research, Sept. 1972.

The Fleischmann Report on the Quality, Cost, and Financing of Elementary and Secondary Education in New York State, Vol. 1, 3 vols. New York: The Viking Press, 1973.

FREDERIKSEN, Norman, and Schrader, William B. *Academic Achievement of Veteran and Non-veteran Students.* Psychological Monographs: General and Applied. Washington, D.C.: American Psychological Association, 1952.

GALLUP, George. "The Third Annual Survey of the Public's Attitudes Toward Public Schools." *United Teachers Magazine,* Nov. 21, 1971.

The Gallup Opinion Index. Nos. 66, Dec. 1970; 73, July 1971; 74, Aug. 1971; 75, Sept. 1971; 77, Nov. 1971; 87, Sept. 1972; 89, Nov. 1972; 119, May 1975. Princeton, NJ: American Institute of Public Opinion.

The Gallup Poll: Public Opinion, 1935–1971. 1st ed. 3 vols. New York: Random House, 1972.

GATES, Arthur I. *Reading Attainment in Elementary Schools: 1957 and 1937.* New York: Teachers College Press, 1961.

GERBERICH, J. Raymond. "The First of the Three R's." *Phi Delta Kappan* 33 (1952).

GINSBURG, Herbert. *The Myth of the Deprived Child.* Englewood Cliffs, NJ: Prentice-Hall, 1972.

GREELEY, Andrew M. *Why Can't They Be Like Us?* New York: Dutton, 1971.

HANDLIN, Oscar. *The Uprooted: The Epic Story of the Great Migrations that Made the American People.* Boston: Little, Brown, 1951.

Harvard Center for Educational Policy Research. "The Effects of High Schools on Their Students," 1972.

HECHINGER, Fred M. "What Happened to the Best and the Brightest?" *Saturday Review/World,* Feb. 9, 1974.

HEINIG, Jean. "A Tale of Two Cities." *The Public Pulse,* Apr. 1970.

HIERONYMUS, A. N., and Lindquist, E. F. *Manual for Administrators, Supervisors, and Counselors.* Levels. Ed., *Forms 5 & 6, Iowa Tests of Basic Skills.* Boston: Houghton Mifflin, 1974.

JENCKS, Christopher, et al. *Inequality: A Reassessment of the Effect of Family and Schooling in America.* New York: Basic Books, 1972.

JENSEN, Arthur R. *Genetics and Education.* New York: Harper and Row, 1972.

JENSEN, Oliver, et al. *American Album.* New York: American Heritage, Ballantine, 1970.

JOHNSON, Elmer H. *Crime, Correction and Society,* rev. ed. Homewood, Ill.: Dorsey, 1968.

JONES, Maldwyn Allen. *American Immigration.* Chicago: the Univ. of Chicago Press, 1960.

KANDEL, I. L. *The Impact of the War Upon American Education.* Chapel Hill, NC: the Univ. of North Carolina Press, 1948.

KLINE, Morris. *Why Johnny Can't Add: The Failure of the New Math.* New York: St. Martin's Press, 1973.

KLINEBERG, Otto. "Life Is Fun in a Smiling, Fair-Skinned World." Quoted in *Policy Issues in Urban Education.* Eds. Marjorie B. Smiley and Harry L. Miller. New York: Free Press, 1968.

KOHN, George C. " 'Grammar Don't Matter'?" *Christian Science Monitor,* July 15, 1974.

LEVISON, Andrew. *The Working Class Majority.* New York: Coward-McCann & Geoghegan, 1974.

LISSANDRELLO, Paul, Jr. "The Last Days of Homework." *Changing Education.* Journal of the American Federation of Teachers, Winter/Spring 1974.

LOBAN, Walter. "A Sustained Program of Language Learning." Quoted in *Policy*

Issues in Urban Education. Eds. Marjorie B. Smiley and Harry L. Miller. New York: Free Press, 1968.

MCCLELLAN, James E. *Toward an Effective Critique of American Education.* New York: Lippincott, 1968.

MCCURDY, Jack, and Speich, Don. *The Decline of American Education.* Los Angeles: *Los Angeles Times,* 1976.

MARSHALL, F. Ray, and Briggs, Vernon M., Jr. *The Negro and Apprenticeship.* Baltimore, Md.: Johns Hopkins Univ., 1967.

MARSHAL, Kim. *Law and Order in Grade 6-E.* Boston: Little, Brown, 1970.

MAYES, Andrew. "Remember, Remember." *New Society,* Nov. 1, 1973. This extract is taken from an article which first appeared in *New Society,* London, the weekly review of the social sciences.

Minutes of the Conference of Directors of State Testing Programs, Nov. 4–5, 1973. Princeton, NJ: Educational Testing Service.

National Assessment of Educational Progress Newsletter, Aug. 1976. Education Commission of the States.

National Report, ATP, College-Bound Seniors, 1975–1976. Admissions Testing Program of the College Entrance Examination Board.

"The 1971 National Reading Difficulty Index: A Study of Functional Reading Ability in the U.S. for The National Reading Center," Aug. 1971 Louis Harris and Associates.

PETTIGREW, Thomas F., et al. "Pierced Armor." Reprinted from *Integrated Education,* Nov.–Dec. 1972, in *Education Yearbook, 1973–74.* New York: Macmillan Educational Corp., 1973.

Philadelphia City Wide Testing Program, 1975–76. *February 1976 Achievement Testing Program, Citywide Summaries,* Report #7692. Office of Research and Evaluation, May 1976.

PHILLIPS, Cabel, ed. *The New York Times Chronicle of American Life: From the Crash to the Blitz, 1929–1939.* London: The Macmillan Co., Collier-Macmillan Ltd., 1969.

POSTMAN, Neil, and Weingartner, Charles. *Teaching As a Subversive Activity.* New York: Delacorte, 1969.

RAVITCH, Diane. *The Great School Wars, New York City 1805–1973: A History of the Public Schools As Battlefield of Social Change.* New York: Basic Books, 1974.

Reading in America, A Perspective of Two Assessments. Education Commission of the States, National Assessment of Educational Progress, Oct. 1976.

ROBERTS, Wallace. "Right to Read: Lost in PR." *The Washington Monthly,* Sept. 1973.

RODERICK, Stephen A. "A Comparative Study of Mathematics Achievement by Sixth Graders and Eighth Graders, 1936 to 1973, 1951–55 to 1973, and 1965 to 1973." Ph. D. diss., Univ. of Iowa, July 1973.

SCHOENER, Allon, ed. *Portal to America: The Lower East Side: 1870–1925.* New York: Holt, Rinehart and Winston, 1967.

SCHRADER, William B. "Test Data As Social Indicators." Statistical Report Nos. 68–77. Princeton, NJ: Educational Testing Service, Sept. 1968.

SCHWAB, Joseph J. *College Curriculum and Student Protest.* Chicago: the Univ. of Chicago Press, 1969.

Science Research Associates. Iowa Tests of Educational Development Forms X-5 and Y-5, 1972.

SHAPIRO, Karl. "Is This Really the Brightest Student Generation?" *Human Events,* July 11, 1970. Speech before the California Library Association, San Francisco.

SLIGO, Joseph R. "Comparison of Achievement in Selected High School Subjects in 1934 and 1954." Ph.D. diss., State Univ. of Iowa, 1955.

SMILEY, Marjorie B., and Miller, Harry L., eds. *Policy Issues in Urban Education.* New York: Free Press, 1968.

Southern Schools: An Evaluation of the Effects of the Emergency School Assistance Program and of School Desegregation, Vol. 2. Report No. NORC-R-124B. Chicago, Ill.: the Univ. of Chicago, Oct. 1973.

SPAHR, Charles B. *America's Working People.* New York: Longmans, Green and Company, 1899.

Student Activism in the High Schools of New York State: A Report to the New York State Commissioner of Education, Mar. 1969. As quoted in the *Student Rights Handbook for New York City.* Published by the Student Rights Project of the New York Civil Liberties Union. New York, 1969.

THAYER, V. T., and Levit, Martin. *The Role of the School in American Society.* New York: Dodd, Mead, 1966.

TUDDENHAM, Read D. "Soldier Intelligence in World Wars I and II." *American Psychologist,* 3 (1948).

WHEELER, Lester R. "A Comparative Study of the Intelligence of East Tennessee Mountain Children." *Journal of Educational Psychology,* 33 (1942).

WILSON, Alan B., et al. "Education of Disadvantaged Children in California: A Report to the California State Committee on Public Education, 1966." Mimeographed. Berkeley, Calif.: Survey Research Center, Univ. of California, 1966.

WORCESTER, D. A., and Kline, Anne. *Reading Achievement in Lincoln, Nebraska, Schools 1921 and 1947.* Lincoln, Neb.: Univ. of Nebraska Teachers College, 1947.

YERKES, Robert M., ed. *Psychological Examining in the United States Army.* Memoirs of the National Academy of Sciences. v. 15, 1921.

U.S. GOVERNMENT PUBLICATIONS

ARNOLD, Mark R. "Public Schools." In *The Federal Social Dollar in Its Own Back Yard.* Ed. Sar A. Levitan. Washington, D.C.: U.S. Bureau of National Affairs, 1973.

COLEMAN, James S., et al. *Equality of Educational Opportunity.* U.S. Office of Education. Washington, D.C.: Government Printing Office, 1966.

HACKNEY, Sheldon. "Southern Violence." *American Historical Review* 74 (1969). As reprinted in *Violence in America,* Vol. 2. Staff Report to the National Commission on the Causes and Prevention of Violence. Washington, D.C.: Government Printing Office, 1969.

LANE, Roger. "Urbanization and Criminal Violence in the 19th Century: Massachusetts As a Test Case." *Violence in America,* Vol. 2. Staff Report to the National Commission on the Causes and Prevention of Violence. Washington, D.C.: Government Printing Office, 1969.

Manpower Report of the President, Washington, D.C.: Government Printing Office, Apr. 1974.

MULVIHILL, Donald J., et al, eds. *Crimes of Violence,* Vol. 12. Staff Report to the National Commission on the Causes and Prevention of Violence. Washington, D.C.: Government Printing Office, 1969.

The Report of the President's Commission on an All Volunteer Army.

U.S. Army Personnel Research Office. "Successive AFQT Forms—Comparisons and Evaluations." Technical Research Note 12, May 1963.

U.S. Bureau of the Census. *Current Population Reports.* "Characteristics of the Population by Ethnic Origin: March 1972 and 1971," P-20, No. 249, Apr. 1973. Washington, D.C.: Government Printing Office, 1973. "Money Income in 1974 of Families and Persons in the United States," P-60, No. 101. Washington, D.C.: Government Printing Office, 1976. "Money Income in 1971 of Families and Persons in the United States," P-60, No. 85. Washington, D.C.: Government Printing Office, 1972.

U.S. Bureau of the Census. *Historical Statistics of the United States: Colonial Times to 1957.* Washington, D.C.: Government Printing Office, 1960.

U.S. Bureau of the Census. *Statistical Abstract of the United States: 1975.* Washington, D.C. Government Printing Office, 1975; *1974,* Wash.: GPO, 1974; *1973,* Wash.: GPO, 1973; *1972,* Wash.: GPO, 1972.

U.S. Civil Rights Commission. *Public Knowledge and Busing Opposition: An Interpretation of a New National Survey,* Mar. 1973, App. 1.

U.S. Congress, House. *Tax Credits for Nonpublic Education.* Hearings before the Committee on Ways and Means. 92nd Congress, Aug. 14–16, 1972.

U.S. Congress, Senate. *Confidence and Concern: Citizens View American Government.* A Survey of Public Attitudes by the Subcommittee on Intergovernmental Relation of the Committee on Government Operations, Part 2, Dec. 3, 1973.

U.S. Department of Health, Education, and Welfare. *The Condition of Education: 1976.* Publication No. NCES 76–400. Washington, D.C.: Government Printing Office, 1976.

U.S. Department of Health, Education, and Welfare. *Digest of Education Statistics: 1975.* Publication No. NCES 76–211. Washington, D.C.: Government Printing Office, 1976.

U.S. Department of Health, Education, and Welfare. *Digest of Educational Statistics: 1974*. Publication No. NCES 75–210. Washington, D.C.: Government Printing Office, 1975.

U.S. Department of Health, Education, and Welfare. *Digest of Educational Statistics: 1973*. Publication No. (OE) 74–11103. Washington, D.C.: Government Printing Office, 1974.

U.S. Department of Health, Education, and Welfare. *Expenditures and Revenues for Public Elementary and Secondary Education: 1970–71*. Publication No. (OE) 73–11407. Washington, D.C.: Government Printing Office, 1973.

U.S. Department of Health, Education, and Welfare. "Literacy Among Youths 12–17 Years: United States." *National Health Survey*, Series 11, No. 131, Dec. 1973. Publication No. (HRA) 74–1613, Appendix I. Washington, D.C.: Government Printing Office, 1973.

U.S. Department of Health, Education, and Welfare. *Patterns of Course Offerings and Enrollments in Public Secondary Schools: 1970–71*. Publication No. (OE) 73–11400. Washington, D.C.: Government Printing Office, 1972.

U.S. Department of Health, Education, and Welfare. *Statistics of Public Elementary and Secondary Day Schools: Fall 1973*. Publication No. 74–155. Washington, D.C.: Government Printing Office, 1974.

U.S. Department of Health, Education, and Welfare. *Statistics of Public Elementary and Secondary Day Schools: Fall 1972*. Publication No. (OE) 73–11402. Washington, D.C.: Government Printing Office, 1973.

U.S. Department of Health, Education, and Welfare. *Statistics of State School Systems: 1969–70*. Publication No. (OE) 74–11421. Washington, D.C.: Government Printing Office, 1973.

U.S. Department of Health, Education, and Welfare. *A Study of the Achievement of our Nation's Students*. Publication No. (OE) 72–131. Washington, D.C.: Government Printing Office, 1973.

U.S. Immigration Commission. *Reports*. 61st Cong., 2nd and 3rd sess. Washington, D.C.: Government Printing Office, 1911. *Abstract of Reports of Immigration Commission*, Vol. 1. S. Doc. No. 747. *Statistical Review of Immigration, 1820–1910*, Vol. 3. S. Doc. No. 756. *Emigration Conditions in Europe*, Vol. 4. S. Doc. No. 748. *Immigrants in Cities*, Vol. 26, S. Doc. No. 338. *Immigration and Crime*, Vol. 36, S. Doc. No. 750. *The Children of Immigrants in Schools*, Vols. 29, 30, 32, 33. S. Doc. No. 749.

STATE PUBLICATIONS

California State Department of Education. *Profiles of School District Performance, California State Testing Program, 1971–72 and 1972–73*. Sacramento, 1974.

Hawaii State Department of Education. Office of Instructional Services, Evaluation Section. *Summary Report of Statewide Testing Program 1972–73*, Report No. 83, Oct. 1973.

Iowa Basic Skills Testing Program, the University of Iowa.

New Jersey Department of Education. Division of Research, Planning, and Education/Field Services. "EAP State Report 1972–1973 Educational Assessment Program."

New York State Education Department, University of the State of New York. Bureau of Testing and Advisory Services, Pupil Evaluation Program.

Ohio Testing Services, State Department of Education. Statewide Reports. Ohio Survey Tests, 1968–73.

South Dakota Education Department. Division of Elementary and Secondary Education, Guidance and Counseling Service. Pierre, South Dakota, Testing Program.

State of Rhode Island, Department of Education. *A Report of Achievement Test Information, Fall 1972, in Grades 4 and 8.*

West Virginia Department of Education. Division of Guidance, Counseling and Testing. *Eleventh Report: State-County Testing Program.* Mimeographed computer printouts. State-County Testing Program.

INDEX

report on functional illiteracy, 192
report on reading skills of 9-, 13-, and
17-year-olds, 65–66 (Table)
National Association for the Advance-
ment of Colored People
(NAACP), 142
National Commission on the Causes
and Prevention of Crime (Lon-
don), 155–156
National Commission on the Reform of
Secondary Education, 115
National Education Association, 25, 94
The National Observer, 119
National Opinion Research Center, 139
National origins *see* Racial/ethnic
groups
Navy Trainability Data, 74
Nebraska
costs per pupil 1974–75, 18
7th and 11th grades compared to
1971 norms, 42
statewide testing program, 231–232
(Tables)
Negroes *see* Blacks
Neighborhood schools
cross-busing and, 122–123
integration/segregation in, 139
survey attitudes toward, 138–139
New Deal
and progressive education in 1940s,
164
social experimentation and, 93
New Jersey
costs per pupil 1974–75, 18; and salaries and fixed charges 1973–74,
20
criterion-referenced tests in, 44–45,
232–233
multiplication/division, in 4th
grades, 190; abilities in 12th
grades, 233
state report on achievement, 233
New Jersey Education Association
blocking of achievement test scores,
26
New math
failure of, as teaching method, 190,
204
and *The Fleischmann Report,* 103
and lack of computational skills, 190
the use of logic in, 103

New Mexico
achievement test scores by racial
background, 234–236 (Tables)
ACT mean scores 1967–68 to 1972–
73, 237 (Table); compared to national, 238 (Table)
apparent falling IQ among 5th grades
in, 76
Department of Education report on
achievement, 236–238
statewide testing program, 233–238
(Tables)
New Orleans, Louisiana, 161
New York City
achievement scores compared to New
York State, 50 (Table)
Bureau of Educational Research on
1958 and 1970 reading abilities,
62
busing in, 123
crime, rates and prosecution in, 153
(Table), by type in 1973, 157
(Table)
discrimination in construction unions
in, 110
elementary and junior high school
reading ability 1965 and 1972, 48
gun laws in, 158
immigrant children in 1909, 82
improved reading 1972 to 1973, 49
murder homicide rates in, 161, in
1900s and 1973, 153 (Table)
new drug laws in, 159
number of policemen in 1900, 1933
and 1973, 154–155
persons charged for crimes 1901 and
1908, 152–153 (Table)
present school conditions in, 115
reading scores compared to new
norms, 62; compared to New
York State 3rd grades and above,
49, 240–242 (Table); 243 (Table)
schools and progressive education, 93
Students Rights Project in, 116
student/teacher ratio, 5–6, 20–21
teachers' self-defense handbook in,
115
New York Civil Liberties Union, 116
New York School Factbook, 118
New York State
achievement scores, 43, 45–50